STATE AND MARKET

STATE AND MARKET
The Politics of the Public and the Private

edited by
Jan-Erik Lane

SAGE Modern Politics Series Volume 9
Sponsored by the European Consortium for Political Research/ECPR

SAGE Publications • London • Beverly Hills • New Delhi

SAGE Publications Ltd
28 Banner Street
London EC1Y 8QE

SAGE Publications Inc
275 South Beverly Drive
Beverly Hills, California 90212

SAGE Publications India Pvt Ltd
C-236 Defence Colony
New Delhi 110 024

British Library Cataloguing in Publication Data

Lane, Jan-Erik
State and market : the politics of the public and the private — (Sage modern politics, vol. 9)
1. Mixed economy
I. Title
330.12′6 HD3611

ISBN 0-8039-9707-8
ISBN 0-8039-9708-6 Pbk

Library of Congress Catalog Card Number 84-052157

Phototypeset by Sunrise Setting, Torquay, Devon
Printed in Great Britain by
J.W. Arrowsmith, Bristol

Contents

Foreword

The rapid expansion of the public sector in the 1960s and the 1970s implied a basic change in the relationship between the public and the private. The strong *process of publicization* meant that the citizens in the welfare state became more reliant on the public budget than ever before. Big government means that a considerable portion of the resources of society is mobilized by the state or local governments and allocated by these bodies to various programmes, thus reducing the scope for markets. Though the problem of the ownership of the means of production is still a salient issue — 'capitalism' versus 'socialism' — and the pros and cons of a planned economy *contra* a laissez-faire economy stimulates much debate it seems that the overriding problem in the 1980s is the issue of how to strike a balance between the public sector and the private sector in the sense of public policy or markets. Basically, this is a *normative* problem concerning the scope for the two fundamental modes for arriving at collective choices. What kinds of criteria can we employ to decide what types of goods and services are to be allocated by means of the budget and through markets? What is an appropriate size for the government redistribution branch? And are there possibilities for mixing public and private modes of interaction? Questions about the size of the public sector and the role of public policy used to be answered mainly in terms of *positive* approaches, searching for the determinants of growth and then displaying the consequences of big government. It may be that the time is ripe for the standard positive models of incrementalism and the demographic approach to be supplemented by more normative deliberations concerning the public and the private. The problem of identifying decision criteria for the demarcation of the public and the private sectors is indeed a formidable question which is relevant for questions about the role of the state and the local government system. The purpose in gathering these articles in a volume on the public and the private is to extend our knowledge of this demarcation problem, which appears to crop up in familiar public policy themes on the determinants of welfare state expansion, the nature of corporatist institutions and the structure and functions of local government.

Social or collective choice in a democracy may basically be of two types: either it is the outcome of a politico-administrative process implementing the decision arrived at in a policy context, or it results from interactions in a market context. Fundamentally, there are only two mechanisms for collective choice: voting, politics and bureaucracy on the one hand, and the variety of markets on the other. How are we to choose between the two? A social choice is a decision as to which social state in a set of alternatives is to be implemented. Formally, the arrival at a collective choice is the specification of a social welfare function:

$$W = W(U^1, U^2, \ldots U^N)$$

where the level of welfare in society is dependent, somehow, upon the utility of its citizens. The pros and cons of policy and market as mechanisms for collective choice are dependent on how well each specifies the social welfare function. A social decision involves two things, a consideration of what is feasible and a deliberation about what is desirable. There are thus two kinds of evaluation criteria that are relevant in deciding between policy and market: the capacity of each choice mechanism to consider *technology*, or to identify the set of alternatives open to participants in the choice process, and *value* (a set of ethical properties), or the capacity of the allocation mechanism to pick the best alternative. The choice between policy or market is typically approached on the basis of the complementarity principle, or the substitution principle. Either it is argued that policy and market should be mixed in some specific way on the basis of their relative advantages, or it is maintained that the one may replace the other. A comparison of public policy as opposed to market must be based on a recognition of the potential pathologies of both mechanisms, not simply on some ad hoc assumption about ideal operations.

The articles included in the volume discuss the nature of any welfare function from three distinct angles; first, there are some papers that investigate arguments to the effect that the content of the social welfare function — the types of goods and services to be allocated — has definitive implications for the employment of one or other of the mechanisms for collective choice — market or public policy. Secondly, there follows a set of articles that analyse the intercation and interpenetration of the public and the private sectors. And finally, the volume includes papers that deal with the nature of collective choice in the public sector. There is an internal consistency in the listing of themes as clarifying the public-private distinction calls for a debate about the analytical criteria for separating the public from the private, as well as involve a search not only for the properties that distinguish the public from the private but also for the interrelationships between the two. Moreover, in order to understand more about the similarities and differences between the public and the private it is not enough to look for some optimal division between the two sectors based on some efficient combination of the allocation mechanisms — public policy and market; it becomes necessary to take a close look at the nature of decision making processes and the implementability of whatever optimal solution to the problem of mixing the public and the private arrived at. Thus, in the logic of public sector decision making, both a static and dynamic perspective is highly relevant to the problem of demarcating the public from the private as well as combining them in various forms on the basis of their differences.

The first section of the volume is oriented towards a discussion of the type of goods and services that one may encounter in the public sector of a welfare state. The paper by Lane contains an examination of the various approaches to a distinction between the public and the private, and it discusses in detail the criteria suggested as the demarcation line: excludability, jointness and externality. It relates various criteria as to the nature of goods and services to the demarcation between market and public policy. Van Mierlo continues this theme looking at the various methods for improving public resource allocation or enhancing the efficiency of public policy. It is often argued that competition characterizes markets whereas hierarchy distinguishes politics and bureaucracies. The paper by Jonsson is a challenge to the standard idiom about the nature of public resource allocation. Sørensen takes a game theoretic approach to the problem of determining the optimal size of the provision of local goods, and shows how the strategic play over spill-over effects and externalities affects the outcome. The second section of the volume deals with the mixes and interactions between the public and the private. It opens up with a thorough discussion of the various economies — public, private and black — in the welfare state. Rose's paper is a penetrating analysis emphasizing the dependencies between the various economies. Williams' paper deals with various strategies for managing urban problems; in particular he illuminates how market and planning approaches may be combined in a complex fashion, looking at recent policy developments under the Reagan administration. Grant makes a careful analysis of a single case of public-private partnership in the UK, attempting to state the pros and cons for this mixture of market and bureaucracy. Konukiewitz gives another example of a public-private partnership, which he evaluates by comparing the partnership with a bureaucratically administered allocation mechanism and a market-type allocation of the same phenomenon. The third section of the volume presents various analyses of public decision making and its implications for the public-private separation. The Lundquist paper is an overview of the trends in public administration theory, showing the development from rationality to anarchy. If public administration cannot be rational, then how can we trust public resource allocation to solve social problems? A probing analysis of the decision problem of determining the size of the public is presented in the Wildavsky paper, which shows that any account of the relative power of the public in relation to the private must recognize the cultural background of society. Finally, the Gurr and King paper contrasts an individual citizen approach with a system-state approach, arguing that the nature of the state interests is of crucial importance to the understanding of the public-private demarcation.

The various papers deal in different ways, using alternative approaches, with the possibility of identifying *criteria* for determining the size of the public sector and the composition of the public basket of goods and services. Thus, there is an attempt to renew the discussion about the nature of public goods and the proper functions of public resource allocation and distribution from the perspective of political science. The focus on decision criteria is elaborated in various analyses of decision mechanisms looking into the possibility of deriving *principles* for determining the structure of the system of public allocation of utilities. Distinctions relating to the separation between market and bureaucracy, hierarchy and competition, planning and laissez-faire as well as between national, regional and local goods in the set of public goods are elucidated from various angles. Whereas some papers deal with the circumstances that result in a choice of either market-type allocation or bureaucracy-type allocation other papers discuss the possibility of public-private partnerships. This book consists of some of the papers presented at the ECPR conference in Freiburg in a workshop with the same title and some manuscripts that have been written specifically for the volume.

I

THE NATURE OF THE PUBLIC SECTOR

1

Introduction: Public Policy or Markets? The Demarcation Problem

Jan-Erik Lane
Umeå University

Much of the literature on the welfare state has focused on the *growth problem* of identifying the factors — environmental, institutional and economic — which determine or are conducive to public expenditure expansion (Tarschys, 1975; Larkey, Stolp and Winer, 1981; Castles, 1982). An increasing part of the literature is now oriented towards the *outcome problem*, or the study of the consequences of governmental expansion and big public budgets. It is argued that unrestrained public sector expansion results in public policy failure due to communication problems, the lack of coordination and of reliable means-end technologies, and revenue satiation (Rose, 1981). The literature also takes up the *problem of shrinking* the public sector, dealing with it basically in two ways. It either outlines alternative ways of delivering services, emphasizing the feasibility of public-private partnerships mixing market allocation forms with bureaucracy (Ostrom and Ostrom, 1977; Bridge, 1977; Savas, 1982), or discusses decision techniques that would contain or impede governmental growth rates (Wildavsky, 1980). Statements to the effect that government or the public sector is too large or that it is vital to find tools to reduce growth rates must somehow be based on ideas about the *proper* size of government, which implies the fact that participating actors do have a *choice* — sometimes forgotten in the huge literature on structural forces conducive to growth in government, which Aaron Wildavsky examines in this book (Borcherding, 1984).

When Anthony Downs argues that the size of the government budget tends to be too small (Downs, 1965), or James Buchanan states that the public sector is too large, the budgetary expansion of the government being beyond control (Buchanan and Wagner,

1977; Brennan and Buchanan, 1980), then it is pertinent to ask for the normative criteria upon which such statements are based. Richard Rose points out that it has been suggested that the public sector should not be larger than some proposed magic figure, Colin Clark's 25 percent in 1945 or Milton Freedman's 60 percent in 1976 (Rose, 1981). While not underestimating the problem of identifying the forces that encourage public sector expansion or the problem of recognizing the myopia regarding outcomes of governmental growth, we would like to deal exclusively with the normative problem to discover if it is indeed possible to formulate arguments that justify some particular size of government or some specific amount of public expenditure: the problem of budget size.

It is no exaggeration to maintain that much of the literature on public policy and political economy has been concerned with the identification of determinants of variation in levels and growth rates in budget expenditures; in the 'Does Politics Matter?' literature, as well as in the study of popularity and political business cycle functions, the emphasis is on the search for positive factors that affect the distinction between the public and the private sectors, which accounts for the employment of econometrics in budget analysis and political economy (Wildavsky, 1975; Hibbs and Fassbender, 1981; Frey, 1978; Whiteley, 1980; Tufte, 1978; Sharpe and Newton, 1984; Lybeck, 1985). However, we may wish to know more about the rationale of public budget-making to look into the reasons why items of expenditure appear on the political budget. Focusing upon choice rather than structure it may be interesting to analyse the kind of *normative* criteria that may be used to make a distinction between the public and the private sector.

The public sector is by no means a single, monolithic entity and consequently the suggested solutions to the size problem will include deliberations about how the structure of government is to be conceived. It is not possible — it seems — to justify a public sector of some specific size without commitment as to how various amounts of national, regional and local goods are to be combined to produce a government of a certain overall size (Tiebout, 1956; Oates, 1972; Buchanan, 1965). The solution to the size problem is a function of the solution to the problems of choosing the proper size for the national government budget, the regional government budget or the local government budget: the problem of budget structure. Speaking generally, a solution to the problem of the proper size for the public sector must be based on deliberations about what the concepts 'public' and 'private' refer to, about the decision criteria that may guide the choice of what is to be public, private or some public-private mixture, as well as how such decisions may be implemented. The demarcation between the public and the private involves semantic questions, issues involved in the derivation of an optimal solution to the problem of what is to be private or public and matters concerning the implementability of any such solution (Margolis and Guitton, 1969).

The concept of the public sector

The debate about the proper size of the public sector is not based on a set of shared and precise concepts that contain an unambiguous definition; our first task is to consider what the concept — public sector — stands for. Most of the time it is taken for granted that the public sector is the budget(s) enacted by political assemblies. The emphasis is on political budgeting, the resources mobilized and disposed of by political assemblies at various levels of government. Such an identifying definition is, of course, only one among several possibilities. It does not recognize another major source of governmental impact on society, legislation. Actually, André Breton argued for a distinction between the *economic* and the *accounting* budget:

> I distinguish between the *economic* and the *accounting budgets* of governments, reserving the first term for the total of government outlays plus the difference between what citizens buy as a result of the legislation and what they would have otherwise freely purchased or to put it differently, plus the difference between the price of the goods that citizens are forced to pay and what it is worth to them (Breton, 1974:19).

The difficulty with the Breton distinction is that it has a counterfactual basis: if there were no legislation about the use of this or that item, which is false, then there would be so much lower costs. How are we to know with any degree of certainty what citizens would purchase 'freely' had they a choice? There are some loose ends in the Breton suggestion; the impact of legislation is difficult to trace *in toto* and how do we calculate the cost implications of choices never made — are we to attempt to estimate the costs incurred as a result of past legislation? Is it always the case that governmental legislation results in a uniform reduction in the freedom of all citizens or that the outcome of such legislation is always an increase in relative cost to the individual compared with free choice?

The definition of 'public sector' implied in the Breton argument may be rendered formally like this:

(DF1) 'Public sector' $=_{\text{def.}}$ 'Government activity and its consequences'

Perhaps the concept of the public sector implicit here is some version of the traditional approach to the public sector as public administration or public authority (Ostrom and Ostrom, 1971); (DF1) may be replaced by

(DF1′) 'Public sector' $=_{\text{def.}}$ 'Government authority and its outcomes'

It must be emphasized that the definition (DF1′) focuses on legislation and authority more than budget and allocation; it is conceivable that the public sector could be all inclusive in the sense (DF1) that the government(s) would lay down complete and detailed directives as to what its citizens should do — directives which they would follow either from belief in the legitimacy of authority or fear of the cost of disobedience (Eckstein and Gurr, 1975). As it is not always the case that the unit that calls the tune also pays the piper, theoretically the public budget could be minimal and the public sector maximal. (DF1) or (DF1′) could be called the *authority interpretation* of the concept of the public sector.

Focusing on the budget, it seems to be reasonable to argue that the public sector consists of government consumption, investment and transfers. Thus:

(DF2) 'Public sector' $=_{\text{def.}}$ 'Governmental consumption, investment and transfers'

The *definiens* expression in (DF2) is reasonably adequate, as specifying a public sector for each and every country would not present insurmountable difficulties. However, it is easy to recognize that (DF2) is amorphous, since its three elements may vary considerably in relation to each other. The distinction between public consumption and investment on the one hand and public transfers on the other, is vital for the solution of the size problem;

one may wish to argue for some particular size of government consumption and investment on the basis of deliberations about the principle of consumer choice, while admitting another size for the transfer part in consideration of an equity argument. (DF2) may thus be replaced by the more precise

(DF3) 'Public sector' $=_{\text{def.}}$ 'Government consumption and investment'

(DF3) would be the *allocation interpretation* of the concept of the public sector. Arguments about the proper size of the public sector would then have to be supplemented by a statement regarding the proper size of public transfer payments. The difference between (DF2) and (DF3) would constitute the *distribution interpretation* of the public sector.

It is a commonplace that it does not follow from the fact that a government allocates resources that it also produces the goods or services thus consumed or invested. A fourth definition of 'public sector' could be like:

(DF4) 'Public sector' $=_{\text{def.}}$ 'Government production'

(DF4) would need clarification as it could refer to two different states of affairs, government provision as well as government ownership of the means of production. Thus, one needs to make a distinction between the *provision interpretation* and the *ownership interpretation*, because the first may rise without affecting the second. Moreover, a further distinction concerning the *employment interpretation* has to be introduced, because governments may provide many services without much government employment as well as employ many people without owning a substantial portion of the capital. Thus, (DF4) is ambiguous as it may refer to government provision (DF4′), ownership (DF5) or employment (DF6). If the various possibilities included under the heading public ownership of capital are recognized, (DF4) becomes even more precarious.

What are the logical relations between the meanings of the word 'public sector' thus far derived: government authority (GA), government consumption (GC) and investment (GI), government transfers (GT), government provision (GP), government employment (GE), and government ownership of the means of production (GO)? First, an increase in (GC), (GI), (GP), (GT),

(GE) or (GO) implies an expansion of (GA), but the reverse is not necessarily true, as the government may increase its authority without expanding its budget, its employment or its ownership. Secondly, (GC) and (GI) are, strictly speaking, independent of (GT), (GE) and (GO). It is, at least theoretically, possible for government to confine itself to the consumption and investment of certain portions of the total resources of society while refraining from any production on its own part. Practically, a certain amount of (GC) and (GI) is often tied to certain levels of (GE) as well as of (GO). Governments increase their consumption in order to employ people and they sometimes use their revenues to increase their ownership share of the means of the production, thereby also expanding their employment. However, the relationship between (GC) and (GI) on the one hand and (GE) and (GO) on the other is in no way a simple or linear one. It is often the case that a government increases its consumption without at the same time producing what it consumes itself. Logically, an increase in public transfers does not imply increased public consumption or public provision. Finally, there is a clear logical connection between government-owned means of production and government employment, such that a socialization of hitherto privately owned means of production leads to an increase in government employment; the opposite is, however, not necessarily the case.

The purpose of these simple distinctions is to emphasize that the public-private distinction is not one distinction but several. If the opposite to the public sector is sought, then we have to admit the possibility that there will be many different entities; actually their number will be a function of the various meaningful ways of specifying the concept of the public sector. In relation to the first concept of the public sector — government authority — we have private autonomy; in relation to the second concept of the public — public consumption and investment — the private would simply be private consumption and investment or net income after the government has taken its share in the form of taxes and reallocated part of these as transfers. That part of the total resources of society which governments use for their consumption and investment purposes constitutes the sphere of governmental choice, the opposite being private choice. The third concept of the public — redistribution — affects private choice but does not replace it. The private counterpart to the fourth, fifth and sixth concepts of the public are, of course, private provision of goods and services, private ownership of the means of production and employment in private organizations. Derivatively, we may now establish that the *size problem* is in reality several different problems; asking about the proper size of the public sector may imply at least five questions:

(1) What is the proper place of governmental authority in society? Or, how much private autonomy are we to recommend? The *problem of individual freedom*.

(2) What proportion of the total resources of society should be left to government choice as regards consumption and investment? And how much should be turned over to private choice? *The allocation problem*.

(3) How large should the governmental budget be? Or how much private income should be generated without governmental influence in the form of transfers? *The distribution problem*.

(4) How much of the means of the production should be owned by government? *The ownership problem*.

(5) How much of the work force should be employed in governmental organizations? *The problem of bureaucracy and of bureau size*.

Market and bureaucracy

Bypassing the semantic distinctions concerning the various meanings of 'public' and 'private' sectors it may be argued that what matters is not the manifestations of the public and the private in various spheres like allocation, income distribution, production and employment. The demarcation problem concerning the proper size of the public vis-à-vis the private is in essence a choice between two fundamentally different modes of social interaction. The *interaction interpretation* of the public-private distinction states that what unites the various public sector concepts is that they assume one model of government action typical of the public, which is very much in contrast to the model of interaction typical of the private sector and its various modes. It remains to be stated what this interaction distinction amounts to. Let us present a few quotations:

> There are two methods for the conduct of affairs within the frame of human society, i.e. peaceful cooperation among men. One is bureaucratic management, the other is profit management (von Mises, 1962: preface).

> The main issue in present-day political struggles is whether society should be organized on the basis of private ownership of the means of production (capitalism, the market system) or on the basis of public control of the means of production (socialism, communism, planned economy). Capitalism means free enterprise, sovereignty of the consumers in political matters. Socialism means full government control of every sphere of the individual's life and the unrestricted supremacy of the government in its capacity as central board of production management. There is no compromise possible between these two systems (von Mises, 1962:10).

Market is not only contrasted with bureaucracy by von Mises; the distinctions between private ownership and public ownership as well as the distinction between planned economy and consumer sovereignty are lumped into the market-command separation. No doubt one classical approach to the public-private distinction is that it is a matter of the separation between market and bureaucracy, but it must be emphasized that the distinction between market and bureaucracy is in no way an easy one nor may we assume that it coincides with other equally important distinctions.

A first step to an increase in conceptual clarity about fundamental concepts may be to identify the variety of concepts employed to describe the interaction distinction between the public and the private. It seems that the following distinctions are considered analytically related to the public-private distinction: exchange and authority, competition and hierarchy, laissez-faire and planning, market economy and command economy, capitalism and socialism, and freedom versus authority. Though this list of concepts may not be exhaustive, it does present an opportunity to analyse in detail the idea that the public-private distinction is the same as the separation between market and bureaucracy. These various distinctions may be contrasted to the market-bureaucracy distinction in order to elucidate the extent to which the market-bureaucracy distinction may be understood in terms of some specific pairs of concepts which also come close to the separation between the public and the private.

The second step would be to cross-tabulate these various distinctions in order to test whether they coincide analytically. It is conceivable that some of these concepts are logically related and that they draw on some of the aspects of the public-private distinction, but it is hardly likely that all these conceptual pairs are reducible to one major conceptual demarcation, that between market and bureaucracy. Actually it may turn out to be the case that the market-bureaucracy demarcation needs clarification in terms of the interaction concepts listed above.

It is often stated that in principle there are only two mechanisms for the allocation of resources, the market and the public budget. How do we characterize the difference between the two? Maybe a promising route to identifying what is distinctive about these two mechanisms of allocation or social choice in general is to try to state how they relate to some of the basic conceptual pairs listed above.

Theoretically, one may easily argue that the ownership distinction — private versus public ownership of the means of production — is different from the separation between market and public budget. The relationship between these conceptual pairs may be visualized in a 2 × 2 figure (see Figure 1).

FIGURE 1
Ownership versus allocation mechanism

	Market	Public budget
Private	I	II
Public	III	IV

Though the ideal-types of capitalism and of communism are oriented towards the combinations I and IV respectively, few argue that combinations II and III are logically possible. Most would state that combination II is also practical but the status of III is a contested issue. Some socialist theoreticians argue that market allocation is feasible even if the means of production are no longer privately owned, whereas some adherents of the market economy deny this. Though this is not the place to enter into the bewildering debate about the concepts of capitalism and socialism, it may be pointed out that combination I is often described as competitive capitalism while combination IV is identified as hierarchical socialism. However, it may be argued that the distinction between types of ownership in no way coincides with the separation between competition and hierarchy (Figure 2).

Private ownership of the means of production is not necessarily tied to a competitive pattern of interaction (I), although the standard welfare economic implication is that such a competitive pattern of interaction will eventually lead to a social optimum (Rowley and Peacock, 1975). Actually, the occurrence of hierarchy in the private sector manifesting itself in trends towards oligopoly and monopoly

FIGURE 2
Ownership versus interaction pattern

	Competition	Hierarchy
Private	I	II
Public	III	IV

has traditionally been considered a target for bureaucratic action by the public (II). The typical defence of hierarchy in the allocation of resources within the private sector is the occurrence of scale economies but it has been argued that hierarchy is often more rational than market when transaction costs are taken into account (Williamson, 1975). From a logical point of view, the occurrence of competition is possible in a system of publicly owned means of production. It is open to debate whether (III) is likely to occur, but in any case the fact that the government owns the means of production does not imply that hierarchy must drive out competition (IV).

Just as it is vital to separate the question of ownership of the means of production from the question of type of interaction pattern, it also seems important that the two basic mechanisms of allocation may be independently combined with the interaction types. Figure 3 shows the possible combinations.

FIGURE 3
Allocation mechanism versus interaction pattern

	Market	Public budget
Competition	I	II
Hierarchy	III	IV

The extent to which markets adhere to the model of perfect competition is not always easily determined and, even more problematic, is the hypothesis that markets on the whole tend to move away from conditions of full competition. In any case, combinations I and III are not simply theoretically possible, they actually exist. The hierarchical interaction patterns between requesters and appropriators is typical of the public budget, but the nature of the budgetary process does not exclude competitive elements. The provision of services may be contracted out to the highest bidder and competition between bureaus may be introduced by means of efficiency-promoting mechanisms that allow the ranking of the various bureaus in terms of output criteria, as Hans van Mierlo and Ernst Jonsson argue in this book.

If public budget-making is the same as planning then perhaps market allocation is the opposite of planning — what may be called 'laissez-faire'. It is far from clear what is to be understood by the concept of planning (Wildavsky, 1973), but one may identify two polar forms of social control. Generally speaking, production and consumption may either be planned or left to the choice of the participants in production and consumption. How do these two types of social control, planning versus laissez-faire, compare with the allocation distinction (Figure 4)?

FIGURE 4
Forms of control and types of allocation mechanism

	Market	Public budget
Laissez-faire	I	II
Planning	III	IV

Since market allocation exchange feeds on diffusion processes and public budget-making (command) expresses the authority of political decision-makers it may be assumed that the only possible combinations are I and IV. Rational budgeting it is claimed must be based on planning and planning is a substitute for the spontaneity and unpredictability of the laissez-faire of markets. However, these formulas equating markets with laissez-faire and public budgeting with planning have been seriously challenged. On the one hand, the idea of a PPB-system has been criticized as uncongenial to the way public budget-making works (Wildavsky, 1975; van Gunsteren, 1976). On the other hand, the relevance of combination III to an understanding of modern society has been pointed out. Charles H. Lindblom frames the concept of planner sovereignty to denote a social state where planners made choices in a market environment (III):

> Market systems, we now know, are not always private enterprise systems. Yugoslavia is a socialist market system of one type; other types not yet in existence can be imagined. We also know that any one of the world's actual private enterprise systems is a mix of several types of market system.
>
> Smith and Marx missed another possibility: the market as an instrument of central planning. We now know that in principle — and in emerging practice — central planning divides into two distinctive methods: administrative or authoritative planning, and market planning (Lindblom, 1977:93).

To sum up, the distinction between the public and the private sector is not the same as the distinction between public and private ownership, nor the same as the separation between a planned economy and a laissez-faire system. The problem of drawing a demarcation line between the public and the private does not totally coincide with the problem of how to mix competition with hierarchy. A large public sector may operate within the confines of markets, and a large private sector may include private bureaucracy. The size of the public sector in the budget interpretation of this concept is a function of how much government allocation or reallocation there is, neither of which necessarily imply a comprehensively planned economy, or public ownership of the means of production. Rather than being mutually exclusive, it appears that a public sector may interact with the market or with a system of privately owned means of production. It is often argued that a public sector of a certain size is a necessary condition for the existence of a market mechanism (c.f. Adam Smith). Government regulation may benefit rather than oppose the workings of the market mechanism. It is equally true that an expansion of the total resources mobilized by the budget does not necessarily imply a weakening of the market mechanism. If these resources are transferred back to the private citizens, then the operation of the markets for goods or services may sustain no damage. Government consumption and investment *per se* do not imply a command economy. First, an increase in public allocation would imply moving consumption and investment decisions from the private sector — citizens and organizations — to public collectives only if the goods so allocated could be allocated by the market mechanism. Secondly, even if budget-making replaces the market in

FIGURE 5
Production and consumption versus market and public budget-making

	Production	Consumption
Market	I	II
Budget-making	III	IV

consumption, then it does not *ipso facto* replace market operations with regard to production. The distinction between consumption and production is, of course, vital (see Figure 5).

Though the reliance on planning in the production or consumption spheres may reduce the scope for the market, two points must be emphasized. When the planning procedure introduces hierarchy or command, it may not actually replace the operation of the market, but it may supersede hierarchy in the private sector or result in the provision of goods that the market could not have allocated anyway (Holler, 1984). Even if the planning procedure may reduce the scope for market interaction, it may be combined with market-type institutions in various ways. Market-oriented production patterns may be combined with planned consumption; or market and planning may be combined in the same sphere of economic activity, as Wyn Grant and Manfred Konukiewitz show in this book. Those who argue that the public sector should be increased may do so, not because they unconditionally favour planning or command to the advantages of the market, but because these two collective choice mechanisms — public budget-making and the market — have their own areas, which may be combined without conflict. Thus, we find that an answer to the problem of choosing between a planned economy or a market economy does not exhaust the possibilities of dealing with the question of mixing the public and private sectors. It is possible to argue for the existence of a large public sector without favouring — carte blanche — comprehensive planning to the market. It could be argued that the public sector has a rationale in that it does what the market cannot do. Let us look at those criteria for determining the size of the public sector that do not imply that planning in general is to be preferred to the market. Thus, we will focus upon the justification for government allocation and reallocation, not the general justification for the use of the planning procedure instead of the market mechanism. Purportedly, there is a set of criteria from which follows a unique size for the public sector — its allocation of resources and its transfer of resources. A public sector exists because it allocates public goods. But what are public goods?

Nature of goods

A social choice mechanism may provide citizens with goods or services they believe they need; of course, citizens may disagree about the quantity or quality to be provided, which means that the choice mechanism must provide for rules of arbitration. However, there seems to be a set of goods which few citizens would not consider necessary: protection of internal and external peace, equality before the law and due legal process, and the enforceability of the principle of the contract. And these goods have to be provided by means of public policy, because they have properties that the market as an allocation mechanism fails to meet. The market mechanism is constructed around voluntary exchange for the interaction between citizens, the applicability of which is constrained by the occurrence of the free rider phenomenon (Buchanan, 1968). Consequently, there is a set of goods or services that has to be provided by means of authority, because a voluntary exchange approach results in a 'prisoner's dilemma' situation as the size of the citizen group increases (Olson, 1965). Thus there must be public policy as a function of market failure (the complementarity principle). A generalization of this argument in favour of policy as against market is the theory of public goods (Samuelson, 1954) or social wants (Musgrave, 1959). According to one theme in the public finance approach (Musgrave and Peacock, 1967), there is a set of goods characterized by non-excludability and jointness that the market mechanism cannot supply but that citizens want. The choice of the collective choice mechanism would thus follow from a consideration of the technical and economic properties of goods (Ostrom and Ostrom, 1977) (Figure 6).

Non-excludability implies market failure because non-excludability is only one side of the more general concept of non-appropriability (Head, 1974) or externality (Pigou, 1962), which means that the price mechanism cannot be employed to appropriate the full social benefits or charge the full social costs. Jointness or

FIGURE 6
Typology of goods

	Jointness	Rivalry
Non-excludability	Pure public goods	Common pool goods
Excludability	Toll goods	Private goods

publicness, however, does not carry any institutional implications as the market may allocate such things in an efficient manner (Demsetz, 1970). Public policy would accordingly be responsible for the allocation of a special set of goods, the purely public goods characterized by the combination of publicness and non-excludability, like defence, whereas the market would take care of the other types of goods. The choice between institutions — voting and bureaucracy on the one hand and market on the other — would be a strict consequence of the citizens' preferences in relation to the possible mixes of purely public goods and other kinds of goods. It has been maintained that this approach to determining the scope of institutions by means of the nature of the goods is the same as the classical minimal theory of the state — the guardian state. However, there is nothing to prevent the allocation of most of the resources of society to the provision of public goods — a maximum theory of the state as it were. If PC is the possibility curve concerning the possible combinations of public goods and private goods given the technology and resources available in a society, then the social welfare function may pick either locus A or B, depending upon the preferences of the citizens and the actual rule of summation of individual preferences employed. If locus A is chosen, then market will dominate over policy and vice versa if locus B is adhered to (see Figure 7).

The difficulty about the theory of purely public goods is that its basic concept — non-appropriability — is not a very precise one. Positive or negative externalities in production and consumption may be identified for almost all goods; there is no such thing as a neatly identifiable set of goods describable as non-excludable, whereas all other types of goods would be characterized by excludability. If externality is a property that occurs to a greater or lesser extent among all types of goods, then there would hardly be

FIGURE 7
The minimum and maximum state

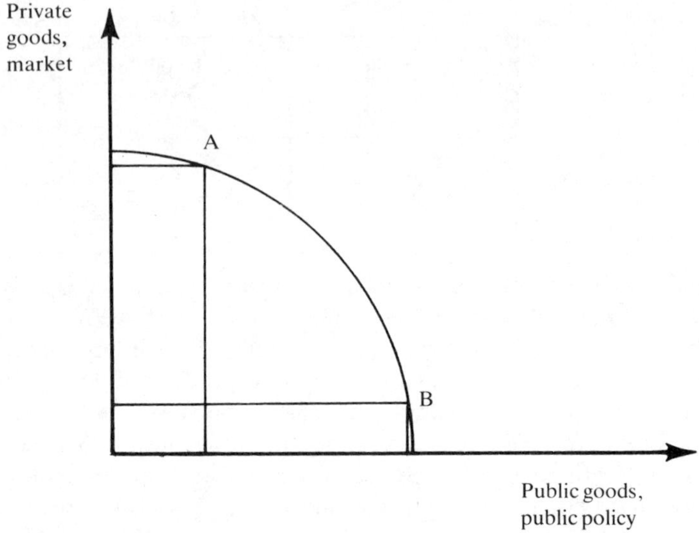

any limit to the size of public policy in relation to market. Actually, we would need an independent criterion that will inform us which externality is to be the target of public policy. Presumably, we could again use some social welfare function that would state how many of the externalities citizens wish to remove or promote by means of public policy and at what cost (Coase, 1960; Buchanan and Stubblebine, 1969). If such a welfare function is available, policy would complement the market in accordance with the citizens' preferences (between loci A and B in Figure 7). It is conceivable that any such social welfare judgement would include considerations not only concerning the relative bad or good of externalities but also concerning the capacity of government to take action. Thus, the existence of non-appropriability in itself can never be a sufficient condition for public policy; not only do we have to know the preferences of citizens in relation to non-excludable goods or social wants, but we must also recognize the cost of implementing public policy. Consequently it is difficult to maintain a sharp distinction between the nature of the goods and the allocation mechanism. If the combination of non-excludability and jointness is an argument for public policy, then is combination of non-excludability and rivalry also one?

The tragedy of the commons

If the nature of goods is to govern the selection of the collective choice mechanism, then it should be the case that institutional considerations should not enter into the description of the salient properties of goods. However, the notion of common pool goods shows how tenuous the distinction is between technical characteristics and properties that derive from the institutional set-up. It has been argued that public policy should be resorted to when exclusion is impossible, but what does 'impossible' mean? Not possible given the present state of technology, or not economically feasible given the present state of economic institutions? Once it is realized that the description of goods in terms of the fundamental 2 × 2 figure is not fixed for all time but is dependent on the evolution of technology and institutions, the idea of a close relationship between goods and allocation mechanisms must be modified. Non-excludability may be a reason for public policy, but it may equally well be an argument for an improvement in technology and institutions so that a good or type of goods may become the subject of exclusion. A large number of resources in society are held in common, for instance exclusion is ruled out, but they are not characterized by jointness in the Samuelson sense: ' . . . each individual's consumption of such a good leads to no subtraction from any other individual's consumption of that good . . . ' (Samuelson, 1954). The problem here is not the provision of goods but the protection of goods. How is such protection to be provided, given that citizens demand or value it? If protection, that is exclusion, does not work, the market mechanism cannot work either. Taking an exchange approach the prisoner's dilemma problem is even more acute in relation to common pool goods than with regard to purely public goods, since consumption by one individual leads to a subtraction from any other individual's consumption. Thus, individual rationality would result in a rapid depletion of the common pool since the free rider would not only get something for nothing but also reduce the benefits of the others. Whereas some citizens may accept the free rider phenomenon in relation to pure public goods because they themselves value the good so highly — the exploitation by the poor of the rich (Olson, 1965) — this cannot be expected in relation to common pool goods. Each and every person will have a strong incentive to use up the pool but not to make any agreement about providing the protection. Are common pool goods, then, a reason for public policy? Where exchange may-fail authority may work, or maybe the solution lies in the transformation of the nature of the goods involved (Hardin and Baden, 1977)? Instead of resorting to public policy the common pool goods problem may be solved by changing the technology and institutions surrounding these resources with the result that exclusion is no longer impossible and market allocation becomes possible. If such goods are definable as private property, then exclusion becomes possible and the prisoner's dilemma situation is removed. Transforming the common pool good into private property may involve other kinds of costs, but it brings out clearly that non-excludability is not a sufficient condition for public policy. What matters is not whether public policy may do what markets cannot do at all, but the relative balance of the two in terms of both pros and cons. Instead of possibility we must look at efficiency.

Non-subtractability

The fact that citizens may be excluded from consuming a good does not imply that market provision is unproblematic. There is a set of goods that is characterized by jointness while simultaneously full exclusion is feasible, so-called toll goods. The collective choice problem vis-à-vis toll goods is to find a choice mechanism that recognizes the public nature of these goods when the principle of exclusion is applied: what is the advantage in excluding citizens from consuming the good if their consumption of the good does not reduce its value with respect to others? Consequently, the provision of toll goods like roads, parks and some types of communication systems involves a paradox; in contrast to purely public goods excludability is not technically or economically impossible, that is, the costs of providing these goods may be covered and there will be no prisoner's dilemma; but on the other hand it is not socially advantageous to exclude citizens since the marginal cost of consuming the goods is nil, or very little. To employ the exclusion principle in relation to toll goods would mean that it would give rise to a considerable negative externality. There would also be the risk that the benefits arising from economies of scale would not be taken advantage of; actually jointness is an extreme version of non-subtractability which may be modelled as an economy-of-scale phenomenon. What allocation mechanism is appropriate in relation to non-subtractability when combined with the principle of exclusion? A distinction between two different types of non-subtractability may be introduced in order to facilitate the discussion of the pros and cons of the two basic allocation mechanisms: public policy or the market.

(1) Economies of scale in consumption

Jointness implies that each citizen consumes the same good and that the variety of citizen preferences regarding the good is expressed in terms of differences in the marginal willingness to pay (Lindahl mechanism). Thus, the social demand curve will be the outcome of a vertical summation of the individual demand curves and the quantity provided will be determined where the supply curve intersects with the vertically derived demand curve. Suppose there are no economies of scale in production; then a market allocation of the toll good will require a system of differential prices in order to match the variety of individual demand curves. Is such a system of price discrimination possible? It has been argued that one type of market allocation mechanism — perfect competition — cannot handle this problem, because in a perfect competition situation the price is supposed to be outside the control of producers and consumers. Thus, according to one authority:

> Perfect competition is simply not capable of generating marginal prices which discriminate between different consumers of a given product (Head, 1974:79)

Another expert on market allocation suggests:

> Price differences for the same good in the world of private goods are inconsistent with perfect competition. But price differences can be consistent with competition because a firm that sells a unit for R_2 or R_1 in markets D_2 and D_1 does not forego the sale of the same unit to market D_3 at price R_3 (Demsetz, 1970:302).

The difficulty with a market allocation of toll goods lies perhaps not so much in what type of market is the proper one — perfect competition or monopolistic competition. Both would face the same problem which becomes increasingly difficult as the size of the citizen group demanding the good becomes larger: How is knowledge about the variety of citizen preferences for the jointly supplied goods to be secured so that a system of differential prices may be employed which reflects these different preferences? Could such an information base ever be devised? Beyond a certain limit for a group of citizens there would no doubt be a strong case for public policy or the public provision of toll goods, as the market allocation of these goods by means of price discrimination may result in considerable social costs. If the price is varied over groups of citizens in a manner that does not correspond to the differences in citizens' preferences, then private cost may be larger or smaller than social cost. If the price varies between groups of citizens reflecting their different demand schedules, then each citizen would have an incentive to distort his/her preferences. Whilst the free-rider problem creates fundamental problems for the market allocation of public goods and common pool goods, the preference distortion problem lies at the core of a market provision of toll goods. Actually, the whole idea of a system of differential prices for jointly consumed goods appears to be unrealistic. When toll goods such as theatres, cable TV or telephone services are provided by markets, then either a homogeneous price is employed or the good is divided up into a variety of goods by means of distinctions such as a seat in the front or a seat at the back in theatres for example.

(2) Economies of scale in production

The provision of toll goods may create another kind of difficulty in relation to market allocation as certain types of toll goods display the phenomenon of decreasing marginal cost (Musgrave, 1959:137). Even if excludability is in principle possible, perfect competition may be impracticable due to the production conditions involved in, for instance, the provision of roads or electricity. The standard analysis of the case for monopoly applies (Bilas, 1971). If there are increasing returns to scale, then the long-term marginal cost will be less than the long-term average cost, meaning that perfect competition cannot be employed (Layard and Walters, 1978). The monopoly mechanism allows for the provision of these toll goods as the price may be made equal to the long-term average cost, thus avoiding losses to the producer (Ramsey optimal price). However, this is not an efficient solution from the point of view of society. Since the price does not equal the marginal cost there would still be a case for public policy intervention in the market. Either the government may pay the monopoly to expand output until price equals marginal cost or there may be public provision of the good financed by means of taxation. Thus, decreasing cost phenomena may be one reason for public policy because the market — either as perfect competition or monopoly — may not meet the standard efficiency condition; however, it must be strongly emphasized that public policy in relation to non-subtractability is not a sufficient condition for social efficiency. Of course, it does not follow from the fact that there is market failure that there will be policy success. Public intervention, in one form or the other with regard to the provision of toll goods will only be an improvement in comparison to market provision if the defects inherent in the public production of these goods are fewer than the standard market failures (too little output at too high a price). What are the difficulties involved in the public allocation of goods? Let us look at the arguments in favour of government allocation of private goods — the debate between socialism and capitalism.

The Barone theorem

Private goods are, of course, the opposite of purely public goods, that is, they satisfy the principle of excludability and the utility derived from their consumption is internalized by the citizen consuming the good. Presumably, these are the types of goods that are suited to the operations of the market as an allocation mechanism: there are no externalities and there is full subtractability, that is, each citizen may act independently of others. What are the conditions for an efficient allocation of this type of good? Does public policy and/or the market satisfy these conditions?

Allocative efficiency has two components following the basic approach in welfare economics (Lange, 1969): exchange efficiency and production efficiency. Exchange efficiency refers to a state where further trade cannot advance the utility of any one citizen without lowering that of another, that is, the marginal rates of substitution between any pair of goods are the same for all the individuals who consume the goods. And efficiency in production means that no change in factor inputs will bring about a larger output of any good without reducing the output of another good, that is, the marginal rates of transformation between any pair of goods is the same for all producers of these goods. A top level optimum — *optimum optimorum* — is reached when the marginal rate of substitution equals the marginal rate of transformation for all pairs of goods in society. It may be shown that, if there is perfect competition, the price system reaches such a top level maximum if the production possibility set is correct. May we then conclude that the provision of private goods should be left to the market as the appropriate allocation mechanism and that public policy should play no part in satisfying individual wants for private goods? Certainly not. Perfect competition is only a sufficient condition for social efficiency with regard to allocation of private goods. It follows from the Barone theorem that public policy may also satisfy the efficiency conditions (Barone, 1935). The ministry of production in the socialist state may achieve exchange efficiency, production efficiency and a top level efficiency to the same extent as the market can, if government has the same information as that utilized by the market. And this is one crux of the matter: is the acquisition of such a vast knowledge of citizen preferences and production possibilities practically feasible (Hayek, 1935)?

The controversy between a planned economy and a market economy boils down to the information and incentive problems: could public policy assemble and process the same amount of information that is contained in a decentralized market system as well as motivate choice participants to find socially rational solutions? According to socialist economists this is indeed possible, not only theoretically, but also from a practical point of view (Lange and Taylor, 1964). This view has been sharply challenged by those who argue that planning is not conducive to efficiency with regard to the allocation of private goods (Caiden and Wildavsky, 1974). Anyhow, the welfare economics theorem about the necessary conditions for efficiency in allocation may be turned against the market and used as an argument in favour of public policy, government planning or ownership of the means of production (Lerner, 1944; Radomysler, 1969; Little, 1973). It is argued that the market as it actually operates in real life falls far short of the perfect competition model with its monopolies, oligopolies and the phenomenon of monopolistic competition. This means that the market allocation of private goods fails to fulfil the efficiency conditions, which could be attained by means of public policy and planning (Bohm, 1976). Thus, in terms of socialist economics the Barone ministry of production should replace the market. Again, we must remind ourselves of the fact that the occurrence of market failure is only a sufficient condition for public policy if it can be shown that public policy entails policy failure less often than markets entail market failure. Nobody has ever been able to prove this, nor does the available empirical evidence concerning the amount of efficiency in planned economies indicate that this is the case.

Efficiency considerations as a foundation for the choice between public policy and the market imply that the principle of citizen sovereignty should be upheld; thus, the question is which mechanism of allocation is the most suitable one, given the preferences of the citizens in a democracy? The starting point in these deliberations and arguments about the complementary or substitution principles is that the preferences of the citizens concerning what goods they need are clear; it is time to look at an approach that states a case for public policy and which bypasses the principle of citizen sovereignty.

Merit goods

To what extent should the outcomes of a collective choice mechanism reflect the preferences of citizens? Some would argue that the principle of citizen sovereignty is inviolable and that social choice is a procedure for the summation or aggregation of individual preferences. Following this approach, it becomes vital to ascertain the extent to which market choice or public policy is in agreement with the preferences of a majority of citizens, or socially consistent. A quite different approach is to demand that social choice be normative, that is, that it satisfies ethical requirements whatever the preferences of the citizens may be. According to one version of this doctrine, public policy must be employed to assure the allocation of merit goods, goods that are meritorious according to some standard set by public policy (Musgrave, 1959). The identification of merit wants, of course, opens up the possibility of extensive public policy making to replace market behaviour and market outcomes. There is no limit to how many merit goods there should be apart from those that the normative standard implies. On the other hand the concept of merit goods identifies a crucial dimension in the concept of a social state or a collective outcome, the fact that as citizens we may wish to consider individual rationality as being different from collective rationality (Hardin, 1982). Even if individual citizens do not value education, culture and art, they may agree that these goods are in the interest of the collectivity and thus should be provided for by means of public policy. The problem is the definition of the concept of individual wants or preferences; is the collective choice rule to be based upon the preferences of the citizens for both private and public wants? Once normative considerations come into the picture alongside the positive deliberations, the problem of demarcation between market and public policy moves into the area of ethics or social justice. It is typical for these to turn up in demarcation criteria as redistribution criteria or in terms of principles of equity.

Justification of public resource allocation

The demarcation problem comprises making a separation in the total set of resources of the society and specifying which goods are to be allocated by government and which are to be allocated by the market. Are there criteria for the identification of these two sets of goods? Instead of talking about how planning or command may replace the market and vice versa, as in the literature on the theme capitalism versus socialism, the demarcation problem looks for the optimal combination of the two allocation mechanisms — market and public budget-making — finding that set of goods for which each has an advantage. The arguments have one end: to show the extent and variety of the occurrence of *market failure*, which then would constitute the argument in favour of the use of the public budget.

What are the implications of the market failure phenomenon for the size problem? According to the public finance tradition the public sector has a proper place in society — a place that may be determined unambiguously through an investigation of the combined technical and economical properties of goods. We do not need to resort to criteria other than technical and economic properties of goods plus citizens' preferences (consumer sovereignty).

If these three entities are known for a society, then we know the size of the public budget. It is a sort of 'theory of the state' where we have

> an attempt to determine which, if any, are the circumstances in which the people composing an economy will find that a particular extension of the authority of their government is requisite for the most efficient pursuit of their own economic interests (Baumol, 1965:51).

Thus, we must see if there is a set of properties that may be employed as decision criteria to derive a set of goods which government is to allocate in accordance with consumer preferences. The preceding examination suggests that the following decision criteria are relevant: non-appropriability and non-subtractability. To what extent do these criteria have more specific implications for determining the proper size of the public sector in so far as public resource allocation is concerned?

In principle, a good is non-excludable when potential consumers *cannot* be excluded from consuming the good. However, with a slight change, the criterion may be economic in nature: it is not economically feasible to exclude potential consumers once the good is supplied to one consumer. However, it matters whether exclusion is to be technically or economically feasible. Whereas the technical criterion indeed delimits a set of goods so that they may properly be designated non-excludable, the economic criterion on the other hand is much less sharply applicable: when is it economically unfeasible to exclude people from consuming a good? The application of the economic criterion appears to require a new criterion— a supplementary criterion that reveals what exclusion is to be allowed to cost. What goods are strictly non-excludable following a definition of the exclusion principle as 'enjoyment of a commodity after paying the price set by its owner' (Musgrave, 1959:9)? The Ostroms mention the following goods:

> peace and security of a community, national defense, mosquito abatement, air pollution control, fire protection, streets, weather forecasts, public TV (V. and E. Ostrom, 1977:12).

One could argue that it is not quite clear in relation to some of the items mentioned — streets, public TV and weather forecasts — whether they are non-excludable on the grounds of a technical or economic interpretation of the principle of exclusion. However, since potential consumers cannot be excluded from the enjoyment of these items if supplied by means of an exchange system of competition with various producers and different prices, the market mechanism must fail. But — and this is the crux of the matter — is non-excludability a necessary and/or sufficient criterion for public resource allocation? As will later be shown, most of the items now included in public budgets hardly satisfy a technical criterion of non-excludability, from which follows that it is an open question whether it is in fact a necessary criterion for public resource allocation. It could not possibly be a sufficient criterion, because there are many goods that are non-excludable by means of the market mechanism— positive and negative ones — and we need a criterion that tells us which of these goods the government should allocate and in what amounts. It appears that non-exclusion is simply the pure type of the concept of externality (Head, 1974:81).

Thus, if we want to use the criterion of non-excludability as an argument for government resource allocation we must have a new criterion that tells us in addition which externality will be the basis for how much of government action. Of course, the non-excludability criterion cannot help us here as it needs for its application the very same criterion that we are looking for.

What are the implications for public policy of non-subtractability or decreasing cost? Jointness in supply or demand seems to imply market failure, because jointness implies a system of differential prices for one and the same good, whereas perfect competition implies uniform prices for different amounts of the good supplied by competing producers. Jointness would thus constitute the second type of market failure. But is jointness a necessary or sufficient condition for public resource allocation? First, very few goods are truly non-subtractable or carry zero marginal cost. In fact, there is a large set of goods often allocated by government that is characterized by limited subtractability or decreasing marginal cost: health care, electricity and gas services, water and sewage systems, education, and so on. Owing to overcrowding, all such goods display non-subtractability up to a certain limit only. We thus need a new criterion which will indicate when the extent of non-subtractability or of the phenomenon of decreasing cost is such as to necessitate public resource allocation. Pure non-subtractability could hardly in itself constitute a necessary condition for public resource allocation, because there are hardly any such goods. Even for such typical Samuelsonian goods as national defence or clean air, there are trade-offs: one part of the country may be supplied with the good so that the availability of the good in other parts of the country decreases or increases. The fact that one subset of citizens consumes a certain amount of such a good may certainly have clear implications for the consumption of the good by other citizens. It seems difficult, not to say impossible, to argue that jointness is a sufficient condition for public resource allocation, because there may be many goods characterized by some non-subtractability or decreasing cost that may conveniently be allocated by the market mechanism: swimming-pools or various kinds of sports facilities, higher education, health care and so on. Obviously, we need a new criterion that will tell us when the amount of jointness reaches a level that indicates public resource allocation. Secondly, even if it followed from the occurrence of market failure in the face of non-subtractability or decreasing cost that a good should be allocated by means of public resource allocation, we still need to know *how much* of the good is to be provided by government action. The criterion of jointness is a *type criterion*, not an *amount criterion*. It will help us understand what kinds of goods are suitable for government provision, but it does not carry any implication whatsoever as to the size of good to be provided. The missing link is, of course, preferences.

In fact, the properties of non-excludability and non-appropriability hardly suffice to delimit a discrete set of goods or services that may be designated the proper sphere of public budget-making, because these properties are better conceived of as ordinal variables, which means that we have two ways of ordering goods in a cartesian space: *extent of externality and extent of jointness*. What are the *public policy implications* of various degrees of externality and various degrees of jointness? The conclusion of the public finance literature is, of course, that government should counteract the effects of externalities and jointness in such a way as to restore the top level optimum. Thus, by talking about degrees of non-excludability and degrees of jointness we may move away from the simplistic notion of a set of goods, some of which the government should allocate. Instead, we focus on some specific properties of whatever goods there are which may constitute criteria for public resource allocation. Two such criteria are central: externality in both the positive sense of impossibility of exclusion and in the negative sense of non-rejectability, as well as the decreasing cost phenomenon.

If goods characterized by the phenomenon of decreasing cost cannot be efficiently allocated by the market, then is decreasing cost a sufficient condition for public resource allocation? Surely, we cannot know the public policy steps to be taken simply from knowing that certain goods display decreasing cost in production. In the first place we must know how much of the good is needed, for instance we cannot derive the size of the good from a knowledge that it is characterized by decreasing cost. The phenomenon of decreasing cost implies government action, but it does not imply a definitive size of public resource allocation. The decisive point is how much citizens demand of the goods that display the decreasing cost property — and not the other way around. Thus, we still need another criterion besides decreasing cost in order to derive a size for the public sector, such as preferences. Taking an individualistic approach, it is a matter of the preferences of the citizens, whereas a collectivistic approach focuses upon the preferences of the state, as Ted Gurr and Desmond King argue in this book.

The occurrence of externalities as the basis for government action is a typical argument in the welfare economics tradition. Baumol only considers externality as the criterion for public resource allocation (Baumol, 1965:52). What is an externality? The phenomenon of externality is usually approached as a divergence between private marginal utility (cost) and social marginal utility (cost) in production or consumption:

(1) positive externality: private marginal utility is less than social marginal utility.
(2) negative externality: private marginal cost is less than social marginal cost.

The government disposes of a number of measures to create equality between private utility and social utility as well as between private cost and social cost (Johansen, 1978:178–84). Are we to conclude that externality is a sufficient condition for public resource allocation? Most fundamental is the objection that government must resort to other criteria in order to arrive at a conclusion as to how to handle the variety of externalities. How is government to know the level of social utility or social cost associated with a good if the market mechanism is not to be trusted? The crux of the matter is that whereas the operation of the market mechanism allows for the aggregation of individual decisions into social outcomes, no corresponding mechanism lies in the hands of government or bureaucracy. In order to arrive at conclusions about the level of marginal social utility, government must know not only how each single individual values the goods in question but also how to aggregate these various individual values. Only if government knows the preferences of the citizens in relation to various externalities (as well as how to add them together) is it possible to arrive at definitive conclusions about how much to allocate. Thus, we end up again with the need for a new criterion — preferences — that will help us sort out the implications of externalities for public policy. If consumer preferences govern the market, then *the symmetry thesis* implies that citizens' preferences may govern the size of the government effort:

> In a democratic society, the decision to satisfy one or another social want cannot be imposed in dictatorial form. It must be derived, somehow, from the effective

> preferences of the individual member of the group as determined by his tastes and his 'proper' share in full-employment income. A political process must be substituted for the market mechanism, and individuals must be made to adhere to the group decision (Musgrave, 1959:10–11).

Thus, we arrive at the obvious conclusion: in order to determine the size of the public sector we need, in addition to the economic and technical criteria, *political criteria* that state how the preferences of the citizens with regard to those goods which satisfy the technical and economic criteria are to be aggregated into a collective decision — what economists call a social welfare function. Market failure occurs in relation to the allocation of goods that display two different types of reciprocities or interdependence between human beings; in the case of externality, reciprocity implies that the actions of one person affect the actions of another person, or

$$U_a = f_a(a_1, a_2, \ldots a_n, b_k); \quad (1)$$

in the case of jointness, the utilities (U) of each person depend upon the consumption of the very same good by several individuals, or

$$a_1 = b_1 = c_1 = n_1. \quad (2)$$

Any society faces a choice with regard to these two types of reciprocities: how much of them do we want? If a society wishes to favour interaction based on jointness, then the public sector will no doubt be large. Similarly, if a society cares about externalities, there will be a great deal of public resource allocation. However, if the actions of independent utility maximizers, bypassing any joint action, are considered more important than reciprocities, then the public sector will be small. The size of the public sector is not a function of properties of goods, nor of the preferences of the citizens, but of the prevailing social welfare function — what Wildavsky calls 'culture' in this book. How to handle the problem of reciprocities versus independence or autonomy is a task for ideologies, and the solution to the problem cannot be derived by investigating 'economic' matters only.

Implementation

Fundamentally, there are two approaches to the choice between public policy and the market, the complementarity principle of the public finance school and the substitution principle of the adherents of a planned economy or a socialist economy. Both approaches share the assumption that public policy is an alternative to the market when, and in so far as, the market fails to operate in accordance with its theory. The disagreement concerns the extent to which there is market failure in reality. To the public finance scholars the market only fails because of the nature of goods — non-appropriability as well as non-subtractability — whereas the believers in a planned economy observe market malfunctioning in terms of institutional deviance, monopoly, oligopoly and monopolistic competition. The weakness inherent in both positions or approaches is that there is no estimation of the likelihood of public policy failure. Theoretically, we cannot compare the probability of market failure with a model of perfect public administration (Hood, 1976). This amounts to an absolute comparison between the market and public policy: when the one fails the other will operate smoothly for certain. Instead we must move to a relative comparison of the pros and cons of each allocation mechanism; thus we must base the choice on some theory about the probability of policy failure. Given the objective of the collective choice, be it efficiency in production or consumption or equity in the distribution of resources, the probability of market failure must be balanced against the likelihood of policy failure as the basis for evaluation of the choice mechanism to be employed. The mere existence of market failure is not a sufficient condition for public policy, because there may also be policy failure. How do we estimate the probabilities of the four types of cases in Figure 8?

The argument that public policy may be superior to the market is

FIGURE 8
Public policy versus market

		Market: Success	Market: Failure
Public policy	Success	I	II
	Failure	III	IV

most often based on the assumption of an ideally perfect fiscal system, the expenditures of which achieve what the market cannot accomplish and the financing of these items is neutral with respect to the market operations (Buchanan, 1967). Recent policy literature has gone a long way towards shattering belief in both the possibility and the desirability of public policy making. If public policy is the attainment of ends by the employment of means (Tinbergen, 1967; Dror, 1974), then doubts have been raised as to the capacity of public policy to pursue ends and means adequately, as Lennart Lundquist shows in this book.

(1) Ends failure

The ends of public policy designate what social states are desirable. In a democracy the set of desirable social states is some function of what the participants in the choice process consider desirable. The social welfare function is the aggregation of the preferences of the participants; it contains a description of social indifference curves according to which it is always possible to make Pareto optimal adjustments. How does one make choices between different social welfare functions? Typically, the participants in a collective choice process disagree about the shape of the social welfare curve with the result that bargaining or the unanimity rule may not do. Public policy making as a choice mechanism specifies the social welfare function by means of majority voting procedures. However, it has been shown that majority voting may result in the minority beating the majority (Downs, 1957) or in outcomes that are irrational (Arrow, 1963). Moreover, majority voting appears to be facing severe difficulties in combining elementary decision properties and is open to strategy-proof difficulties (Sen, 1970; Mueller, 1979; Moulin, 1983), though the likelihood of these defects should not be exaggerated (Ferejohn, McKelvey and Packel, 1984).

The evaluation of the capacity of public policy decision processes to satisfy basic, ethical choice properties proceeds from the assumption that ends are precise and clear, the problem lies in the aggregation difficulty. However, a more fundamental version of the ends failure argument is the statement that ends in public policy, whether those of the participants or the collectivity, are anything but clear and precise. Ends are ambiguous and have a more symbolic than real function in public policy making (Wildavsky, 1979).

(2) Means failure

Even if it is possible to arrive at socially desirable ends it does not follow that public policy will work. The availability of technologies that identify which ends may be accomplished in terms of what means is crucial to policy making. Technology is knowledge about the causal connection between ends and means in public policy. And technologies may be anything but certain. There is an abundance of literature which argues that public policy or public administration lacks reliable technologies (Rose, 1984). Even if policies know their objectives they do not know how to achieve these or how to accomplish them in an efficient manner. It appears that the larger the organization, the larger the technology problem (Hedberg, Nyström and Starbuck, 1976) though organizations, including the state and its modes, operate under a rationality assumption (Thompson, 1967). One consequence of the difficulties in arriving at reliable means-ends technologies is an increase in the probability of implementation failure. Again, experiences with implementation seem to accord poorly with the model of perfect implementation (Dunsire, 1978). Some argue that implementation is almost bound to fail to fulfil its objectives (Pressman and Wildavsky, 1984). In any case the implementation of public policy is not a simple task and may require complicated action patterns including bargaining and implementation tactics (Bardach, 1977).

Combining the ends failure argument with the means failure argument we arrive at the possibility of extensive garbage-can processes in public policy (March and Olsen, 1976). Thus, we have Figure 9:

FIGURE 9
Typology of policy failure

		Ends: Unambiguous	Ends: Ambiguous
Means	Reliable	Policy success	Policy diffuseness
	Unreliable	Policy uncertainty	Policy failure, garbage can processes

It used to be argued that there should be as much public policy as there was common interest among the citizens. Individual wants would then be handled by the market where each citizen could act by him/herself to maximize individual utility. Social wants were to be provided for by means of a politico-administrative procedure in which neutral politicians and bureaucrats would allocate resources in accordance with citizen preferences aggregated according to some proper rule. However, there is no longer much adherence to the theory of common interest. The objective function of politicians and bureaucrats comprises not simply the provision of some goods according to a budget restriction, but the individual wants of these actors, the goal of reelection and the search for scale also play a part (Breton, 1974; Phelps, 1962; Niskanen, 1971; Tullock, 1970). If it is in the very nature of a bureaucracy to attempt to allocate resources wastefully, then how could there be policy success? If politicians attempt to maximize a utility function consisting of the probability of reelection and personal gains such as pecuniary rewards, power and prestige, how could public policy have the advantage over the market as regards the efficient allocation of resources? If it is true that tax policies are not devised to optimize common interest aspects such as neutrality or efficiency (Musgrave, 1959) but to satisfy the needs of a revenue-maximizing Leviathan (Brennan and Buchanan, 1980), then maybe all the paraphernalia of constitutional reform and constitutional constraint on public policy are necessary in order to avoid the negative effects of public policy? Efficiency in public policy is a function of bureaucratic behaviour; it may be true that bureaucracies, relatively speaking, do better when it comes to the redistribution of income than in the allocation of goods and services. However, governments mix allocation and redistribution policies in a manner that makes bureaucracies crucially important, not only with regard to a small set of purely public goods, but also as the providers of merit goods on a large scale. If it is true that bureaucratic behaviour implies waste (Tullock, 1965), then how can we be certain that a large public policy provision of goods and services will bear any relation to the common interest? Though bureaucracy in the public sector may deliver, it may deliver at staggering opportunity cost. Yet, a fundamental objection to the idea of a common interest is that citizens may differ in their preferences for the common interest. If citizens are grouped into two homogeneous groups demanding different portions of the public budget, what will be the common interest? What would stop the majority from using the public budget or public policy to their own advantage? This holds true not only with regard to redistribution policies, where the possibility of exploiting the minority need not be doubted, but it may also be true for public goods — pure or impure. Citizens demand public goods as a function of their willingness to pay, but there will only be a Lindahl equilibrium between two homogeneous groups (for example, rich versus poor) if they are equally strong. If not, there is nothing in theory to prevent the majority from imposing upon the minority a common interest that it does not want and also placing the burden of financing it on the minority.

If the question is asked whether we should use the market or public policy as the collective choice mechanism in order to arrive at social choice the usual approach is to compare the relative advantages of each with the other. However, the focus should include the relative disadvantages. If the ideal models do not work in either case, which is worse: market or public policy? Is it more difficult to handle policy failure than market failure? If the markets fail, there is always the exit option, whereas policy failure has to be countered with voice. And exit tends to be more efficient than voice (Hirschman, 1970). Though this may be true generally, there are limits to exit in certain market-type situations and voice may be quite effective where the principles of contestation of power operate fully. However, public policy displays an inertia to an extent that the market does not, which makes public policy much less flexible than the market; a programme on the public budget tends to remain an item of public expenditure. And public policy tends to be very insensitive to signals of change, meaning that processes of adaptation are slow. It is impossible to arrive at any final, overall judgement as to whether policy failure is worse than market failure, as this would depend on the decision involved, the types of goods and services to be provided. The choice between market and public policy, if based on the advantages and disadvantages of each choice mechanism, could thus be expressed in the two equations:

$$V(M) = PXB - PXC \tag{1}$$

$$V(PP) = PXB - PXC \tag{2}$$

where the market is to be preferred to public policy only if:

$$V(M) > V(PP) \tag{3}$$

The value of the market exceeds that of public policy if its probable benefits minus its costs exceed the expected value of public policy.

It may well be the case that public policy can deliver where markets fail; market failure may be extensive in relation to goods and services which are very much in demand by citizens, meaning that there is a real necessity for public policy. The public household has a rationale, no doubt; we only have to point to some purely public goods, common pool resources and toll goods involving considerable non-excludability or jointness in order to state a case for public policy; many would argue the redistribution case of equity for public policy. But policies have their costs. How do we pay for the public household? Markets have their revenue logic, which implies the identification of a budget constraint for the provision of goods as well as a natural way of eliminating whatever does not meet the criterion of fiscal solvency. Whilst there may be a case for public expenditure because of market failure, the revenue aspect of the public household is much less impressive. Basically, public policy may be paid for by means of benefit taxation, the ability to pay taxation or deficit spending (Musgrave and Musgrave, 1980; Buchanan, 1967, Brennan and Buchanan, 1980). Benefit taxation is only possible to a limited extent, because total application of the principle of benefit taxation to pay for public policy would require an elaborate information system that would indicate each citizen's willingness to pay in relation to each good. This is not feasible, (preference revealing problem), nor are redistribution policies possible under benefit taxation. Resorting to the principles of ability to pay implies that the relationship between sacrifice and benefit becomes obscure in public policy. Moreover, even if it is true that there are Laffer curve limitations on the extracting capacity of governments (Laffer, 1981), the combination of benefit and ability to pay taxation does not imply a budget constraint on public policy owing to the extensive use of deficit spending.

Justification of redistribution

The attempt to derive implications about public resource allocation from an argument about the properties of public goods is based on the idea of aggregating individual and technical efficiency into social efficiency. The argument contains three elements:

(a) the Pareto principle

(b) the market mechanism and the public budget-making mechanism
(c) the principles of externality and jointness.

It is assumed that the application of (a), (b) and (c) will give an optimum allocation of resources, which will result in a distribution of income. However, a fundamental idea is that the resulting distribution of income may not be just because the initial income distribution was not equitable. Though the workings of the efficiency criteria are neutral, the outcome may still be socially unacceptable. The application of the allocative principles requires that matters of equity be relegated to the distribution branch, which may secure a just, initial distribution of income before the beginnings of exchange and public goods provision (Lindahl and Wicksell in Musgrave and Peacock, 1967). The idea of an *ex ante* welfare distribution criterion has the same function as the general idea of a social welfare function that is a necessary complement to the efficiency framework (Bator, 1957; Bergson, 1938). The social welfare function in the perspective of the welfare economist is supposed to supply the *equity* criterion, which may, of course, also be employed as an *ex post* criterion. In the words of Head:

> In welfare maximization analysis for *both* a private goods world *and* a world with a public good, we obtain a utility possibility locus or infinite set of Pareto-optimal points corresponding to different distributions of welfare. In both cases the choice of unique optimorum or optimum optimorum requires the strong value judgements of a social welfare function (Head, 1974:94).

Whether the social welfare function is to be employed *ex ante* or *ex post* the operation of the allocative principles is a contested issue; here, the important point is that the efficiency argument is supposed to govern the size of the public sector in the allocation interpretation, whereas the equity argument expressed in a social welfare function is assumed to solve the problem of arriving at a size for the public transfer. Technically speaking, the problem of deciding how equity is to be combined with efficiency is usually approached in terms of a utility possibility curve and a social welfare function applied to that curve (Figure 10). This means employing an *ex post* procedure to solve the problem, the equity consideration being applied after the resources have been allocated and the incomes distributed by whatever decision mechanism is considered efficient (T). All discussions about the equity-efficiency combination proceed on the basis of the assumption that the private goods world is to be regulated

FIGURE 10

***Ex ante* and *ex post* equity**

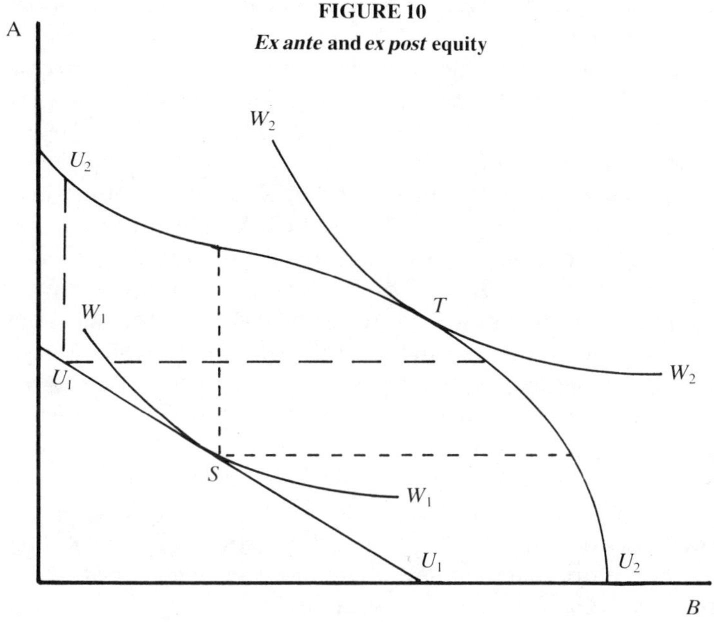

by the market with the government supplying the public goods. Obviously, if we know the welfare function we could apply it *ex ante* making sure that the working of the efficiency principle does not exacerbate the original inequities (S).

From a political science stand-point, using the social welfare function construction as a tool to bridge the gap between the allocation branch (efficiency) and the distribution branch (equity) of the public budget raises important theoretical issues concerning the relationship between the principle of social justice (equity) and the nature of collective choice. First, the working out of the efficiency principle following, basically, consumer preferences for public goods and private goods would depend for its final outcome on the initial distribution of incomes. If the initial distribution of income is not in accordance with the equity principle, how can we apply a social welfare function *ex post*? If the initial distribution of income is equitable, then we do not need a social welfare function *ex post*. If the resulting distribution of income is not in accordance with the principles of equity, then of what use would the *ex ante* criterion be? The problem is that in determining how much income redistribution there should be, no distinction can be made between the *ex ante* and *ex post* application of a social welfare function. When a government decides how much equity it wants in terms of income distribution it has to face the fact that the prevailing outcomes are efficient only in a conditional sense, given the initial distribution of income; moreover, it necessarily changes the efficiency operations when it redistributes income. In a dynamic perspective, including both *ex ante* and *ex post* situations, efficiency and equity cannot be separated. Suppose we have a society of two individuals A and B, whose utility situations *ex ante* and *ex post* are depicted in Figure 10. If A and B are at S and the *ex ante* equity criterion is considered satisfied, then we do not need to make a new equity decision *ex post* (T). If A and B are not at S at some non-equitable point — a 'false start' — the outcome of the efficiency principle may constrain the *ex post* choices in such a way as to make an optimal *ex post* situation impossible. But how is government to know what would have followed had we started from S or outside S? Moreover, the *ex ante* and *ex post* criteria do not have to be the same as we may wish to apply a Rawlsian maximin rule to the outcomes of a primary state of equity. But if we want to employ two equity criteria why bother about *ex ante* equity? Secondly, there is the even more fundamental problem of specifying a principle of equity in the first place. What is social justice?

Equity

The standard approach to equity is to argue that efficiency considerations are only necessary but not sufficient for the derivation of a social state. Allocative efficiency offers a number of efficiency loci, the choice amongst which has to be made on the basis of redistributive criteria or social justice (Samuelson, 1958; Mishan, 1981; van de Graaf, 1957). How are principles of social justice to be identified? If equity is interpreted as equality we get the famous distinction between equality *ex ante* and equality *ex post* (Thurow, 1980). Of course, the market cannot afford these equity principles, since they are supposed to be relevant to collective choice before or after (or both) the operations of the market. However, this does not imply that equity must be at odds with the market principles. It is possible to conceive of principles of equity which legitimize the market. If the established order of rights and duties is accepted as the starting point for the derivation of an efficiency locus, then public policy may be dispensed with. It can be shown that perfect competition tends to distribute income in accordance with the marginal product value of the factors (Henderson and Quandt, 1958). It could be argued that the profits derived in other market situations might be regarded as justified because they may be used for risk-prone activities.

In any case, the quite correct analysis that any social welfare function involves equity considerations does not imply that public policy must replace or complement market activities. This is an ethical question, the solutions to which are contested. The equity consideration as a basis for the choice between market and public policy is indeterminate; the implications to be derived from the principles of equity depend on the principles one adheres to. Such principles may offer a straightforward defence for the market, the contractarian man of Buchanan (1977) or the minimal state of Nozick (1974), or they may suggest far-reaching intervention in either the presuppositions of the market or the outcomes of the market, as in the Rawlsian maximin and difference principles (Rawls, 1971). Ultimately, the choice between market and public policy with regard to social justice depends upon the valuation of merit versus equality of result and will in each situation be determined by some combination of ideological considerations and expediency deliberations (the equity-efficiency trade-off). Thus, the choice between market and public policy as a function of equity would depend on how much redistribution of income and wealth society wants and is prepared to pay for (Okun, 1975). Basically, there are two types of definitions of the equity principle in a social welfare function: the *derived* and the *absolute* definition.

Perhaps the social welfare function is an enlightened decision principle, the rationale of which everybody would recognize once they accept the right perspective; if people assume a veil of ignorance, they will find the difference principle (Barry, 1972) or a utilitarian solution (Harsanyi, 1977); if they pursue a contractarian perspective, they will see the attractiveness of the unanimity principle or the Pareto Rule. The difference principle and the contractarian perspective are merely versions of the *ex ante* equity criterion, because they start from the idea that a choice of a preferred social state should not be based on the actual preferences that people hold in relation to present-day activities. The welfare function containing the equity principle should follow from the preferences people would hold before they become immersed in the interests of the present-day world. But how are we to know what the veil of ignorance and the contractarian state really imply if these states are fictions? The ideal welfare function, whether in the form of the Rawlsian maximin principle or the Buchanan Pareto Rule, introduces a political maxim into the attempt to derive a government size from the preferences of the consumers/citizens. It may, of course, be challenged by other ideological principles.

Only if the social welfare function is derived by means of some aggregation rule from individual welfare functions is the public finance requirement of consumers' sovereignty satisfied.

> The basic rule is that resources should be allocated in response to the effective demand of consumers, determined by individual preferences and the prevailing state of distribution. Indeed, social wants are quite similar in this fundamental respect to private wants (Musgrave, 1959:13).

Even if it were possible to allocate public goods in strict accordance with the diversity of individual preferences by means of an intricate system of differential prices, the applications of the distribution principle changing the outcome of the allocation by means of transfer payments must be zero-sum. In order to move along the utility possibility curve, the social welfare function must contain criteria for how conflicting interests are to be accommodated. Consequently, we need political criteria that will inform us as to when it is proper for a majority of citizens to implement a social welfare function against the will of the minority. We will need metacriteria to arrive at criteria for the aggregation of citizen's preferences — and these criteria cannot be justified merely by referring to the principle of consumer sovereignty. Actually, the idea of a functional correspondence between private goods and public goods — supply follows demand — is abandoned by the acceptance of a third category — merit goods. According to Musgrave:

> They (social wants) become public wants if considered so meritorious that their satisfaction is provided for through the public budget, over and above what is provided for through the market and paid for by private buyers (Musgrave, 1959:13).

Merit goods may be interpreted as redistribution. Redistribution may be in cash or in kind. Various kinds of redistribution may be identified: broad horizontal, life cycle and insurance type, vertical as well as fragmented horizontal redistribution among minority groups, besides redistribution to organized interests (Lindbeck, 1984:1). The existence of categorical equity has implications for the distinction between the public and the private. We may wish to make a sharp distinction between the allocative and redistributive branches of government, the former providing goods and services in accordance with the criteria of externality and jointness whereas the latter would concentrate on *ex ante* or *ex post* transfer payments. Redistribution in kind means that we cannot make a simple distinction between efficiency and equity, between public resource allocation and public resource distribution. The public provision of goods and services has clear distributive implications whatever the nature of the goods involved. It is not only the case that the public allocation of private and semi-public goods carries redistributive consequences but also the provision of pure public goods may be employed for redistribution (Tullock, 1959). Under majority rule there is no guarantee that the groups that benefit from the composition of the budget are the same groups that pay the costs or that benefit equals sacrifice. The simple framework of efficiency and equity in determining the proper size of the state is muddled by the recognition that public resource allocation is not neutral in relation to considerations of social justice. It is not only a matter of efficiency in relation to public goods, but it involves redistributive criteria, as budgetary provision may discriminate either on the benefit or on the cost sides.

The admission of merit wants into the framework has two important implications; we will need two additional criteria:

(1) the criterion for meritoriousness

(2) the criterion for how many merit goods there should be.

It appears that it is not so easy to derive a social welfare function (SWF) from individual preferences; as a matter of fact the SWF may have to contain much more than individual values and some aggregation rule — an equity criterion. If a cardinal utility aggregation is impossible because the utility rankings of individuals are not strictly interpersonally comparable (Samuelson, 1965) and if the political decision process cannot generally devise an aggregation rule that satisfies a few elementary choice criteria, then how do we arrive at the necessary criterion? Will the actual workings of the political process suffice? Of course not, because social outcomes may fail to satisfy ethical criteria that make collective choice a function of individual values. E.J. Mishan is explicit on this point:

> . . . a SWF for society giving expression to a distributional ordering is *not* to be regarded as a sort of synthesis of the individual SWF's of a society of economic men

> or political men; not, that is, of men in the material circumstances of the world where choices are guided by self-interest no matter how far-seeing or enlightened. For the purpose of normative economics, at least, society's SWF ought to be regarded as a synthesis of the individual SWF's of men in their capacity as ethical beings, in which capacity their deliberations are guided solely by considerations of what is right and just (Mishan, 1981:130).

Thus, we are back to the ideal interpretation, but a solution to the size problem concerning the public sector cannot await the future arrival of ethical reasoning at some principle of equity that will meet with acceptance among men — reasonable men, contractarian man or man in the state of veiled ignorance. The obvious solution is the one employed by Samuelson: we simply assume that there is a SWF, that it is ethical and that it satisfies the Pareto principle for being a function of individual preferences:

> What is the best or ideal state of the world for such a simple system? . . . To answer this ethical, normative question we must be given a set of norms in the form of a *social welfare function* than renders interpersonal judgements. For expository convenience, let us suppose that will be supplied later . . . (Samuelson, 1955:351–52).

We may wish to know who is to give us the SWF and how the SWF is going to handle zero-sum situations.

Macro- and micro-solutions

Instead of starting from the properties of goods and bearing in mind that the possibility of exclusion and the existence of jointness are decisive for the use of allocation mechanisms, the failure perspective to the demarcation problem means that properties of the allocation mechanisms themselves will determine the demarcation problem. If public policy has the properties ascribed to it by Tullock — bureaucratic waste — and by Buchanan — revenue-maximizing Leviathan — then why not devise a solution to the demarcation problem by restricting the scope of public policy as much as possible? The traditional approaches to the demarcation problem proceed along a micro perspective, taking each type of good and service by itself and discussing the relative merits of the two allocation mechanisms, seeking a solution that is adequate in terms of efficiency and equity. The weakness of the micro solution is that it implies a public policy preference; if public policy is *prima facie* to do what markets cannot do, then there is hardly any limit to what public policy may be trusted to do. The outcome is that public policy will drive out markets if there is no awareness of the danger of policy failure or the weak financial restrictions on policy making. A macro-solution would be: tie public sector growth to economic growth so that the public-private balance will not be upset. If the number of resources in society grows then public policy may expand, but not otherwise except in national emergencies (Wildavsky, 1980). The strength of the macro-solution to the demarcation problem is that it identifies another dimension in the problem, the system level. The use of allocation mechanisms has, from the point of view of a systems level, profound implications for basic values in society, including the confrontation between individualism and collectivism. Those who adhere to a macro-solution, by fixing the public policy sector once and for all, argue that markets are an essential ingredient in a free society as they are based on the exit option. Fundamentally, public policy rests upon authority not exchange, and authority may be backed by power and coercion, however large the voice option may be. Moreover, collectivist allocation mechanisms like public policy feed on fiscal illusions that make citizens blind to bureaucratic strategies and to overspending by politicians (Buchanan and Wagner, 1977). A constitutional spending limitation decision would curb those forces conducive to overexpansion in the public sector.

The disadvantage of the macro-solution is that there is no way of knowing if the fixation of the size of public policy is a desirable decision in terms of efficiency. Maybe the actual preferences of consumers in combination with some criterion of efficiency in allocation imply that markets ought to be expanded and public policy reduced, or that public policy should be used even more. Will policy failure diminish if the rate of expansion of public policy is limited? It seems important not simply to identify some overall desirable size for public policy but to identify the causes of policy failure in each circumstance in order to discover whether the market could have performed better. If taxation or inefficiency is the major problem in public policy then it is not absolutely certain that a spending limitation decision will be the answer. Even after a constitutional amendment, which would limit the decision-making capacity of parliaments in a way that might be difficult to accept, we would still be looking for ways of solving the demarcation problem in order to put the allocation mechanism to its most efficient use in providing goods and services for the citizens. The macro-solution may be an important step towards such objectives as saving markets, but it does not solve the demarcation problem. Besides, such a demarcation solution does not solve the problem of the proper size of the domestic economy and the unofficial economy which may substitute for the official economy at times — as Richard Rose shows in this book.

Conclusion

It is often argued that the distinction between the public and the private sectors has become more diffuse in the mixed economies of the rich countries with representative governments (Johansen, 1979). Public policy is about to drive out the market, intervening in several different ways with the operations and outcomes of market allocation mechanisms. The traditional approach to the demarcation problem — how to separate and mix market and public policy — can no longer be used, whether it results in a complementarity principle or in a substitution solution. One cannot simply state a case for public policy over and above market failure; the probability of policy failure has to be taken into account, but is it feasible to calculate the expected value of the market and of public policy in order to arrive at an acceptable system solution? Perhaps we ought to try a constitutional solution to the demarcation problem, fixing in some way the relative sizes of public policy and market once and for all. But will this macro approach to the demarcation problem help us to make efficient adjustments and to replace public policy with markets whenever possible considering the fiscal crisis of public policy in the eighties. The macro-perspective in the search for constitutional decision making may divert attention from the various ways in which the gulf between the market and public policy could be narrowed. Market-type aspects like competition and consumption charges may be introduced into public policy to a much greater extent. If policy failure is so extensive, then we should focus both on a better division between market and public policy and also on improvements in the performance of public policy. In fact we may face a situation where markets will fail because it is a matter of providing goods that display a great deal of non-excludability of jointness, but where policy reform and the introduction of more market-type features are feasible.

There is not one single way to make the private-public distinction; it seems important to remember several interpretations of the public:

(a) bureaucracy
(b) planned economy
(c) authority
(d) public resource allocation
(e) public distribution of income
(f) public ownership
(g) public employment

Focusing on the allocation and distribution branches of the public we have inquired into whether a *positive* determination of the size of the public budget is possible on the basis of a symmetry between the private and public worlds. The symmetry thesis asserts that public resource allocation can satisfy efficiency and equity to the same extent as a well-functioning market mechanism does for a world of private goods. Actually, the symmetry thesis states that the size of the allocation branch follows from the technical and economic properties of goods and the preferences of citizens. Similarly, the size of the distribution branch would complement, not replace, the market operations on the basis of a social welfare function expressing the preferences of citizens in relation to equity.

It seems that a crucial element has been left out when deriving a size for the public sector: political criteria. The implications of technical or economic properties of goods for public resource allocation are indeterminate without criteria that state how government is to handle various degrees of externality and jointness. To derive these decision criteria on the basis of an aggregation rule from the preferences of the citizens is not in general possible, because such an aggregation rule may not always satisfy elementary ethical criteria. We need in both branches of the public finance system, social decision criteria or a so-called social welfare function. However, the implication that the social welfare function is only political decision-making is not in accordance with the symmetry hypothesis. Then, what is the SWF? A positive derivation of a definite size for the public sector using only goods' properties and citizens' preferences is not possible. The missing link is the idea that the SWF is 'given', but as political scientists we must take the next step and try to understand how and who is or should be 'giving' the SWF.

REFERENCES

Arrow, K.J. (1963) *Social Choice and Individual Values*. New Haven: Yale University Press.

Arrow, K.J. and Scitovsky, T. (1969) *Readings in Welfare Economics*. London: George Allen and Unwin.

Bardach, E. (1977) *The Implementation Game*. Cambridge: the MIT Press.

Barone, E. (1935) 'The Ministry of Production in the Collectivist State' in Hayek (1935).

Barry, B. (1972) *The Liberal Theory of Justice*. Oxford: Oxford University Press.

Bator, F.M. (1957) 'Simple Analytics of Welfare Maximisation'. *American Economic Review*, 47: 22–59.

Bator, F.M. (1958) 'The Anatomy of Market Failures'. *Quarterly Journal of Economics*, 72: 351–79.

Baumol, W.J. (1965) *Welfare Economics and The Theory of The State*. London: Bell and Sons.

Baumol, W.J., Bailey, E.E. and Willig, R.D. (1977) 'Weak Invisible Hand Theorems on the Sustainability of Multiproduct Natural Monopoly'. *American Economic Review*, 67: 350–65.

Bergson, A. (1938) 'A Reformulation of Certain Aspects of Welfare Economics'. *Quarterly Journal of Economics*, III: 310–34.

Bergson, A. (1954) 'On the Concept of Social Welfare'. *Quarterly Journal of Economics*, 68: 233–52.

Bilas, R.A. (1971) *Microeconomic Theory*. New York: McGraw-Hill.

Bohm, P. (1976) *Social Efficiency — A Concise Introduction to Welfare Economics*. London: Macmillan.

Borcherding, T.E. (1977) *Budgets and Bureaucrats: The Sources of Governmental Growth*. Durham: Duke University Press.

Borcherding, T.E. (1984) 'A Survey of Empirical Studies about Causes of the Growth of Government' (memo). Paper presented at the Nobel Symposium on the Growth of Government. Stockholm.

Breit, W. and Hochman, H.M. (eds.) (1969) *Readings in Microeconomics*. New York: Holt, Rinehart and Winston.

Brennan, J.M. and Buchanan, J. (1980) *The Power to Tax*. Cambridge: Cambridge University Press.

Breton, A. (1974) *The Economic Theory of Representative Government*. London: Macmillan.

Bridge, G. (1977) 'Citizen Choice in Public Services: Voucher System' in Savas, E.S. (ed.) (1977).

Browns, C.V. and Jackson, P.M. (1978) *Public Sector Economics*. Oxford: Martin Robertson.

Buchanan, J.M. (1965) 'A Theory of Economic Clubs'. *Economica*, 32: 1–14.

Buchanan, J. (1967) *Public Finance in Democratic Process*. Chapel Hill: University of North Carolina Press.

Buchanan, J. (1968) *Demand and Supply of Public Goods*. Chicago: Rand McNally.

Buchanan, J.M. and Stubblebine, W.C. (1969) 'Externality' in Arrow and Scitovsky (1969).

Buchanan, J.M. (1975) *The Limits of Liberty: Between Anarchy and Leviathan*. Chicago: Chicago University Press.

Buchanan, J. and Wagner, R.E. (1977) *Democracy in Deficit*. New York: Academic Press.
Buchanan, J. (1977) *Freedom in Constitutional Contract*. College Station: Texas A&M University Press.
Caiden, N. and Wildavsky, A. (1974) *Planning and Budgeting in Poor Countries*. New York: John Wiley and Sons.
Castle, F.G. (ed.) (1982) *The Impact of Political Parties*. Beverly Hills: Sage.
Coase, R.H. (1960) 'The Problem of Social Cost'. *The Journal of Law and Economics*, 3: 144.
Demsetz, H. (1970) 'The Private Production of Public Goods'. *The Journal of Law and Economics*, 13: 293–306.
van den Doel, H. (1979) *Democracy and Welfare Economics*. Cambridge: Cambridge University Press.
Downs, A. (1957) *An Economic Theory of Democracy*. New York: Harper and Row.
Downs, A. (1965) 'Why the Government is Too Small in a Democracy' in Phelps, E.S. (ed.) (1962).
Dror, Y. (1974) *Public Policymaking Reexamined*. New York: Leonard Hill Books.
Dunsire, A. (1978) *Implementation in Bureaucracy*. Oxford: Martin Robertson.
Eckstein, H. and Gurr, T.R. (1975) *Patterns of Authority. A Structural Basis for Political Inquiry*. New York: John Wiley and Sons.
Ferejohn, J.A., McKelvey, R.D. and Packel, E.W. (1984) 'Limiting Distributions for Continuous State Markov Voting Models'. *Social Choice and Welfare*, 1: 45–67.
Frey, B.S. (1978) *Modern Political Economy*. London: Martin Robertson.
Galbraith, J.K. (1967) *The New Industrial State*. London: Hamilton.
van de Graff, J. (1957) *Theoretical Welfare Economics*. Cambridge: Cambridge University Press.
van Gunsteren, H. (1976) *The Quest for Control*. New York: John Wiley and Sons.
Hardin, G. and Baden, J. (1977) *Managing the Commons*. San Francisco: Freeman.
Hardin, R. (1982) *Collective Action*. Baltimore: Johns Hopkins University Press.
Harsanyi, J. (1977) *Rational Behavior and Bargaining Equilibrium in Games and Social Situations*. Cambridge: Cambridge University Press.
Hayek, F.A. (ed.) (1935) *Collectivist Economic Planning*. London: Routledge and Kegan Paul.
Head, J.G. (1974) *Public Goods and Public Welfare*. Durham: Duke University Press.
Hedberg, B.L.T., Nystrom, P.C. and Starbuck, W.G. (1976) 'Camping on Seesaws: Prescriptions for a Self-Designing Organization'. *Administrative Science Quarterly*, 21.
Henderson, J.M. and Quandt, R.E. (1958) *Microeconomic Theory*. New York: McGraw-Hill.
Hibbs, D.A. and Fassbender, H. (eds.) (1980) *Contemporary Political Economy*. Amsterdam: North-Holland.
Hibbs, D.A. and Fassbender, H. (1981) *Contemporary Political Economy*. Amsterdam: North-Holland.
Hirschman, A.O. (1970) *Exit, Voice and Loyalty*. Cambridge: Harvard University Press.
Holler, M. (ed.) (1984) *Coalitions and Collective Action*. Würzburg: PhysicaVerlag.
Hood, C.C. (1976) *The Limits of Administration*. London: John Wiley and Sons.

Johansen, L. (1978) *Public Economics*. Amsterdam: North-Holland.

Johansen, L. (1978) *Lectures on Macroeconomic Planning*. Vols. 1–2. Amsterdam: North-Holland.

Johansen, L. (1979) 'The Bargaining Society and the Inefficiency of Bargaining'. *Kyklos*, 32: 497–522.

Laffer, A.B. (1978) 'Taxation, GNP, and Potential GNP'. *Proceedings of the Business and Economics Statistics Section*: 1978. Washington: American Statistical Association.

Laffer, A.B. (1981) 'Government Exactions and Revenue Deficiencies'. *Cato Journal*, 1, 1: 1–21.

Lane, J-E. (1983) 'The Concept of Implementation'. *Statsvetenskaplig Tidskrift*, 1: 17–40.

Lange, O. and Taylor, F.M. (1964) *On the Economic Theory of Socialism*. New York: McGraw-Hill.

Lange, O. (1969) 'The Foundations of Welfare Economics' in Arrow and Scitovsky (1969).

Larkey, P., Stolp, C. and Winer, M. (1981) 'Theorizing about the Growth of Government: A Research Assessment'. *Journal of Public Policy*, 2: 157–220.

Layard, P.R.G. and Walters, A.A. (1978) *Microeconomic Theory*. New York: McGraw-Hill.

Lerner, A.P. (1944) *The Economics of Control. Principles of Welfare Economics*. New York: Macmillan.

Lindahl, E. (1919) 'Just Taxation — A Positive Solution' in Musgrave and Peacock (1967).

Lindblom, C.H. (1977) *Politics and Markets*. New York: Basic Books.

Lindbeck, A. (1984) 'Redistribution Policy and the Expansion of the Public Sector' (mimeo). Paper presented at the Nobel Symposium on the Growth of Government. Stockholm.

Little, I.M.D. (1973) *A Critique of Welfare Economics*. Oxford: Oxford University Press.

Loerhr, W. and Sandler, T. (eds.) (1978) *Public Goods and Public Policy*. Beverly Hills: Sage.

Lybeck, J. (1985) 'A Simultaneous Model of Politico-Economic Interaction'. *European Journal of Political Research* (forthcoming).

March, J.G. and Olsen, J.P. (eds.) (1976) *Ambiguity and Choice in Organizations*. Oslo: Universitetsforlaget.

Margolin, S.A. (1963) 'The Social Role of Discount and Optimal Rate of Investment'. *Quarterly Journal of Economics*.

Margolis, H. (1982) *Selfishness, Altruism and Rationality*. Cambridge: Cambridge University Press.

Margolis, J. and Guitton, H. (eds.) (1969) *Public Economics*. New York: St Martin's Press.

von Mises, L. (1962) *Bureaucracy*. Westport: Arlington House.

von Mises, L. (1963) *Human Action. A Treatise on Economics*. New Haven: Yale University Press.

Mishan, E.J. (1981) *Introduction to Normative Economics*. New York: Oxford University Press.

Moulin, H. (1983) *Strategy of Social Choice*. Amsterdam: Elsevier.

Mueller, D. (1979) *Public Choice*. Cambridge: Cambridge University Press.

Musgrave, R.A. (1959) *The Theory of Public Finance*. New York: McGraw-Hill.
Musgrave, R.A. and Peacock, A.T. (eds.) (1967) *Classics in the Theory of Public Finance*. New York: St Martin's Press.
Musgrave, R.A. and Musgrave, P. (1980) *Public Finance in Theory and Practice*. New York: McGraw-Hill.
Nath, S.K. (1969) *A Reappraisal of Welfare Economics*. London: Routledge and Kegan Paul.
Niskanen, W.A. (1971) *Bureaucracy and Representative Government*. Chicago: Aldine-Atherton.
Nozick, R. (1974) *Anarchy, State and Utopia*. New York: Basic Books.
Oates, W. (1972) *Fiscal Federalism*. New York: Harcourt, Brace Jovanovich.
Okun, A.M. (1975) *Equality and Efficiency*. Washington: Brookings.
Olson, M. (1971) *The Logic of Collective Action*. Cambridge: Harvard University Press.
Ostrom, V. and Ostrom, E. (1971) 'Public Choice: A Different Approach to the Study of Public Administration'. *Public Administration Review*, 31: 203–16.
Ostrom, V. and Ostrom, E. (1977) 'Public Goods and Public Choices' in Savas (ed.) op. cit.
Phelps, E.S. (ed.) (1962) *Private Wants and Public Needs*. New York: Norton and Co.
Pigou, A.C. (1962) *The Economics of Welfare*. London: Macmillan.
Pressman, J. and Wildavsky, A. (1984) *Implementation*. Berkeley: University of California Press.
Radomysler, J. (1969) 'Welfare Economics and Economic Policy' in Arrow and Scitovsky (1969).
Rawls, J. (1971) *A Theory of Justice*. Cambridge: Harvard University Press.
Riker, W.H. and Ordeshook, P.C. (1973) *An Introduction to Positive Political Theory*. New Jersey: Prentice-Hall.
Rose, R. (1981) 'What if Anything is Wrong with Big Government?' *Journal of Public Policy*, 1: 5–36.
Rose, R. (1984) *Understanding Big Government: The Programme Approach*. London: Sage.
Rowley, C.K. and Peacock, A.T. (1975) *Welfare Economics*. London: Martin Robertson.
Samuelson, P.A. (1954) 'The Pure Theory of Public Expenditure' in *The Review of Economics and Statistics*, 34: 387–9.
Samuelson, P.A. (1955) 'Diagrammatic Exposition of a Theory of Public Expenditure'. *The Review of Economics and Statistics*, 37: 350–6.
Samuelson, P.A. (1958) 'Aspects of Public Expenditure Theories'. *The Review of Economics and Statistics*, 40: 332–8.
Samuelson, P.A. (1965) *Foundations of Economic Analysis*. New York: Atheneum.
Savas, E.S. (ed.) (1977) *Alternatives for Delivering Public Services*. Boulder: Westview Press.
Savas, E.S. (1982) *Privatizing the Public Sector*. New Jersey: Chatham.
Sen, A. (1970) *Collective Choice and Social Welfare*. San Francisco: Holden-Day, Inc.
Sharpe, L.J. and Newton, K. (1984) *Does Politics Matter? The Determinants of Public Policy*. Oxford: Clarendon Press.
Tarschys, D. (1975) 'The Growth of Public Expenditure: Nine Modes of Explanation'. *Scandinavian Political Studies*, 10: 9–31.

Thompson, J.D. (1967) *Organizations in Action*. New York: McGraw-Hill.
Thompson, E.A. and R.L. Faith (1981) 'A Pure Theory of Strategic Behavior and Social Institutions'. *American Economic Review*, 71: 366–80.
Thurow, L.C. (1980) *The Zero-Sum Society: Distribution and the Possibilites for Economic Change*. New York: Basic Books.
Tiebout, C. (1956) 'A Pure Theory of Local Expenditure'. *Journal of Political Economy*, 64: 416–24.
Tinbergen, J. (1967) *Economic Policy. Principles and Design*. Amsterdam: North-Holland.
Tufte, E. (1978) *Political Control of the Economy*. Princeton: Princeton University Press.
Tullock, G. (1959) 'Some Problems of Majority Voting'. *Journal of Political Economy*, 67: 571–9.
Tullock, G. (1965) *The Politics of Bureaucracy*. Washington: Public Affairs Press.
Tullock, G. (1970) *Private Wants, Public Means*. New York: Basic Books.
Whitely, P. (1980) *Models of Political Economy*. London: Sage.
Wicksell, K. (1896) 'A New Principle of Just Taxation' in Musgrave and Peacock (eds.), op.cit.
Wildavsky, A. (1972) 'If Planning is Everything, Then Maybe it is Nothing'. *Policy Sciences*, 4: 127–53.
Wildavsky, A. (1975) *Budgeting: A Comparative Theory of the Budgetary Process*. Boston: Little, Brown and Co.
Wildavsky, A. (1978) 'Changing Forward Versus Changing Back. Lindblom: Politics and Markets: The World's Political-Economic Systems'. *The Yale Law Journal*, 88: 217–34.
Wildavsky, A. (1979) *Speaking Truth to Power. The Art and Craft of Policy Analysis*. Boston: Little, Brown and Company.
Wildavsky, A. (1980) *How to Limit Government Spending*. Berkeley: University of California Press.
Williamson, O. (1975) *Markets and Hierarchies*. New York: The Free Press.

2

Improvement of Public Provision of Goods and Services

Hans J.G.A. van Mierlo
Erasmus University, Rotterdam

The aim of this chapter is to criticize the methodological foundations of the dominant thinking about existing modes of provision of goods and services and to make some suggestions for the improvement of public provision on the basis of the results of this survey. In the public debate of the 1980s, the explosive expansion of the public sector is considered to be an enormous problem, which threatens the achievements of the welfare state and the survival of the democratic political system. Public choice theory can explain how this point has been reached and what can be done to solve some of the problems.

Some suggestions for improvement

Using the paradigm of 'consumer sovereignty in politics', the only criterion for over- or underexpansion of the public sector lies in the individual preferences of the citizens. It is not clear how individual preferences relating to the public sector should be interpreted at the present time. Some indicators point in the direction of overexpansion, such as the popularity of 'reaganomics' and 'deregulation', the existence of the 'black circuit', mass tax avoidance, evasion and fraud, and increasing civil disobedience in the economic relation between the state and the individual. Other indicators point in the direction of underexpansion, such as the ongoing cry for government intervention as the one and only 'problem-solving method'.

However, we notice that the political process as a transformation mechanism between individual preferences and policy output also has its serious defects, by which individual preferences as well as policy output are distorted. On the demand side, every decision-making model, be it a democracy or a bureaucracy, influences in some way individual preferences. On the supply side, problems of government intervention mainly arise because of the technical characteristics inherent in the public goods which are provided and because of the organization of the provision. It can be argued that the mere existence of these problems leads to overexpansion of the public sector, but one need not draw that conclusion in order to make suggestions for the improvement of the functioning of the public sector in Western democracies. The following suggestions for improving public provision need further exploration: (a) the application of the benefit-principle in financing, (b) competition in production through self-management by civil servants and (c) competition in consumption through exit options.

The benefit-principle in financing

The benefit-principle for taxation was originally developed by classical public-finance theorists such as Lindahl and Wicksell (in Musgrave and Peacock, 1967). The principle can also be derived from Bowen's vertical addition of demand curves for collective goods, as used by Samuelson in his famous polar presentation of the collective good / individual good dichotomy. Musgrave and Musgrave (1976: 55–6) add a caveat to the usefulness of this principle for taxation of 'pure collective' goods. In their opinion, it is misleading to suggest that the provision of collective goods might be implemented by a market mechanism of demand and supply, with equilibrium at E, as in the case of an individual good. This interpretation implies that consumers will bid as they do for individual goods and thus overlooks the crucial fact that preferences for collective goods (or willingness to bear sharing of the cost in line with marginal benefits) will not be revealed voluntarily in the absence of exclusion possibilities.

Where the number of participating consumers is large, it is in their interest to act as free riders and the action of the market breaks down, as is demonstrated by Olson (1971). Where a small number is involved, bidding will indeed occur, but the outcome will be determined by bargaining and may deviate from the competitive result. The demand schedules of Samuelson's representation do not come into play. They are so-called pseudo-demand schedules, based on the unrealistic assumption that individual preferences are revealed. A political approach, that is a kind of voting system, must be taken to compel preference revelation. Individuals, knowing that they must comply with the decision made by the collective choice via the voting process, will find it in their interest to vote for that solution which will bring the outcome closest to their desires. In this way they will be forced to reveal their preferences. By serving as a mechanism for preference revelation, the voting process connects tax and expenditure decisions with each other.

The voter must be confronted with a choice between budget proposals which carry a price label in terms of his or her own tax contribution. This price label will depend on the total cost for the community as a whole as well as on the share to be contributed by others. The individual's choice is thus contingent on his own knowledge that others must also contribute in line with the adopted tax plan. It is this mandatory nature of the budget decision which induces preference revelation and permits the determination of collective good-provision. Wolfson (1979: 193–5) goes a step further. He stresses the point that the benefit approach to distributing tax burdens considers the relation between taxpayer and government in *quid pro quo* terms.

The public sector is seen as a market for (quasi-)collective goods where taxpayers offer user charges for the exact quantity of goods and services demanded. As a theory of exchange, the benefit approach has the conceptual advantage of providing for a simultaneous determination of public services and tax shares, thus combining both sides of the budget. Unlike the ability-to-pay approach, which considers taxes as compulsory payments and the revenue-expenditure process as a planning problem to be solved by policy makers, the benefit-principle ties the choice of public services to the preferences of individual members of the community. In this way, the benefit approach would not be restricted to distributing the financial burden of a given budget, but would also provide a vehicle for determining the size of the budget. On the basis of comparable arguments Bird (1976) concludes that the theoretical case for the benefit-principle of taxation would be far stronger than that for the more favoured ability-to-pay doctrine (Bird, 1976: 10).

Although the point is well taken with regard to quasi-collective goods, the contribution of the benefit approach to determining the size of the budget remains only notional where pure collective goods are at stake. Wolfson also points out the problem that, since nobody can be excluded from the benefits of a pure collective good, consumers will be most unlikely to reveal their true preferences. Thus, the entire intellectual effort of Wicksell, Lindahl and others to specify an optimal size for the public sector and to design tax prices equal to marginal benefits, provides in his opinion no more than a useful heuristic model. Besides the logical problem of application of the benefit approach to pure collective goods, it is generally argued as a major objection that benefit taxation is fair only in so far as the primary distribution of income is acceptable, since benefit taxation would, at best, have no progressive redistributive potential and, at worse, might be outright regressive. But this position is exaggerated, since user charges, like excises, can be structured to have a progressive incidence.

On the other hand, there is the danger of allocative efficiency-distortions. However, it must be granted that benefit taxation, with its incidence mostly on the user's side of income, generally cannot take account of needs that arise from taxpayers' family circumstances and individual conditions in a way that taxes at source, based on the ability to pay, can (with school fees as a notable exception). It seems on balance that systems based on the ability to pay leave more scope for upward graduation (by raising progression for redistribution purposes) than systems based on the benefit-principle. And if economic theory cannot provide much guidance in identifying the conditions for equal proportional sacrifice (see Keller and Hartog, 1977: 321–32), that cannot be helped.

In spite of the logical problem of application to pure collective goods and the empirical observation that it has regressive effects on income distribution, which arguments are excellently treated in Haselbekke (1981: 125–55), there remains a considerable number of public goods which are not pure collective and thus are suited for the application of a kind of benefit financing. Musgrave and Musgrave (1976: 212–15) give a brief overview of the possibilities. After rejecting, on logical grounds, a general benefit tax, they see the possibility of practical applications of benefit taxation where particular services are provided on a benefit basis.

This may be the case where direct financing is made via fees, user charges, or tolls. Alternatively, certain taxes may be imposed indirectly in lieu of charges, as is done on the taxation of gasoline and other automobile products for purposes of highway finance. This technique is feasible and desirable where the goods or services provided by government are in the nature of individual goods, that is where consumption is wholly rival. Where benefits are internalized, the government may act in a capacity similar to that of a private firm and the same pricing principles are appropriate. In other instances, where imposition of direct charges is desirable but too costly (perception costs, collection costs), a tax on a complementary product may be used in lieu of charges. Gasoline or automobile taxes may be viewed in this light. Other illustrations are certain uses of the property tax and social security taxes. By using a market mechanism, a more efficient determination of the appropriate level of supply becomes possible.

Competition in production: self-management by civil servants

The problem that the bureaucracy, according to the analysis of Niskanen (1971), does not work at an optimum, is further explored by van den Doel (1979: 133–43). He explains the bureaucratic oversupply by two factors: on the one hand the aims of leading bureaucrats, on the other the possibility of realizing these aims, which results from the monopoly position of a department. If remedies are to be found, they must be sought in the removal of these causes. In order to start the discussion on this subject, van den Doel launched the revolutionary idea of self-management by civil servants in 1973 (van den Doel, 1973: 28–30). In the same year Faludi (1973: 250), too, had concluded 'that departments formulating programmes, instead of being hierarchically structured, ought to be of a collegiate, self-directing type'.

The characteristics of self-management by civil servants, are defined by van den Doel as follows: (1) all civil servants in a department are equal from an organizational point of view in so far as they choose representatives on a majority vote, who decide on the department's policy and on the appointment of departmental heads; (2) the department is financed exclusively by a budget authorized by the politicians; (3) the politicians negotiate with the departmental representatives about the tasks to be performed for the budget to be provided, and they secure the co-ordination between the departments; (4) no single department has the exclusive right to provide specific public goods.

The fact that the aims of departments are directed at expansion results, according to this model, from the hierarchical structure of a department. The prestige, the salary or the power of the head of the department are increased by raising the output or the budget. Irrespective of idealistic considerations, it is also in his own interests to maximize the output or the budget. The pattern of behaviour of the department in the model changes radically if the hierarchical structure is destroyed. In so far as the civil servants are motivated largely by selfish and not altruistic considerations, the decisions will be made to suit the interests of the lower-ranking rather than of the more senior civil servants. An increase in output or in the budget will have consequences for a lower-ranking civil servant different from those which would have applied to his seniors in the previous hierarchy. An expansion of a department will inevitably mean that the work can no longer be overseen and that there will be a loss of social contacts for the lower-ranking civil servant. On the other hand, he can benefit in three respects from expansion. First, the number of supervisors per civil servant will grow so that the freedom for the individual to pursue his own policy increases. Moreover, he will have more chance of promotion. Finally, the existing amount of work can be divided among more civil servants.

However, in the opinion of van den Doel, many of the advantages of expansion will be lost in a model of self-management by civil servants. For a lower-ranking civil servant the gain in policy freedom is wholly compensated for by the loss of power, because he must share his authority with his colleagues when his section is expanded. In a model of self-management of civil servants, 'promotion' occurs mainly when some civil servants are elected as representatives. It is probable that a civil servant who desires such a 'promotion' will hold up expansion because he fears competition from his new colleagues. When departmental expansion is not expressed in a greater output but in less effort per civil servant, this will be punished in the model of self-management not only by politicians but also by competing departments. The managers appointed by the civil servants will also strive for expansion in a situation of self-management. But within their departments these managers do not possess the monopoly of information about the real cost schedules. Thus the stimulus for a large departmental expansion will be reduced if it does not disappear altogether.

Vanek (1970, 1977) analysed the economic consequences of self-management within the firm. In a firm with a hierarchical structure, too, the benefits (that is, the financial benefits) of the production process will primarily be of advantage to the managers and the shareholders. As soon as there is a workers' autonomy, however, the benefit will be shared among all participants in the firm. A number of hypotheses are possible in respect of a workers' collective in such a situation (Vanek, 1977: 30, 32). In a wide, but vague, concept the workers' collective has many aims as regards income, effort, collective consumption, the environment, and community service. In a less wide, but more operational, concept, the members of the workers' collective strive after their own interest, confining themselves mainly to matters connected with their income. In this last concept, profit (or output) is not maximized, but the profit (or output) per worker (Vanek, 1970: 2).

However, an increase in profit (output) is not possible without an increase in the number of workers. The extra profit must therefore be divided among more workers. This leads Vanek to the conclusion that a self-managing firm does not tend towards overexpansion (Vanek, 1970: 119). By changing some mathematical equations in Vanek's model, Meade (1972: 417) has shown that lessening of the tendency to expand is solely the result of the introduction of a co-operative element in the aims. The simple mathematical model which was at the basis of van den Doel's idea about self-management was published by him in 1974. We do not represent it here. The conclusion of that model is that after self-management has been established, the civil servants no longer strive to maximize the total output or the total budget, but to maximize the output or the budget per civil servant.

The second main problem of bureaucracy is the monopoly position each department has. This monopoly position makes it possible for bureaucrats to make politicians choose between all or nothing, thus forcing them to buy their services at a loss. Political reformers, confronted with the power of a bureaucracy, are always trying to solve this problem by making proposals to tighten the external control of the bureaucracy. Van den Doel summarizes such devices: organization of parliament should be improved, members of parliament should concern themselves more with their departments, ministers should give more guidance, an ombudsman should be appointed, systematic policy analysis should be applied. These measures will have little effect: internal control is limited. So is external control. Only by stimulating competition between bureaucrats can the foundations of bureaucratic power be demolished. For this reason, the fourth characteristic of self-management by civil servants is that no single department should have the exclusive right to provide specific public goods. This implies that other departments will have free entry or that existing departments can take over the tasks of other departments on condition that the government finances these initiatives. This condition allows a government to pursue a policy of entry which makes it possible to avoid waste from duplication.

Under conditions of perfect competition in the administration, politicians are able to confine their executive task to comparing the various plans drawn up by a number of competing departments and choosing the best: they have an exit option (Hirschman, 1970). In practice, competition will never be perfect because it is difficult to set up a new bureaucratic department. Yet the possibility that a new department can be set up will work preventively. For fear of a potential competitor the existing departments will be more sensitive to the wishes of the politicians. The market for administrative services will no longer be characterized by a bilateral monopoly between the politicians and the bureaucrats, but will become an asymmetrical structure because one group of politicians will be able to negotiate with competing departments.

In the second characteristic of self-management it is laid down that in such a market structure the politicians will be the sole buyer (monopsony) which will give them a strong bargaining position. Although van den Doel himself admits that the significance of the model of self-management by civil servants is largely heuristic, the model indicates the direction in which bureaucratic reforms for securing optimal supply of public goods and services should go. More internal and external control, which do not change the hierarchical organization structure but strengthen it, will not solve the problem but will make it worse. Only the building-in of competitive elements in bureaucracy will improve its performance from the viewpoint of the individual preferences of citizens.

Competition in consumption: the exit option

The model of 'perfectly competitive capitalism' can only work in a market with separable, per unit divisible goods. Goods which technically cannot be split up in separate units for reasons of non-exclusiveness and non-rivalry, are not marketable: prices cannot be calculated, the rational price system is not possible and exclusion of consumption cannot be imposed. Subsequently the classical argument concludes with the impossibility of any competitiveness in the public provision of these goods. But in this conclusion two analytically completely different features are mixed up: on the one hand there is the technical characteristic of pure collective goods, on the other hand there is the political decision of public provision of goods. And, as we have seen, there is no logical relation between both features. Technical characteristics can be used as arguments for public provision, but welfare economics offers more arguments. In reality, all goods which are provided publicly are public goods, but not all public goods are pure collective goods! Many public goods contain elements of divisibility, and if this is the case, the conclusion of complete non-competitiveness in public provision breaks down. Elements of competition, price-calculations and marketability have to be considered then. Even competition in consumption of public goods becomes possible in the presence of elements of divisibility.

We start the argument with the so-called 'exit option', which concept has become well-known from Albert Hirschman's book *Exit, Voice and Loyalty* (1970). In this book the useful distinction is developed between processes in which individuals express their preferences via entry or exit decisions, and processes in which some form of written, verbal or voice communication is employed. An example of the first is a market for a private good in which buyers indicate their attitudes toward the price-quality characteristics of the good by increasing or decreasing (entry or exit) their purchases. An example of the exercise of voice to influence a price-cost nexus would be a complaint or commendation of the product delivered to the manufacturer. A necessary condition for the effective use of exit is that the potential users of this option be mobile. Full mobility of both buyers and sellers (free entry and exit) is an assumption underlying all demonstrations of market efficiency in the model of fully competitive capitalism.

In contrast with this, the literature focusing on voting processes, public choice and political science, has, as Mueller (1979: 125 ff.) asserts, almost exclusively assumed (most often implicitly) that exit is not an option. The boundaries of the polity are predefined and inclusive, the citizenry is supposed to be fixed. A citizen is at most allowed to abstain from participating in the political process, but he cannot leave the polity to avoid the consequences of its decisions. This is an extreme case of pure collectiveness of the good involved in the decision-making process. Given the assumption of fixed boundaries and citizenry, the characteristics of a pure collective good require that a collective *voice* or non-market decision process be used to reveal individual preferences and achieve Pareto efficiency as is emphasized by Samuelson (1954). For many public goods however, the non-exclusion principle and/or the non-rivalry property may not be applicable over the full range of possible production and distribution alternatives. For the quasi-collective or local-collective goods the possibility may exist for employing exit as an alternative or complement to the voice process. These possibilities are excellently reviewed in Mueller (1979: 126–47).

Following Mueller, the first exit possibility is *voting-with-the-feet* with regard to local-collective goods. This has to do with a relaxation of the non-rivalry property (economics of scale). Let us consider a collective good with no production costs, for example the proportion of tulips in the public square where bulbs are free. If the dimensions of the policy coincide with the population of consumers, the problem of preference revelation persists. However, let us assume that more than one polity can exist. Within any polity all must consume the same collective good (flower bed), but there are no spillovers between polities. With this limited degree of excludability, people can reveal their preferences for a local-collective good by moving into the community providing the most desirable fraction of tulips. Considering only the whole percentile options, 101 polities suffice to achieve Pareto optimality. Ballots need not be cast. All preferences are revealed through the silent voting-with-the-feet of individuals entering and exiting communities. This possibility is first noted in Charles Tiebout's *Pure Theory of Local Expenditure* (1956) and further explored in the theory of local-collective goods and the theory of fiscal federalism. In contrast to the disappointing promise of majority rule, unanimity and other traditional voting procedures, and the imposing complexity of newer, more sophisticated procedures for revealing individual preferences like the Clarke-tax, Tiebout's voting-with-the-feet procedure seems to accomplish the task via the surprisingly simple device of allowing people to sort themselves out into groups of similar preferences. Strategizing is eliminated and the voluntary association approach is operationalized through the assumption of full mobility between communities.

The Tiebout model is based on a number of extreme assumptions. The example above assumes no economies of scale, which is quite important to Tiebout's argument. The most important and at the same time questionable assumptions are the following: (1) full mobility of all citizens; (2) full knowledge of all of the communities' characteristics; (3) a full range of community options available spanning the range of collective good possibilities desired by the citizens (101 different polities in our example!); (4) no spillovers across communities; (5) no geographical constraints imposed on individuals with regard to their earnings. Every assumption of this list meets severe objections. Assumptions (1) and (4) tend to work at cross-purposes: assumption (1) requires small communities and assumption (4) large ones. Assumptions (2) and (3) raise complementary issues. The basic argument assumes a full range of possible baskets of collective goods available at the start. But how is this spectrum of opportunities established (the constitutional problem)?

An additional problem arises as the number of local-collective goods is expanded. Consider the consequences of introducing a second collective good in our example above; the proportion of oaks in the public square. This issue's solution requires the further separation of individuals into groups of identical preferences, now with respect to both flowers and trees. The number of polities necessary for Pareto optimality leaps to 101 squared. Each additional collective good raises the number of communities required to a higher exponent. If the number of collective goods is very large, one ends up with a situation in which the number of polities equals the size of the population. Each community-individual becomes a polity with a basket of public-private goods (gardens, woods) tailored to his own tastes, which possible consequence Tiebout himself observed from his model. Voting-with-the-feet achieves Pareto optimality by grouping individuals together in competing polities of homogeneous tastes. At the extreme, it satisfies the severe condition for consistent majority rule decisions, that all individuals have identical indifference maps, through the imposition of a silent unanimity rule. It can realistically be assumed to come close to satisfying this condition when, in relation to the size of the population, (1) the number of collective goods is small, and/or (2) the number of distinct preferences for combinations of collective goods is small. Since the task of public choice is the revelation of differing individual preferences for collective goods, voting-with-the-feet in part solves the public choice problem by significantly limiting its scope.

The second exit possibility distinguished by Mueller, regards the *theory of clubs*. Let us consider the effect of non-rivalry without non-excludability. That is, assume that exclusion is possible, but addition of a new member lowers the average cost of the good to all other members, that is they are economies of scale (the case of an impure or quasi-collective good). If average costs fall indefinitely, optimal club size is the entire population and the traditional collective good problem is present again. If they eventually rise, either because scale economies are exhausted (full capacity is reached) or from the additional costs of crowding (congestion costs), an optimal club size smaller than the whole population may occur.

J.M. Buchanan was the first to explore the efficiency properties of voluntary clubs using a model in which individuals have identical tastes for both collective and individual goods (1965). Buchanan first employed the example of the formation of a swimming club. Assume first that the size of the pool, and thus its total cost, is fixed and the only issue to be decided is the size of the club. For the members already in the club, the marginal benefits from an additional member decrease and the marginal costs increase. Given identical tastes and incomes, it is reasonable to assume equal sharing of the costs. The marginal benefit to the first member from adding the second member to the club is the saving of half the cost of the pool. The marginal benefit of the third member is the additional savings of one third of the cost of the pool. The additional benefits from adding new members, the saving to the other members from further spreading the fixed costs, continue to fall as the club size increases. The marginal costs of a new member are psychic costs. If individuals prefer to swim alone, these costs will be positive over the entire range. If individuals enjoy the company of others in small enough number, the marginal costs of additional members will be negative over an initial range of club sizes. Eventually, the positive costs of crowding will dominate and the optimal club size is determined where the marginal cost of an additional member from enhanced crowding just equals the reduction in the other members' dues from spreading the fixed costs over one more club member.

This kind of analysis can also be used for the polar cases of pure individual and pure collective goods. For a pure collective good, the addition of one more member to the club never detracts from the enjoyment of the benefits of club membership to the other members: marginal costs are zero, the optimal club size is infinity. For a pure individual good, crowding begins to take place on the first unit. If a consumer experiences any consumer surplus from the good, the utility lost from giving up half of his unit will exceed the gains from sharing its cost and optimal club size is one. But even with pure individual goods, as for example bread, co-operative consumption may be optimal. If the unit price of bread is lower when sold by the bushel, the distribution of bread will exhibit joint supply characteristics and might dictate optimal-sized buying clubs of more than one individual. The theory of clubs can be extended to take into account the choice of quantity and other characteristics of the collective good. The disutility imposed on the other club members from the addition of one more club member, must equal the proportion of the good's costs he pays, weighted by the marginal utility of individual goods to the representative member. Under normal assumptions changes in taste or technology leading to an increase in the amount of one of the variables will lead to an increase in the other. An increase in collective good quantity will increase each individual's share of the costs, raise the marginal disutility from additional club membership, and thus encourage a larger club size (Buchanan, 1965: 6–10).

The assumption that individuals have identical tastes and incomes is not as innocuous as it first might appear. As in the Tiebout model, it is inefficient to have individuals of differing preferences in the same club, if this can be avoided. If all individuals are identical but some prefer rectangular pools and others oval ones, then the optimal constellation of clubs will sort out individuals into oval and into rectangular pool clubs. The ideal constellation of clubs is one in which all members of any club have identical preferences. If the number of differing preference functions is small relative to the population size, this ideal can be met. An efficient allocation of these quasi-collective goods through the voluntary association of individuals into clubs of homogeneous tastes can be envisaged. The rules or charter of a club can be compared to a social contract unanimously accepted by all members (Pauly, 1967: 317). Under these assumptions, the theory of clubs is obviously much in the spirit of the contractarian voluntary exchange approaches to public choice and public finance. With a large number of alternative clubs available, each individual can guarantee himself the equal benefits for an equal share of the costs assumed above, since any effort to discriminate against him will induce his exit into a competing club, or the initiation of a new one.

If optimal club sizes are large relative to the population, discrimination is possible, and stable equilibria may not exist. With an optimal club size of two thirds of the population, for example, only one such club can exist. If it forms, those not in it have incentives to lure members away by offering disproportionate shares of the benefits gained from expanding the smaller club. But the remaining members of the larger club have incentives to maintain club size, and can attract new members by offering the full benefits of membership in the big club. And so on. No stable distribution of club sizes and benefits need exist (Pauly, 1967, 1970). Analytically the problem is identical with the cycle problem in coalition-formation. The two farmers forming a winning majority constitute an optimal-sized club, but one farmer left out has an incentive to try and form an optimal club too, and his efforts to form a new club can lead to an unstable equilibrium, a cycle. Even when stable equilibria are reached, the equal sharing of benefits may no longer occur if the optimal club size is large relative to the number of people having a given preference function. The threat of exit to another club will be weak if an individual's preferences are such that only a small and relatively inefficient club could be formed by individuals of identical tastes. Thus individuals with 'majority' preferences are in a better position to threaten withdrawal to optimal-sized clubs than those with 'minority' preferences, and coalitions with discriminatory sharing of the benefits from cooperation can be expected even when stable, Pareto-efficient club sizes are obtained.

Thus, the conclusion is similar to the voting-with-the-feet model. The voluntary formation of clubs to allocate collective goods is most attractive when the optimal size is relatively small, that is, when the quasi-collective goods have a limited degree of collectiveness. Despite this qualification, the voluntary formation of clubs is at least conceptually a more promising means for revealing individual preferences for collective goods than voting-with-the-feet, for it does not require geographic proximity of club members (Mueller, 1979: 134). In practice, most clubs do provide their benefits to a subset of a local population, as in Buchanan's swimming club example. But even here, it is not necessary for members of the local swimming club to join the golf club, and the problems associated with voting-with-the-feet are reduced through the formation of limited membership clubs.

Nevertheless, it should be remembered that the two devices are not interchangeable. Where local-collective goods are involved (limited excludability in combination with non-rivalness), competition between providing communities, allowing voting-with-the-feet, leads to Pareto optimality in public provision. Where quasi-collective goods are involved (excludability in combination with limited non-rivalness), competition between providing clubs, allowing voluntary membership, leads to Pareto optimality in public provision. The first refers to a geographical dimension of competition between different areas, the latter to a social dimension of competition between different clubs in the same area.

This brings us to the third possibility, the provision of local-collective goods which are produced with economics of scale. In this case it is even more unlikely that individual mobility suffices to achieve Pareto optimality. It is then necessary that there be 'just the right number of individuals' with identical preferences to satisfy the optimality conditions for each collective good. The complications of determining 'just the right number of individuals' are treated extensively by Mueller (1979: 134–42). Voting-with-the-feet in the presence of jointness of supply (economics of scale) is not discussed here further. Exit options, be it in the form of voting-with-the-feet between competing communities or in the form of voluntary membership of competing clubs within the community, are a direct and frequent response to local conditions. Further support for the Tiebout hypothesis is provided by econometric studies linking migration patterns to the levels of local public services and tax rates (Cebula, 1974, 1977). Exit options can be practised in the consumption of public goods by decentralizing public provision towards the level of local communities which compete with each other, or towards competing voluntary membership clubs. This building-in of exit options implies once more a relaxation of the budget-market dichotomy. If centralized public provision does not work satisfactorily, there are other ways out besides market provision.

Conclusion

The first policy-implication is concerned with critical examination of existing modes of government intervention and public provision, ending with a search towards possibilities for escaping from the fatal dichotomy, market-budget. The second policy-implication aims at improvement of the degree of competitiveness of the market mechanism in the private sector and at more use of the market mechanism for objectives decided upon in the public sector. The third policy-implication contains the following: the appraisal of market price-similar pricing techniques in public provision, that is, the benefit approach; the appraisal of self-management of civil servants, directed towards more competition in thus far hierarchical, monopolistic bureaucracies employed with public provision; the appraisal of competitive devices in the consumption of public goods in the form of competing local communities or competing voluntary membership clubs.

REFERENCES

Bird, R.M. (1976) *Charging for Public Services: A New Look at an Old Idea*. Toronto: Canadian Tax Foundation.

Buchanan, J.M. (1965) 'An Economic Theory of Clubs'. *Economica*, 32: 1–14.

Cebula, R.J. (1974) 'Local Government Policies and Migration'. *Public Choice*, 19: 85–93.

Cebula, R.J. (1977) 'An Analysis of Migration Patterns and Local Government Policy towards Public Education in the United States'. *Public Choice*, 32: 113–21.

Doel, J. van den (1973) 'Ekonomie en demokratie in het staatsbestuur', inaugural lecture, Nijmegen, Deventer: Kluwer Press.

Doel, J. van den (1974) 'Baten en offers in het bestuurlijke systeem'. *Acta Politica*, October, 423–31.

Doel, J. van den (1979) *Democracy and Welfare Economics*. Cambridge: Cambridge University Press.

Faludi, A. (1973) *Planning Theory*. Oxford: Pergamon Press.

Haselbekke, A.G.J. (1981) 'Het profijtbeginsel en de beheersing van de collectieve sector', in D.J. Wolfson (ed.) (1981), 125–55.

Hirschman, A.O. (1970) *Exit, Voice and Loyalty*. Cambridge, Mass.: Harvard University Press.

Keller, W.J. and Hartog, J. (1977) 'Income Tax Rates and Proportional Sacrifice'. *Public Finance*, 32: 321–32.

Meade, J.E. (1972) 'The Theory of Labor-Managed Firms and Profit Sharing'. *Economic Journal*, 82: 402–28.

Mueller, D.C. (1979) *Public Choice*. Cambridge.

Musgrave, R.A. and Musgrave, P.B. (1976) *Public Finance in Theory and Practice*. New York: McGraw-Hill. (First edition, 1973.)

Musgrave, R.A. and Peacock, A.T. (eds.) (1967) *Classics in the Theory of Public Finance*. New York: St. Martin's Press. (First edition, 1958.)

Niskanen, W.A. (1971) *Bureaucracy and Representative Government*. Chicago: Aldine-Atherton.

Olson Jr, M. (1974) *The Logic of Collective Action: Public Goods and the Theory of Groups*. Cambridge, Mass.: Harvard University Press.

Pauly, M.V. (1967) 'Clubs, Communality and the Core: An Integration of Game Theory and the Theory of Public Goods'. *Economica*, 35: 314–24.

Pauly, M.V. (1970) 'Cores and Clubs'. *Public Choice*, 9: 53–65.

Samuelson, P.A. (1954), 'The Pure Theory of Public Expenditures'. *Review of Economics and Statistics*, 36: 386–9.

Tiebout, C.M. (1956) 'A Pure Theory of Local Expenditure'. *Journal of Political Economy*, 64, 416–24.

Vanek, J. (1970) *The General Theory of Labor-Managed Market Economies*. Ithaca: Cornell University Press.

Vanek, J. (1977) *The Labor-Managed Economy*. Ithaca: Cornell University Press.

Wolfson, D.J. (1979) *Public Finance and Development Strategy*. Baltimore: Johns Hopkins University Press.

Wolfson, D.J. (ed.) (1981) *Naar een beheersbare collectieve sector*. Deventer: Kluwer Press.

3

A Model of a Non-Budget-Maximizing Bureau

Ernst Jonsson
Stockholm University

Introduction

According to economic theory the private firm seeks to maximize its profit, but what characterizes the behaviour of public bodies financed out of taxation? What determines the way the activities of central government or municipal bureaucracies develop over time? One view advanced by various researchers is that the public body tends to expand its own sphere of operations. There is — as for example Northcote Parkinson (1958) and Downs (1967) asserted — a built-in dynamic that results in the public body becoming larger and larger. In a well known analysis from 1971, William A. Niskanen elaborated these ideas, by advancing an economic theory of the public body, what he refers to as the 'bureau'. The bureau is defined as a body with a specific identifiable budget that is financed through appropriations granted by the political assembly (what is called the sponsoring organization). In Niskanen's theory the bureau's activities centre on one single individual, namely, its head/manager, and the assumptions include that this person seeks to maximize his own utility, which depends on such things as: salary, reputation, power and the ease with which the bureau can be shaped and administered.

It is assumed that the first three of these factors — but not the last — increase along with an expansion of the budget of the bureau. Thus the head of the bureau has a vested interest in maximizing the budget. This is why every bureaucratic organization has an inherent tendency to request an ever-widening budgetary framework for its operations and to make that framework increasingly complex. According to Niskanen's theory the bureau will certainly be more difficult to administer the larger it is, but as the bureau grows, the manager is in a position to delegate administrative tasks to newly created posts.

At the same time as the manager is assumed to maximize his budget, Niskanen maintains that the political, appropriation-granting assembly adopts a passive role. It has neither the incentive nor the possibility to acquire information about the minimum level sufficient to enable the bureau to provide the prescribed quantity of services in an efficient manner. As the bureau is in a monopoly position in its area it is furthermore impossible for any outsider to demonstrate that the work can be carried out more simply or more cheaply. According to this theory it is difficult for the political assembly to resist the demands made for increased appropriations which in practice leads to bureaus becoming too large, that is to say, in relation to the efficient minimum level. This applies not least to head office units.

Gordon Tullock (1974) has presented a variant of this theory. In order to be able to demand higher salaries at a later date it is in the interest of the top management of the bureau to ensure its expansion. In Sweden the economist Ingemar Ståhl (1976) has maintained that the bureaucracy endeavours to maximize the size of its own organization, because everyone within the organization gains from such an increase in size: through promotion to a higher post and salary level in the growing hierarchy, and through less work and more congenial working conditions. On the other hand, the individual official has almost no chance of directly increasing his salary level through an increased budget. As Ståhl maintains, the salary level for a certain post is usually more or less given.

Competition as a means of promoting efficiency

Niskanen states that if the pressures to maximize the budget are to be restrained the personal interests of the bureau manager must be brought more into line with those of the public at large. To this end he suggests that bureaus providing similar services be allowed to compete with each other concerning the provision of a specified amount of services; this could be done by requiring them to submit tenders specifying what such an amount would cost. Such a procedure would give the bureau a bigger incentive to use simpler and more efficient methods of production; thanks to such competition the parliamentary body that is to consider the budget proposals of the various bureaus will also be in better position to identify bureaus that are inefficient.

Niskanen adds that the bureau manager could also be given a reward of some kind to encourage him to maximize, not the total budget, but the difference between the approved budget and the minimum total costs of the bureau's services. For example, the manager of a bureau who succeeds in reducing his budget might be allowed to retain some part of the budget reduction as a bonus.

A more radical proposal is that social welfare is provided by a number of competing and financially independent producers. The tax revenues to the public body would be placed at the disposal of the consumers in the form of service vouchers worth a certain fixed sum per year. The consumers would then be able to choose freely among the producers who compete with one another. The producers of, for instance, medical services would then be allowed to earn their revenues by attracting patients in competition with other producers. The producer whom the consumers decide to rely on would be paid by vouchers (Olsen, 1969; Niskanen, 1973; Ståhl, 1976).

A model of a non-budget-maximizing bureau

The proposals presented by Niskanen and other economists aim to deprive the public body of its monopoly position, and require it to compete with other public or private producers about the provision of a certain service. However, if the aim is to generate competition designed to promote efficiency, it is not necessary to deprive public administration of its monopoly position. Instead of introducing market solutions attempts could be made to encourage bureaus to compete with each other about who is the most efficient, and in what follows a model is presented of how such competition could be generated. The model is based on the same assumptions as those found in Niskanen's theory.

If competition designed to promote efficiency is to come about, then the political assembly (or its representative, for example, a ministry or a board) must in the first place be able to obtain continuous information about how efficient a certain bureau is in relation to other bureaus performing similar functions. It will be necessary to have some form of recurrent efficiency measurement that permits the ranking of various bureaus in order of efficiency.

In the second place, the political assembly must change the incentive of the bureau manager so that he strives to improve the efficiency of his bureau (rather than maximize its size). How is this to be done? Let us assume that the welfare of the bureau manager himself is affected by the same factors that Niskanen listed. If the manager's salary, reputation and power were to be affected positively by a behaviour that promoted efficiency, it would be possible to ensure that his own interest coincided with that of the public at large. To realize such an effect, the sponsoring organization could start to implement the following procedure. At regular intervals (say once or twice a year) a ranking list could be published showing where the various bureaus stand as regards efficiency. This ranking list would then be discussed at regular conferences with representatives of the bureaus concerned, and particular attention would be directed towards the differences between bureaus as regards efficiency. For the sponsoring organization the purpose of the conferences would be to seek to encourage bureaus, especially those low down on the ranking list, to increase their efficiency. To reach this goal the sponsoring organization would employ the following means: the promotion prospects for the bureau manager (including heads of sections under him) will improve, the higher up the bureau is ranked, and bureaus that always tend towards low ranking run the risk of a special audit designed to uncover the reasons for the low level of efficiency. To ensure that efficiency does improve, the sponsoring organization may also have reason to pay special attention to and supervise the future development of such bureaus. Bureaus with permanent efficiency problems also run a greater risk than others of having the budget scrutinized more rigorously and reduced.

The application of both the carrot ('pull') and the whip ('push') would therefore encourage bureaus to improve their efficiency. The higher up on the ranking list the bureau moves the greater will in fact be the manager's prospects of promotion and a higher salary; reputation: the more efficient a bureau is the higher will be the reputation of the manager in the eyes of his colleagues and those of the sponsoring organization; power: the more efficient a bureau is the less risk it runs of having its freedom of action and power restricted by special audit measures instituted by the sponsoring organization.

The more efficient the bureau is the easier it will be to administer, and this consequence coincides with the personal interest of the manager. Thus, by means of a combination of measures (including efficiency measurement and comparisons) it is possible to encourage bureaus that perform similar functions to compete in order to promote efficiency. Those bureaus which at a certain point of time find themselves low down on the ranking list will endeavour to climb to the upper half, and for this reason they will seek to minimize rather than maximize their budgets.

The bureaus on the upper rungs of the ranking list will be aware that those lower down try to improve their positions and so the highly placed bureaus themselves will be concerned to retain or – if possible — improve their own positions. Such bureaus will be unlikely to seek to maximize their budgets since this might lead to a worsening of their positions. As long as positions in the upper half of the list are not threatened by the bureaus lower down, bureaus in the upper half will be unlikely to strive to minimize their budgets. The higher up on the ranking list the bureau lies the more pronounced this attitude will be.

According to the model the bureaus in the lower half of the list will therefore endeavour to minimize their budgets, and those in the upper levels will at any rate not want to maximize them. In time this competition will lead to an increase in the average level of efficiency as well as a decrease in the differences in efficiency between bureaus. Can a system which includes recurrent comparisons between similar authorities produce the desired effect of promoting efficiency? To obtain an answer to this question an evaluation is made of the continuous classification of work and performance undertaken since 1972 by the regional social insurance offices in Sweden.

Regional social insurance offices' work and performance measurement[1]

In Sweden the general social insurance system (health, occupational injury, dental services, old-age pensions, supplementary pensions, child allowances, advance payments, etc.) is administrated by 26 regional, independent bodies known as social insurance offices. Since 1972 these offices have been subjected to continuous work and performance measurements. All tasks carried out are grouped together to form cases that are assigned standard times (including an addition for administration, that is, staff management, internal administration, dealing with mail, reading circulars and group consultations). In 1980 there were standard times for 13 different cases (e.g. notification of illness, training allowance) and these were based on frequency studies undertaken at 13 local branches during a period of two weeks in 1979.

If the number of cases during a certain period is multiplied by the corresponding standard times one arrives at the number of 'case-time days' achieved by the local branch. This number may be viewed as a measure of the performance volume during the period in question, and is intended to serve as an indicator of the number of employees the local branches should have. The performance measurement has enabled the central authority (the National Social Insurance Board) to make regular productivity comparisons between the regional offices. As a complement to the productivity comparisons the National Board also tries to provide itself with an overall picture of how efficiency is developing at the various regional offices and for this purpose makes regular inspections of these offices. The results of these comparisons and inspections have been presented and discussed at annual conferences of top officials of the various regional offices.

The analyses and comparisons carried out regularly by the Board are for the express purpose of encouraging improvements in efficiency. As a result there is an implicit link between promotion prospects and the relative efficiency position of the regional office. The more efficient a regional office is considered to be in relation to other offices the more favourable will be the promotion prospects of the regional office's managerial staff, that is, the manager and the section heads. Officials at this level are appointed by the National Board.

Results of the evaluation

It is obvious that the system of continuous work and performance measurement has led to competition that promote efficiency, especially among the county offices (that is, excluding the four regional insurance offices in the major conurbations, e.g. Stockholm). It appears that it is precisely those regional offices that proved less efficient than the average to start with, which have endeavoured to improve their positions. Among the factors that suggest that this is the case the following should be mentioned. The number of persons employed at regional offices has almost without exception increased more slowly than the 'case-time' volume during the years 1973–1980. This is also true of staff costs calculated at fixed prices. Moreover, the higher the number of employees per 'case-time day' in 1973 the greater the fall in that number down to 1980

FIGURE 1

Total number of net employees per 1000 matter time days at regional social insurance offices (RSIO) in 1973 and 1980. Horizontal line = mean value

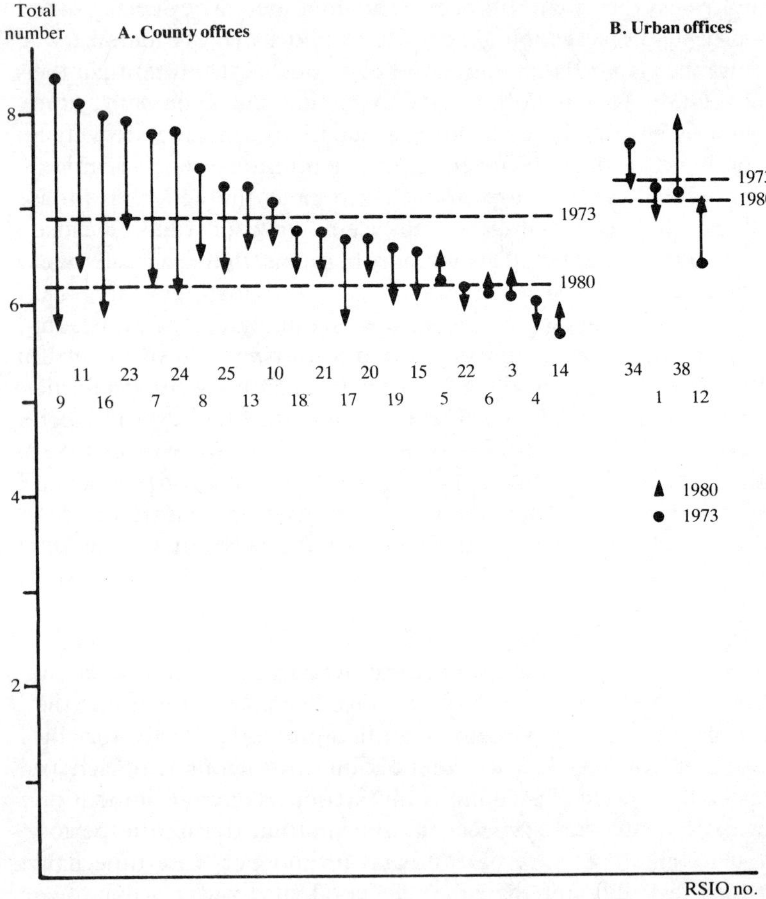

(Figure 1). This trend applies to both regional and local offices. Thirdly, during the period 1973–1980 the administration costs per 'case-time day' of those regional offices which in 1973 had higher than average costs have on average fallen by 14 percent on a fixed price basis. As regards those regional offices which in 1973 had lower than average costs there has been an average increase per 'case-time day' of 8 percent. Consequently the reductions in costs achieved by the first group of regional offices were a good deal greater than the cost increases typical of the latter group. Just over 75 percent of the differences in the percentage cost change during the period in question are explained by the different positions of the regional offices at the start of the period (Figure 2). A similar link is to be found as far as the four main regional offices are concerned. Because of their high density of population it seems that each of them measures its performance in relation to those of the other three and not with any of the county regional offices. Finally, the differences in productivity at the start of the period have been halved by 1980, which applies to the four main urban regional offices as well as the twenty-two county regional offices (Figure 3). The reduced differences are mostly due to the fact that those regional offices that at the start of the period had higher than average costs, approached or even recorded lower costs than the 1980 average. This trend is not the outcome of significant reductions by the central authority in the appropriation requests of these regional offices, but is rather a result of the efforts made by the regional offices themselves.

The productivity comparisons made over the years have applied mainly to the number of persons employed by the various regional offices. No equivalent comparisons have been made regarding the size, equipment and standard of office premises. Partly for this reason it seems that the costs of premises and fittings (=12 percent of administration costs) have not been the object of any competition aimed at promoting efficiency. It appears that during the period 1973–1980 the costs of premises and fittings per 'case-time day' incurred by regional offices (calculated at fixed prices) have increased by 17 percent at the same time as the number of net employees per 'case-time day' has fallen by 9 percent. It is also the case that the rate of increase in the costs of premises and fittings per 'case-time day' has no obvious connection with how large the administration costs of each of the regional offices were at the start of the period. Besides, the variations in the costs of premises and fittings per 'case-time day' that existed between the regional offices

FIGURE 2

Connection between the relative change in administrative costs per matter time day expressed as a percentage of the average change between 1973 and 1980 (Y) and administrative costs per matter time day in 1973 expressed as a percentage of the average value (X) for regional social insurance offices (excl. the four RSIO in the major conurbations).

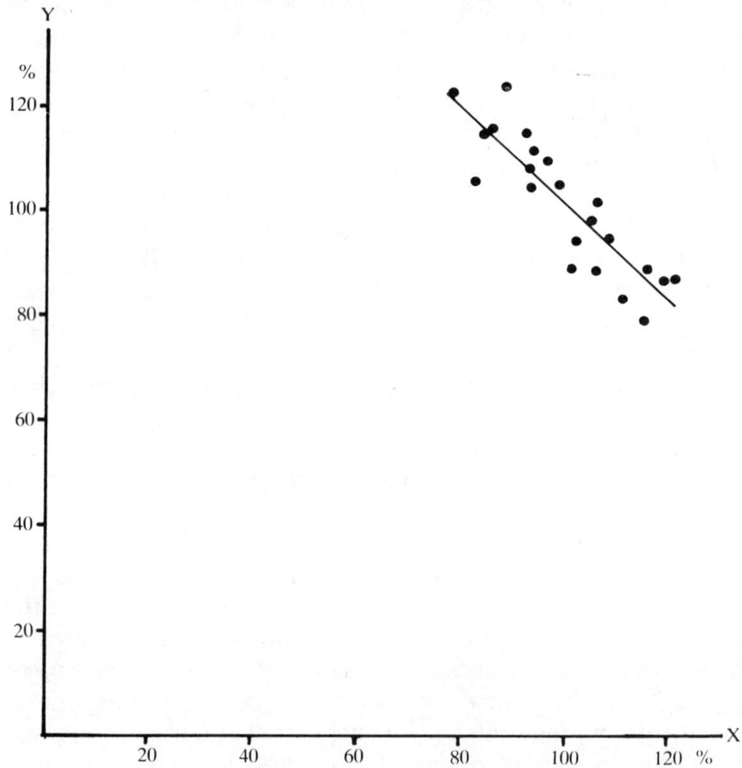

$Y = 194.9 - 0.933\,X$
$R^2 = 0.77$

FIGURE 3

The relative distribution (= coefficient of variation) of the number of net employees per 1000 matter time days (1) and of administrative costs per matter time day (2) at regional social insurance offices (excl. the four RSIO in the major conurbations) during the period 1973–1980. Semilogarithmic scale.

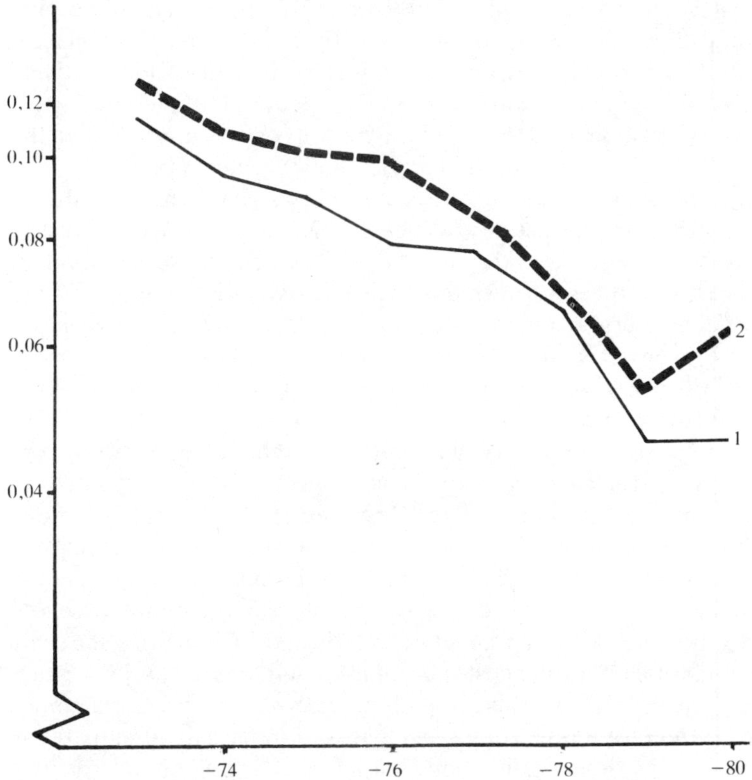

in 1973 were not reduced by 1980, in contrast to what took place concerning the major portion of administration costs.

As a result of the productivity-promoting competition generated between the regional offices, administration costs (excluding costs of premises and fittings) per 'case-time day' fell by an average of 5 percent between 1973 and 1980. Compared with what would have happened if continuous performance measurement had not been introduced, the productivity improvement is probably much greater. How great is this improvement? To obtain an answer one would have to know the cost increases that would have taken place if there had been no performance measurement. One could tentatively suggest that the regional offices in the upper half of the ranking list have in fact increased their administration costs by no more than the rate that would have applied had no measurements taken place. If the trend of these regional offices is used as a measuring stick, then it seems that the productivity between 1973 and 1980 rose by at least 10 percent. According to the supervisory authority there is nothing to suggest that this improvement in productivity has been won at the cost of a deterioration in 'case' quality (e.g. an increased frequency of mistaken decisions or less control of social insurance payments) or level of service (e.g. longer waiting time for decisions) during the period in question.

Similarly, a comparison with authorities that do not employ continuous performance measurement suggests that the cost trends of regional social insurance offices between 1973 and 1980 in Sweden were favourable. For instance, the administration costs of municipalities have developed along totally different lines. Calculated at fixed prices, municipal administrative cost per inhabitant increased on average by 175 percent between 1969 and 1979. During the same period total operating costs per inhabitant increased by 75 percent. This means that municipal administrative costs increased much faster than total operating costs. The differences in administrative costs per inhabitant between the various municipalities increased between 1969 and 1979 (Lane et al., 1982).

During the period 1973–1980 new managers have been appointed to take charge of eleven of the twenty-two county regional offices. Most of these promotions came during the latter half of this period. Nine of the appointed managers came from regional offices that had improved their position on the ranking list during this period and in five cases the improvement was very great indeed.

Conclusion

In order to counteract the urge to expand operations, economists recommend competition within public administration, meaning that if it is to become more efficient, the Bureau must lose its monopoly position. Instead — it is suggested — it must compete with private firms or other public bodies regarding who is to provide the services in question. Those competing can, for example, submit tenders specifying what the public services cost to produce. However, the generation of competition that promotes efficiency need not entail the public administration losing its monopoly position. Instead of introducing market solutions, it is possible to seek to stimulate public bodies providing similar services to compete among themselves and establish which is the most efficient. To bring about such a competition, the political assembly (or its representative) can make recurrent comparisons of their productivity and efficiency. In this way those that prove to be comparatively less efficient will be given a special incentive to improve their position. Such recurrent comparisons have generated an efficiency-promoting competition between the regional social insurance offices in Sweden.

NOTE

1. From this paragraph onwards this article has previously been published in *Public Choice*, 42, 2, 1984. The permission of the publisher of *Public Choice* has been obtained for the inclusion of the article in this volume.

REFERENCES

Downs, A. (1967) *Inside Bureaucracy*. Boston: Little Brown and Co.

Lane, J.E., Magnusson T. and Westlund, A. (1982) 'Kommunernas byrakratisering (Bureaucratization of Municipalities) in *Tvärsnitt* 2, Stockholm.

Niskanen, W.A. (1971) *Bureaucracy and Representative Government*. Chicago: Aldine.

Niskanen, W.A. (1973) *Bureaucracy: Servant or Master*? London: The Institute of Economic Affairs.

Olsen, E. (1969) *Some Theorems in the Theory of Efficient Transfers*, P–4018–1, The Rand Corporation.

Parkinson, C.N. (1958) *Parkinson's Law or the Pursuit of Progress*. London: John Murray Publishers Ltd.

Ståhl, I. (1976) 'En ekonomisk teori för blandekonomin' (An economic theory of the mixed economy) in *Erfarenheter av blandekonomin* (Experiences of the Mixed Economy), Stockholm: Skandinaviska Enskilda Banken.

Tullock, G. (1974) 'Dynamic Hypothesis on Bureaucracy' in *Public Choice*, 19: 127–31.

4

Economic Relations between City and Suburban Governments

Rune J. Sørensen
Oslo University

Introduction

The theory of collective or public goods can trace its roots back to John Stuart Mill's classical *Principles of Political Economy*. Mill discusses the market in terms of efficiency, and argues that it has a limited capacity to supply certain goods and services. Later on, economists like Sax, Wicksell, Lindahl, Musgrave and Bowen, elaborated on the idea that certain goods and services ought to be provided by government, and financed by general taxes. In the 'Pure Theory of Public Expenditures' (1954) Paul Samuelson gave an extensive theoretical treatment of the problem of collective goods.

Samuelson defines collective goods by two characteristics: joint consumption and non-excludability. That is, as one person consumes a collective good this does not reduce the amount available to others, and it is impossible to exclude anyone from enjoying the benefits — as well as disbenefits — of a collective good.[1]

Samuelson's mathematical treatment of the problem gives conditions for optimal supply of public and private goods. Simply stated, the condition of optimality is that the aggregate marginal utility across all members in society shall equal the costs of producing the collective good.

The question remains whether this model has any relevance to, or is fruitful in the *empirical* study of public economics. I shall suggest that the theory of collective goods can generate falsifiable hypotheses of substantial interest in the study of urban economics. Collective goods are produced both in central cities and surrounding municipalities. Goods supplied by one local government are often available to the population in neighbouring municipalities. The non-excludability of collective consumption involves spillover effects across local jurisdictions, and causes interdependencies between suburbs and cities. I propose that this might create conflicts between the local governments involved. The externalities can also pose problems of optimal supply of collective goods in urban areas. Before I proceed to this issue I should like to draw attention to the general state of urban finances.

Urban finances

Historically, cities were *the* wealthy municipalities — and it is probably fair to say that they still are wealthy. The international recession has, however, struck the urban communities hard. And even more important, this acute recession-situation has accentuated other latent difficulties in urban society: crime, unemployment, problems of housing-decay and expenditure cuts in health services and social care.

These factors have contributed to a shift in the political attention regarding regional economics and distribution. Until recently, the focus has been on the rural problems, the relatively lower standard of living in peripheral districts, the migration from sparsely populated communities and problems stemming from insufficient municipal tax-revenues. For decades, such political preferences have materialized in a large number of laws, rules and programmes — all designed to strengthen local communities in peripheral regions.

The cities — and especially the central cities — argue that existing systems discriminate too hard against central urban areas. For instance, urban politicians demand that the transfers from central to rural municipalities through the tax equalization system must be reduced.

In short, central cities have established a new offensive self-consciousness. Urban politicians claim renewed attention to city-problems. In addition, the distributional conflicts inside city, and between urban government and outside actors, are further strengthened by the general economic recession. The old lesson that conflicts tend to harden during economic crises, seems to hold for the suburban-central city relationships as well.

The recession, and the 'new' urban consciousness have increased the intensity of disputes between suburbs and cities. The economic crisis has made the conflict more visible. In the next section of the chapter we intend to show that at least some part of this conflict ought to be analysed by the theory of collective goods. Then, in

Section 3, we shall formulate a model to describe the dependence-structures between the local governments. Section 4 is the empirical part of the chapter suggesting one way of testing the model of suburban-city relationship.

The relevance of 'Public Goods-Theory' to the study of local expenditures

The main result in Samuelson's treatment on collective consumption is perhaps *not* the mathematical conditions for optimal supply. Even more interesting is his analysis of preference registration and policy implementation. Each member in community will pay a 'tax-price' to finance the public supply proportional to his or her relative preference for collective goods. And accordingly, Samuelson states that

> . . . it is in the selfish interest of each person to give false signals, to pretend to have less interest in a given collective consumption activity than he really has (Samuelson, 1972: 93–4).

Misrepresentation of preferences — and the closely related problem of free riding — will, of course, only arise when model conditions are fulfilled.[2] In empirical analysis of public budgeting, we shall carefully have to review the assumptions on which the theory rests.

Leif Johansen (1977: 147–152) examines the apparent contradiction between the logical problem of correct revelation of preferences and, on the other hand, the difficulties in finding evidence which show the practical significance of the problem. Johansen argues that this lack of correspondence is chiefly due to the open political decision-making process. We do *not* have a political system where voters 'signal' their preferences to a central agency, which in turn carries out the calculations needed in order to supply collective goods, and impose taxes on the inhabitants. This kind of process seems to be implicit in the Samuelson decision-model. We do, however, have a two-tier system where elected representatives decide on public expenditures and taxes without any exact knowledge of preferences, and without the objective of taxing according to individual preferences. It is hard to imagine that a politician will mask his preferences in a decision-making body in order to reduce the cost or tax-share levied on the group which he or she represents. The institutional assumptions on which current theory rests seems not to be fulfilled. In this kind of *representative* democracy, the problem of hiding preferences will be of minor relevance. Within other institutional contexts, related problems may arise. Johansen suggests an example:

> I suggested above that it is hard to find empirical evidence which shows the relevance of the revelation issue. The best examples (in Norway) are probably to be found in decision-making about public goods which require joint undertakings by more than one municipality, but which are not referred to the national level . . . Some of the factors which counteract the tendency towards misrepresentation of preferences in ordinary processes are then more or less removed: the connection with elections and competition for votes across the boundaries of the municipalities; the groups behind the negotiators are well defined by geographical boundaries, and have more or less common interests in the issue; and the division of the total burden is a clear-cut issue, any pattern of burden-sharing being implementable through the tax and transfer system and the agreements concerning the financing of the joint undertakings (Johansen, 1977: 151).

Johansen's example is explicitly based on the cooperative approach; the actors are supposed to *bargain* on the provision and payment of collective goods. Misrepresentation (in our model) will *only* occur when municipalities negotiate over the subject. This point seems to be somewhat obscured in the literature on preference registration.

Olson (1965) makes use of a non-cooperative approach to the analysis of collective goods provision. His well known thesis is that rational actors will not act to realize their common interests through participation in voluntary associations. The members of society may have a common interest in obtaining the collective benefit, but they have no common interest in paying the cost of providing the collective services.

The discussion on public goods provision in small groups is particularly relevant here. First, Olson argues that ' . . . the larger the group, the farther it will fall short of providing an optimal amount of collective goods' (Olson, 1965: 35). Secondly, groups of actors of unequal size or intensity of interest, have a better chance that collective goods will be provided. This is due to the relatively great interest which the dominant actor(s) have in collective goods provision. The sub-optimality will decrease as size-distribution gets unequal, and increase as the number of group members rise. Thirdly, in small groups the great actors will pay a disproportionate cost of producing the collective goods. In Olson's colourful formulation, ' . . . : there is accordingly a surprising tendency for the "exploitation of the great by the small"' (Olson, 1965: 35).[3]

Olson's *Logic of Collective Action* is mainly devoted to the study of organization-formation, but he indicated that the model might give insight to other fields as well — such as urban economics:

> It would also suggest that neighbouring local governments in metropolitan areas that provide collective goods (like commuter roads and education) that benefit individuals in two or more jurisdictions would tend to provide inadequate amounts of these services, and that the largest local government (e.g. the one representing the central city) would bear disproportionate shares of the burdens of providing them (Olson, 1965: 36).

Of course, this example resembles Johansen's, and both authors have seen the usefulness of collective goods theory in this area. This point towards further theoretical elaboration and empirical testing.

The spillover problem between municipalities can in principle be cured by adjusting the local borders. It is necessary to have correspondence between the area where people enjoy the benefits from the collective supply, and the area where local government legally taxes the inhabitants. This is the principle of '*fiscal equivalence*' (Olson, 1969: 479; Oates, 1972). An efficient system of local government requires that each government can tax as far as its collective supply reaches. Normally it is impossible to obtain such ideal conditions. Different goods have unequal reach. According to the theorem of fiscal equivalence, this implies that there is a need for a separate government for each good. In addition, there are practical difficulties stemming from increasing population-mobility. This has rapidly enlarged the consuming population outside municipal jurisdictions.

Urban areas are characterized by a high degree of economic integration. They are common markets for a number of private goods and services, including housing and work. This causes frequent crossing of municipal borders, very often in the form of a day-visit to central cities in order to work or shop. Such activities can easily affect the consumption of collective goods provided by the central-city government.

A number of jurisdictional changes in urban areas can be interpreted in terms of fiscal equivalence. The enlargement of the city-territory has, however, not resolved the spillover problem. Other attempts have been implemented, such as the establishment of a new tier of regional government with a wider responsibility.

In concluding this part, I shall present the hypotheses: if there is a number of local government units in a highly integrated urban area, and these units provide collective goods with significant spillover effects, then we shall expect two different mechanisms to be activated. The first is the cooperative rationale of 'tuning down' preferences. The resulting supply of collective services will be suboptimal. The second mechanism is the non-cooperative logic analysed by Olson. Here, the outcome will be suboptimal, dependent on the number of municipalities involved, and the cost-distribution might be an 'exploitation' of the big city by the surrounding municipalities.[4]

A model on inter-municipal relations in urban areas

We shall assume that a local government (city or suburban municipality) can rank two types of public services against each other. First, there are collective goods and services which is provided in an amount K. Secondly, the municipality is providing private goods which are consumed individually. A local government supplies an amount P_c of such goods. We assume that local preferences can be expressed by a simple welfare function W_c:

$$W_c = K^a P_c^b \qquad 0 < a, b < 1 \tag{1}$$

Then we turn to a basic assumption in our model. The population in the municipality has two sources of collective supply; the amount provided by its own government and the goods provided by its neighbour-municipality.

The kind of collective goods we discuss here are somewhat different from the pure case discussed by Samuelson. We shall assume that our population does not have equal benefits from goods which are produced outside their own municipality. That is, we assume that the population only enjoys a fraction z_c $(0 < z_c < 1)$ of the collective goods provided by neighbouring government. This implies that our concept of collective goods has an important spatial dimension: geographical distance reduces the availability of collective supply. In this way we have modified the pure case, because distance to a certain extent will exclude the population from collective goods consumption (Bennett, 1980: 220). The reason might be that travelling is costly and time-consuming.[5]

The collective goods variable K above does not have a subscript c

(referring to city) because it consists of two components: one component which has to be financed by municipal taxes, and in addition the goods provided freely by the neighbouring governments. The first component is measured by the variable K_c, and the second by the variable K_s so that local collective consumption K is written:

$$K = K_c + z_c K_s \qquad 0 < z_c < 1 \tag{2}$$

Finally, we shall incorporate a budget-restriction in the model. We assume that the local government enjoys a total income r_c. The cost of providing both collective and private goods is conventionally fixed at unity. As we assume that no fees are charged on collective consumption, and that collective goods provided outside municipal jurisdictions are free, the budget restriction is:

$$r_c = K_c + P_c \tag{3}$$

We imagine that the welfare-function represents the preferences of the municipality or its electorate, and assume that the local government acts as to maximize the welfare of its inhabitants. It is also possible to interpret the preference-function as the decision maker's preferences, and thereby avoid the problems connected with the concept of society's 'welfare-function'.

We shall first present *the non-cooperative analysis*, that is, using the assumption of autonomous decision making. First, we incorporate the 'overspill'-function (2) and the budget-restriction (3) into the welfare-function (1). Independent decision making implies that the municipality will adapt its policy assuming the budget-allocations by neighbouring governments as given. By derivation the individual optimal policy (K_c, P_c) (K_s being the independent variable) may be calculated. The resulting optimal budget-allocation becomes:

$$K_c = \frac{a \cdot r_c}{a+b} - \frac{b}{b+a} \cdot Z_c \cdot K_s \tag{4}$$

It follows from this that the optimal supply of collective goods K_c in a municipality is a linear decreasing function of the supply outside its borders, K_s. If outside government increase its supply with 'one unit', our government will react with a decrease in its supply. This supply reduction will depend on the municipality's relative preference between collective and private goods ($b/(b+a)$), and the overspill-coefficient z_c (Williams, 1966).

Next, we shall assume that our urban region is composed of two municipalities, the central city and one suburb. According to general knowledge on the urban travelling-pattern, it is reasonable to assume that spill-ins into the suburbs are far greater than spill-outs from suburbs to city. Normally, the suburban population finds it attractive to travel across city borders in order to enjoy the varied supply of public and private goods provided there. The assumption is that:

$$0 < z_c < z_s < 1, \qquad \begin{array}{ll} c: & \text{city} \\ s: & \text{suburb} \end{array} \tag{5}$$

We are now able to formulate a complete noncooperative model, a model assuming no attempts to coordinate or negotiate any joint solution. The only element missing is the suburban analogue reaction-function to (4), which is the condition for optimal supply in the city. K_s is the amount of collective goods supplied in the suburb.

The a' and b' variables of the suburban reaction-function represent the suburban welfare-parameters, and its total revenue is r_s. The complete reaction model is:

$$\left.\begin{array}{lr} K_c = \dfrac{ar_c}{b+a} - \dfrac{b}{b+a} \cdot z_c \cdot K_s & \text{(a)} \\[2ex] K_s = \dfrac{a'r_s}{b'+a'} - \dfrac{b'}{b'+a'} \cdot z_s \cdot K_c & \text{(b)} \end{array}\right\} \tag{6}$$

Before completing this discussion of this reaction-model, it is useful to illustrate the logic imbedded in the cooperative model. Let us assume that public officials from the city and the suburb agree to coordinate their policies. The motive might be that individual decision making leads to a kind of stable suboptimal solution for both parties. Therefore, the officials agree that the possible outcomes of the negotiations must be better to both parties than no agreement, that is the status quo solution. Secondly, the agreement must have the property that no other possible outcome is better for both municipalities. All possible outcomes which satisfy these conditions belong to the 'negotiation set' (Luce and Raiffa, 1958). All solutions within this set will (of course) be Pareto-optimal. We can easily deduce this condition:

$$\frac{r_c+(b/a)\cdot Z_c\cdot K_s+K_c((b/a)-1)}{Z_c(r_c-K_c)}=\frac{Z_s\cdot(r_s-K_s)}{r_s+(b'/a'),Z_s,K_c+K_s((b'/a')-1)} \quad (7)$$

Here, b/a annd b'/a' can be interpreted as the two actors' relative interest in collective goods. Assume first that the spill over coefficients ($z's$) is one. Then we have the polar case of a pure collective good. It can be shown that the total amount of collective goods that ought to be provided depend on both actors' relative interest in collective goods. And the total amount $K = K_c + K_s$ ought to be provided according to relative interests. The municipality having the greatest interest in collective goods will produce the higher share to achieve an optimal solution. This is the rationale behind the masking of preferences — the attempt to avoid paying a high price or cost-contribution to finance the collective good. The resulting outcome will in this case be far from optimal. Therefore, in negotiations we shall expect the actors to pretend to be less interested in collective consumption than they really are.

Assume then that $b/a = b'/a'$, and also that the spill-coefficients are somewhat less than one. In this case the actors ought to produce collective goods according to the spillover effects. If city-provision spills over to a wider area, then optimality requires that this is taken into consideration during the negotiations.

This is in principle a technical problem, and the production problem can of course be separated from its distributional aspects. We shall, however, suspect that the 'technicalities' will enter the negotiations. Spill-outs represent a legitimate claim on financial support from neighbour municipalities, especially when collective production are extended well beyond the local-optimality level. Because of the asymmetrical nature of city-suburb relationships, where the city population does not enjoy great benefits from suburban supply, the suburban local government might dispute a claim that city produce collective externalities. In some cases, the suburban government will resist any negotiations, because the expected gains beyond status quo are small compared to future expected costs. Implicit in a cooperative approach is an acceptance of the spill-problem as such. It might — from a suburban point of view — be a rational self-interest not to acknowledge the existence of externalities at all. This indicates that the non-cooperative approach, which we have discussed earlier, may be a more realistic point of departure. We shall therefore return to our reaction-model (6) in the empirical part of this chapter.

Model testing and interpretation

We have so far established the non-cooperative reaction-model which we think will represent *one* aspect of the inter-municipal relations. The model is heavily dependent on a number of assumptions. First, at least a certain amount of the local expenditures has a joint — or collective — character. A number of important local goods are obviously private in character, such as health-care and most social-services. Secondly, we assume that local governments have some autonomy of action. The centrally imposed regulations and other kinds of bindings are assumed not to be so strong and extensive that local discretion is virtually out of the question. Thirdly, we assume that local government is a purposeful, rational actor. We have already assumed that its aim is to maximize a local welfare function. The assumption of rationality also implies that externalities are visible, and that the other municipalities in the 'game' are identifiable. Implicit in this approach is the view that public decision making and budgeting is a product of conscious calculations of a unitary actor. This is the conventional 'public choice' assumption.

Even though this is an analytical simplification, the reader should be warned that local governments are *not* unitary (Wildavsky 1975). On the contrary, they are complex actors in which administrative and political actors pursue different goals, and act to maximize a combination of personal, professional and centrally imposed values. In addition, the budget-process is not rational as we have conceptualized the term. Ample empirical evidence seems to support the incremental model, which views decision making as 'muddling through' by means of 'successive, limited comparisons'. There is of course no guarantee that the outcome of this process can be understood or predicted within our 'rational-comprehensive' framework (Lindblom, 1959; March and Olsen, 1976).

This lack of realism ought to be justified by a corresponding high degree of fruitfulness. I hope that we shall be better enabled to cope with inter-municipal relations within a rational-choice approach than within a model incorporating a large number of unpredictable and irrational features.

The testing is tentative in three respects. Our data are limited to 43 Norwegian cities and twice the number of suburbs (86). Secondly, the data stem from one year, 1978. It may be better to test a model based on diacronic data. Finally, I have no information of the preferences of the decision makers or the actual decision process. The aim is therefore to illustrate the potential of statistical estimation and testing, not to give any conclusive answers to the questions presented.

We shall turn to the empirical analysis by examining the proposition that the central cities will provide a larger amount of collective goods. If this hypothesis is supported, we can proceed with the analysis of the reaction-functions. The proposition that cities provide a larger amount of collective goods can be considered an *a priori* assumption on which the estimation of the reaction-functions rests. We may then ask whether our reaction-model can generate the resulting budget-allocations in cities and suburbs. Then we shall suggest two models for interpreting our results, the Nash and the Cournot models.

We suggest that at least two types of local expenditures can be labelled 'collective'; expenditures to building and housing, and on cultural goods. Building and housing involves investments in infrastructures, such expenditures contributes to maintenance and growth in industry and trade and may also reduce the migration to other municipalities. Even though we hypothesize that a local government may decrease its efforts in this sector because of rising expenditures in neighbour municipalities, we do not find strong theoretical arguments in favour of it. Cultural goods may be a better category. It includes goods such as theatres, concert-halls, libraries, sporting-facilities, parks and public swimming-pools. These are goods which are potentially available to a large population outside local borders.

In both cases, we think that the budget-policy in one municipality is one decision-premise in the neighbouring local governments. In Table 1 we present the per capita expenditures for relevant Norwegian municipalities.

Table 1 indicates that the cities have higher expenditures for collective goods. If we accept the collective nature in the expenditures analysed, this seems to be in accordance with the predictions in the Olson-model.

We shall then turn to the analysis of reaction-functions. In order to estimate the coefficients in model (6), we must include exogenous variables. The population base is a useful control-variable in the model. A number of goods, such as museums, theatres, concert-halls and infra-structure (local roads and public transport) might be joint in supply over specific levels of demand. As demand exceeds a

TABLE 1
Expenditures on 'culture' and building and housing (Kroner per capita) 1978

	Culture	**Building & Housing**	(*N*)
City—municipalities	242	1291	(43)
Suburban municipalities	227	871	(86)
Difference	15[x]	420[x]	

[x] Differences are significantly greater than 0 at 5 percent level. One-tailed T-test.

specific level, the goods will suffer from crowding effects.[6] In the long run, queues and excess demand will increase the pressure on local government for additional supply. On the other hand, a sufficient population base might be necessary to reduce initial costs. At low levels of demand, fixed costs might be prohibitively high.

Secondly, the municipal income influences decisions on collective supply. We shall enter average personal net-income in each municipality as an exogenous variable in the model. In Norway, this income is taxed with a fixed percentage (municipal taxes).

Variable list:

K_c, K_s Per capita expenditures to collective goods in the city (c) and the suburbs in the urban area (s).

P_c, P_s Population in the city (c) and the suburb (s).

I_c, I_s Personal net-income in the city (c) and the suburb (s).

Our revised model is

$$\left.\begin{aligned} K_c &= \alpha_1 \cdot K_s + \alpha_2 \cdot P_c + \alpha_3 \cdot I_c + R_c \qquad \text{(a)} \\ K_s &= \beta_1 \cdot K_c + \beta_2 \cdot P_s + \beta_3 \cdot I_s + R_s \qquad \text{(b)} \end{aligned}\right\} \qquad (8)$$

We shall analyse these structural relationships by the method of maximum-likelihood estimation. LISREL is a computer program for estimating the coefficients in a set of linear structural equations, and is particularly well designed to handle models with reciprocal causation (Jöresskog and Sörbom, 1978). It can be shown that the parameters in our model are identified.

We shall now proceed to the hypothesis about the structural parameter in our model. An obvious solution concept is the *Cournot equilibrium*. The model is based on successive reactions between the actors. Each actor takes the opponent's choice as given, and calculates his best reply to this choice. This reply is easily found by using the reaction-function already presented. We shall then have a sequence of adjustments between the municipalities. This process will hopefully converge towards a stable equilibrium. The actors use rather simple 'rules-of-thumb' in the sense that they assume that their own strategies will not influence the opponent's choice.

A better solution is the game-theoretical one. In the Cournot case the behavioural assumptions are mechanical and somewhat inconsistent. The game-theoretical solution consists of pairs of strategies, one for each player, which have the property of being optimal against each other. Here, the concept of optimality implies that a city-strategy K_c is the best possible as the suburban government chooses K_s — and vice versa. An equilibrium strategy has to be located on the actor's reaction-curve. This game-theoretical equilibrium — the *Nash-solution* — will coincide with the Cournot equilibrium. Both will fall at the intercept between the reaction-curves.

We now assume that our data are generated through a Cournot or Nash decision-process, and that the budget allocations represent stable equilibria. Each urban area has a specific city-suburb budget-allocation. An infinite number of different pairs of reaction-curves can be drawn through each of these. It is, however, possible to estimate the underlying functions from the data. We assume that our exogenous variables (income and population base) have produced variations or shifts in each reaction-curve. We estimate the true function by 'levelling out' these individual shifts in reaction-curves. Our estimation presupposes that equilibrium is obtained. Our hypothesis is:

$$0 > \alpha_1 > \beta_1 \qquad (9)$$

Table 2 gives the estimated effects in Model 8.

Let us first examine Model 8a; per capita expenditures on cultural

TABLE 2
Maximum likelihood estimates for the models 8a (cultural expenditures) and 8b (expenditures to building and housing)

Parameters	Estimates	
	Model 8a	Model 8b
α_1	0.435 (0.203)	0.079 (0.262)
β_1	−0.381 (0.179)	−0.085 (0.262)
α_2	0.225 (0.164)	−0.127 (0.051)
α_3	0.197 (0.164)	0.241 (0.161)
β_2	−0.262 (0.115)	−0.201 (0.150)
β_3	0.202 (0.161)	0.170 (0.147)
($N = 159$)		

Note: The standard error of the estimates are given within parenthesis.

goods. The interaction-effects are considerable, both types of municipalities react significantly as the opponent adjusts his policy. The suburb reduces its supply as we expected. But, expenditures in the city do not decrease as the suburban supply increases.

In Model 8b, per capita expenditures on building and housing, we find a similar reaction-pattern. The estimated parameters are not significantly different from zero. The city-reaction curve seems, however, to rise, while the suburban curve tends to fall. The chi-square test indicates that our models are poorly fitted to the data.

It is difficult to give a clear-cut interpretation of these results. A number of possibilities are open. Obviously, radically different models may do a better job. Budget-allocations can perhaps be explained as simple learning-processes, as non-strategic adoption to a complex environment, as a product of political and bureaucratic games within local government or even as the outcome of a democratic system where 'justified needs' are given high priority.

The rational choice framework should perhaps be modified to incorporate other actors, strategies and decision-premises. It is also possible that the actors play another game than the one we have suggested here. Perhaps it is rational city-policy to increase supply when the suburbs decrease their supply?

Anyhow, the empirical results do not rule out the potential value of the presented model. First of all, some authors argue that all science can do is falsify theories. Secondly, the lack of empirical support might be due to the special setting, that is the non-urban character of the Norwegian society. Thirdly, the regional organization might be successful in the sense that it satisfies the 'fiscal equivalence' requirements rather well. The spillovers might simply play a minor role. This is of course an optimistic conclusion.

Conclusion

The concept of collective goods has prevailed in the literature on public budgeting. In normative theory, the problem of preference-registration has gathered much interest. Implicitly this approach rests on a cooperative decision process. We have elaborated on this point and have suggested a model in which local government will adapt its policy to the budget in neighbouring municipalities according to the 'reaction-function'. The tentative empirical testing on Norwegian data supports the hypotheses in the sense that cities have somewhat higher collective expenditures than suburbs. The estimated reaction-curves do not support the theoretical argument. Contrary to the model-prediction, the city-supply increases as a function of the suburban collective output.

NOTES

1. The criterion of non-excludability is the crucial element in my later discussion. It is the missing ability of local government to exclude 'outsiders' from consumption which causes dependencies between municipalities. John G. Head argues that the impossibility of exclusion is the more significant characteristic of public goods. It is this factor that makes for difficulties in public finance (Head, 1972). Snidal (1979) gives an excellent discussion of definitions of concepts of public goods.

2. Charles Tiebout (1956) has suggested a solution on this registration-problem. He assumes that the citizens are fully mobile, that within each polity all must consume the same amount of collective goods, and that there are no spillovers between communities. People can then reveal their preferences for a local public good by moving into the community providing the most desirable types and amounts of collective goods. Cebula (1974) finds empirical support for the Tiebout-model in an analysis of American data.

3. The Olson propositions are, of course, controversial. A number of authors have elaborated on the theory. Thomas C. Shelling and Russell Hardin have explicitly connected the theory of the *n*-person prisoners' dilemma with the problem of collective action. Russell Hardin suggests that the greater success of small groups may be due to a 'statistical fluke'. John Chamberlain argues that group size should not be

an obvious determinant of group success or failure in collective action. The level of collective production will, under reasonable conditions, rise as the number of participants increases (Hardin, 1982: 107–195).

4. A number of authors has discussed the 'exploitation thesis'. Bennett (1980) is rather negative in his evaluation. The contributions of Heilbrun (1972) and Kasarda (1972) seem to support the hypothesis.

5. The theory of urban hierarchies are closely connected with this assumption. The classical geographers like Lösch and Cristaller suggested a ranking of the cities. The cities having the higher rank supplied goods and services to a wide 'hinterland' which also included the lower-ranking cities. The smaller region cities supplied a relatively smaller region outside their own borders (Mills, 1972; Johnston, 1980).

6. The theory of clubs explicitly incorporates crowding effects. A pure public good does not require a kind of exclusion. The club theory determines the need for exclusionary zoning. Impure public goods are partially rival, and exclusion is feasible owing to crowding and congestion (Sandler and Tschirhart, 1980).

REFERENCES

Bennett, R.J. (1980) *The Geography of Public Finance*. London: Methuen.

Cebula, R.J. (1974) 'Local Government Policies and Migration: An Analysis for SMSA's in the United States 1965–1970'. *Public Choice* XIX: 85–93.

Chamberlin, J. (1982) 'Provision of Collective Goods as a Function of Group Size' in Hardin, R. and Barry, B., op. cit., pp. 197–212.

Coase, R.H. (1974) 'The Lighthouse in Economics'. *Journal of Law and Economics* 17: 357–77.

Friedman, J.W. (1977) *Oligopoly and the Theory of Games*. Amsterdam: North-Holland.

Hardin, R. and Barry, B. (1982) *Rational Man and Irrational Society*? London: Sage.

Heilbrun, J. (1972) 'Poverty and the Public Finance in the Older Central Cities' in Edel, M. and Rotenburg, J., *Readings in Urban Economics*. New York: The Macmillan Company.

Johansen, L. (1977) 'The Theory of Public Goods: Misplaced Emphasis?' *Journal of Public Economics*: 147–52.

Johansen, K. (1981) 'On the status of the Nash type of non-cooperative equilibrium in economic theory', Memorandum fra Institutt for Sosialøkonomi, Oslo.

Johnston, R.J. (1980) *City and Society: An Outline for Urban Geography*. Harmondsworth: Penguin Books.

Jöresskog, K. and Sörbom, D. (1978) *LISREL. Analysis of Linear Structural Relationships by the Method of Maximum Likelihood*. Uppsala.

Kasarda, J.D. (1972) 'The Impact of Suburban Population Growth on Central City Service Functions'. *American Journal of Sociology*, 77: 1111–25.

Lindblom, C.E. (1959) 'The Science of "Muddling Through"'. *Public Administration Review*.

Luce, R. and Raiffa, H. (1957) *Games and Decisions*. Wiley: New York.

Mueller, D.C. (1979) *Public Choice*. Cambridge: Cambridge University Press.

March, J.G. and Olsen, J.P. (1976) *Ambiguity and Choice in Organizations*. Oslo: Universitetsforlaget.

Mills, E. (1972) *Urban Economics*. London: Scott, Foresman and Company.

Oates, W.E. (1972) *Fiscal Federalism*. New York: Harcourt Brace Jovanovitch.

Olson, M. (1965) *The Logic of Collective Action*. Cambridge, Mass.: Harvard University Press.

Olson, M. (1969) 'Strategic theory and its applications. The principle of "fiscal equivalence": The division of responsibilities among different levels of government.' *American Economic Review*, IIX.

Samuelson, P.A. (1954) 'The Pure Theory of Public Expenditures'. *The Review of Economics and Statistics* 1954, pp. 387–9.

Samuelson, P.A. (1972) 'Towards a Pure Theory of Public Expenditure', pp. 74–110 in Sahni, B.S. *Public Expenditure Analysis*. Rotterdam: Rotterdam University Press.

Sandler, T. and Tschirhart, J.T. (1980) 'The Economic Theory of Clubs: An Evaluative Survey'. *Journal of Economic Literature*, XVIII: 1181–521.

Schelling, T.C. (1982) 'Hocey Helmets, Daylight Saving, and Other Binary Choices' in Barry, R. and Hardin, B., op. cit.: 110–19.

Snidal, D. (1979) 'Public Goods, Property Rights and Political Organizations'. *International Studies Quarterly*, 23: 532–66.

Tiebout, C.M. (1956) 'A Pure Theory of Local Expenditures'. *Journal of Political Economy*, 64: 416–24.

Wildavsky, A. (1975) *The Politics of the Budgetary Process*. Boston: Little, Brown and Company.

Williams, A. (1966) 'The Optimal Provision of Public Goods in a System of Local Government'. *Journal of Political Economy*, 74: 18–33.

II

PUBLIC AND PRIVATE INTERACTION

5

Getting By in Three Economies: The Resources of the Official, Unofficial and Domestic Economies

Richard Rose
University of Strathclyde

> The increase of the black economy shows that people do not, once they are free of their companies, their unions and to a certain extent their government, shirk the idea of work
> Prince Charles (1981).

> The black economy can be large enough to yield a rich vein of anecdotes without necessarily being a phenomenon of quantitative significance
> Dilnot and Morris (1981).

Fiscal stress affects both governors and governed, but it does not affect them equally. When the national economy is growing more slowly than expected and public expenditure is growing fast, government is under pressure to raise more money in taxes. When the economy is not growing and government's tax claims are growing, ordinary citizens have difficulty in getting by, that is, maintaining individual consumption. The contradiction in priorities is common to most Western nations and it can force post-tax income to contract.

The conflict between fiscal priorities and domestic priorities leads to political anxiety when economic difficulties are expected to create political trouble. Yet troubles did not come in the 1970s; individual life satisfaction remained high (Rose, 1980). Ordinary people appeared more satisfied with their conditions than was often predicted. Because ordinary citizens could get by, government too could get by. But that does not necessarily mean that the 1980s will be trouble free. We must understand why macro-economic pressures upon individual income have not produced individual protest, in order to understand the likely future consequences of continuing fiscal stress.

Prince Charles, a person with as great a stake as anyone in institutional stability, offers good news for individuals but bad news for government. Two economists, Dilnot and Morris, conclude that the black economy is much overrated. Novelty not only accounts for an upsurge of anecdotes, but also is an indication of relatively small scale. The fact that a taxpayer 'bites' the tax collector by evading taxes is news, precisely because the tax man can still sink his teeth into much of what an ordinary individual earns. The sceptical conclusions of Dilnot and Morris have been borne out by many other surveys in Britain, the United States, and most other OECD countries (see, e.g., Smith, 1981; Barthelemy, 1981, and Blades, 1982).

The practical policy implications of this debate are important and immediate. If the sceptics are correct, then the political authority of government is secure under conditions of fiscal stress. The good news is that government will continue collecting more and more tax revenue to finance public expenditure rising with economic recession. The bad news is that individual consumption will be eroded, as increased taxes leave most people with less purchasing power than before. If, however, Prince Charles is correct, then reports of a fall in individual consumption are misleading because they omit the value of work in the Unofficial Economy. There is more money in most pockets than official statistics note because government is being defrauded of revenue. The controversy not only concerns morality; it also affects the management of the economy, whether by neo-Keynesian or monetarist techniques (cf. McGee and Feige, 1982). It is relevant too to the electoral calculations of politicians trying to give voters what they want. Voters may prefer *less* effective government revenue collection rather than more effective spending programmes.

To answer the question — how do individuals get by in times of fiscal stress? — we must broaden the discussion from two to three economies: the Official Economy recorded in the national income accounts; the Unofficial (alias black, shadow or cash-only) Economy operating outside the national income accounts; and the Domestic Economy, whose products are neither recorded in the national income accounts nor are they exchanged for money. The three economies are interrelated; each can produce some of the goods and services that individuals consume each week. Policy makers will want consumption to be maintained — but not at the expense of the tax base represented by the Official Economy. When the Official

Economy is in difficulty, the important question for individuals is: can one get by making more use of the other two economies?

I
Three ways to maintain consumption: the view from the bottom

This paper starts from the point of view of the ordinary individual, rather than from the top-down perspective of national policy makers. When management of the economy is the issue, policy makers deal in large-scale statistical aggregates recorded in money terms, such as the Gross National Product. Policy makers cannot ignore or repudiate the evidence reported by their own institutions. By contrast, ordinary citizens look at economic questions in terms of how they can get by as individuals, being primarily concerned with their own standard of living (Alt, 1979: chapter 5), whether or not the things they consume are reported in the national income accounts.

The goods and services that collectively constitute individual consumption come from three analytically distinct sources, the Official, the Unofficial and the Domestic Economies.

The Official Economy (OE): the economy of concern to policy makers is the Official Economy, which is measured in money terms and recorded by government departments, especially tax offices. Strictly speaking, the national income accounts are no more and no less than a measure of activities observed and recorded in the national accounts according to conventions agreed by economists. The invention of national income accounts is very recent. Long before economists devised this summary measure, there was lots of economic activity, even though much of it was not officially recorded. The further back in time economic historians seek to extend their knowledge, the greater the gap between the Official Economy and what is meant to be measured. Since government today is itself responsible for much of what happens in a mixed economy, there is today a good data base. But conventions for treating this data still present problems, such as the standard assumption that there is nil change through time in the productivity of the public sector.

The Unofficial Economy (UE): in this economy all goods and services can readily be measured in money terms, because they involve cash-only transactions. In principle, the Unofficial Economy is just as observable as the Official Economy; both can be reduced to the measuring rod of money. The primary difference is that transactions in the Unofficial Economy are not reported to or recorded by government. Within OECD countries the principal reason for this is tax avoidance; in less developed countries administrative inadequacy can also be a reason. Because transactions in the Unofficial Economy involve both producers and consumers and have a money trace, they are commensurable with data compiled in the first economy, even though they are not officially reported.

The Domestic Economy (DE): goods and services produced and consumed by the same individual (a person who bicycles to work instead of taking a bus) or within the confines of a single household (a meal prepared for a family of four, or a do-it-yourself repair to a common household utility) are products of the Domestic Economy (Hill, 1979:34). From a sociologist's perspective, there is no fundamental problem in measuring the Domestic Economy: the activities involved are commonplace and readily observable. Time-budget studies have measured and compared activities in the Domestic Economy across a wide range of societies in Eastern Europe, Western Europe, and North America (Szalai et al., 1972). But from an economist's point of view, measurement problems are intrinsic to the Domestic Economy. Because its goods are not bought and sold in the market, they are not immediately recordable in money terms. Even if notional shadow prices are imputed to domestic activities, it does not follow that these imputed prices reflect the value of such 'priceless' activities as a mother's care for a child. There is no public record of activities in the Domestic Economy, nor could a non-totalitarian government ask every household to provide an annual return of all the goods and services that it produced and consumed itself.

An individual trying to get by is more concerned with securing food, shelter, transport, clothing and leisure amusements than in reducing all of these consumption goods and services to the single measuring rod of money. In total, Individual Consumption is the sum of goods and services produced in three very different economies.

$$IC = OE + UE + DE \qquad (1)$$

From an analytic point of view, the Official and Unofficial economies both involve money transactions; they differ because transactions in the Official Economy are subject to taxation, whereas taxation is evaded in the Unofficial Economy. The Domestic Economy differs from both the Official and the Unofficial economies, because the goods and services are produced without cash transactions. There is no legal obligation to pay taxes, because activities are not monetized. To maintain a given standard of consumption, an individual can add together goods and services produced in three different economies.

Estimating the size of each of these economies is in principle practicable, because it involves what is a pre-eminently empirical phenomenon, the production and consumption of goods and services. But it is not easy, for the methods required to estimate the size of the Official Economy (which themselves are problematic) are not immediately transferable to the other two economies. A variety of measures have been devised to estimate the size of the Unofficial Economy, drawing upon monetary data, data about the composition of the labour force, and occupational status. Opinion surveys can be used to estimate attitudes toward taxation and exchanges in the Unofficial Economy. To estimate the scale of the Domestic Economy involves different methods, such as time-budget studies of the population. The fact that money values cannot reliably be imputed to what is produced therein presents significant problems of commensurability with conventional economic indices based solely upon money values.

For an individual, changes in the relative importance of the three economies are most likely to be caused by changing position in the life-cycle. An infant will be heavily dependent upon the goods and services produced by the mother in the Domestic Economy. A young unmarried person, given a job and no family responsibilities, can concentrate activity in the Official Economy. A husband and wife invest more time in the home, producing and exchanging household goods and services. Having children will cause a radical shift, often moving a wife from work in the Official Economy to working overtime in the Domestic Economy. The departure of children to form their own households will alter a family's use of consumption sources again (Gershuny, 1982). As long as the age structure of a nation's population does not change radically, then the movement of individuals within the life-cycle has a limited effect upon national aggregates.

Of greater relevance here are changes in the technology of production and in welfare state programmes that affect the family as well as the economy. From the perspective of centuries, the Domestic Economy has been the source of most of the goods and services consumed by most people in Europe. It is not necessarily so today, because of the rise of the money-oriented industrial economy and the decline of a domestically oriented peasant economy (Franklin, 1969). Welfare state measures have a mixed impact upon activity in the three economies. For example, agricultural price supports may make it possible for more people to remain in agricultural employment, with greater input of labour outside the Official Economy. The provision of nursery care for pre-school children and of part-time public employment for women encourages women to monetize their work. But high marginal tax rates on the second income in a family can discourage wives from working in the Official Economy (Kay and King, 1980:32ff.).

Since 1945, the political economies of Western nations have changed significantly, and each stage has altered the relative significance of the three economies for individual consumption.

(1) *The economy in Year Null*. At the end of the second world war physical shortages were the primary problem in Europe; most production recorded in national income accounts was pre-empted by government for military use. The shortage of consumer goods was an incentive for households to get by through producing as much as they could domestically. Insofar as rationing and price controls kept official prices low, there were incentives to buy goods in the black market at a higher-than-official price. In extreme cases, transactions were demonetized, when cigarettes became the medium used to facilitate multilateral exchange on black markets. This primitive economy does not operate today in Western Europe, but everyone age 50 or above will have memories of it. Moreover, in Eastern Europe there are 'second' or 'coloured' economies (Grossman, 1977; Katsenelinboigen, 1977) with many of the characteristics found in Western Europe at a time of great scarcity.

(2) *Further industrialization and affluence*. In the 1950s and 1960s two processes were common to all Western societies. The first was a continuing decline in agricultural employment. Given the propensity of farm households to rely more upon the Domestic and Unofficial economies than urban families, this substantially reduced the proportion of the labour force outside the national income accounts. The affluence that drew people from farms to cities gave people more money to spend, and there was more money for

government to tax in the Official Economy. Measures of the Official Economy became of growing significance in the management of the economy. But the validity of these measures is contingent upon conditions that vary in time (as between agricultural pre–1914 and industrial post–1950 Europe) and place (as between Europe and Africa today).

(3) *Fiscal stress.* In the 1970s two things happened concurrently: Western governments continued to increase demands for tax revenue in order to finance growing welfare state commitments, and the rate of growth of the Gross National Product started to decline. In consequence, it became more and more difficult to finance additional tax revenue painlessly from the fiscal dividend of growth. In the absence of strong political commitment to rising levels of public consumption, citizens could turn to work in the Unofficial Economy to avoid taxation (Rose and Peters, 1978). Significantly, most attempts to estimate the size of the Unofficial Economy assume nil or very little activity during the boom times of the 1960s; it is assumed that fiscal stress increases effort in the Unofficial Economy.

(4) *Economic stagnation.* In the 1980s Western economies are growing very slowly and in some years contracting — or so it is reported in national income accounts. The demand for productive work in the cash-only Unofficial Economy could also slow down or contract, since it requires that consumers have the discretionary income to buy its goods and services. In conditions of economic stagnation, the Domestic Economy may boom as people have more time to invest in producing goods and services for their own consumption than money to spend on products of the Official or Unofficial economies. People can still get by, but there is a change in the mix of the three economies.

From the viewpoint of policy makers, three questions are of basic importance. First, what is the absolute size of each economy, and the share that each contributes to total national output, whether or not officially recorded or monetized? The second question concerns the direction and rate of change: which economies are growing, which are contracting, and how fast or how slow is change occurring? Thirdly, what are the interdependencies between the three economies? If all three expand or contract in the same direction at more or less the same rate, then movements in the Official Economy would be a valid indicator of rates of change in Individual Consumption in total. On the other hand, if interdependencies result in the economies changing in different directions, the Official

Economy will be misleading. In boom times, measures of the Official Economy will tend to overstate rates of economic growth, and in periods of economic recession like the 1980s, to understate the level of economic wellbeing.

II
The continuing strengths of the Official Economy

Reports of the death of the Official Economy are much exaggerated. The sustained growth of the Official Economy in the post-war era is a matter of record. The Gross National Product of the average OECD nation as measured by its national accounts has increased by several hundred percent in volume terms in the past quarter century. Even in the difficult 1970s the cumulative growth of Official Economies in OECD nations was 38 percent, and the Official Economy usually grew in nine out of ten years (OECD, 1982: Table 3.1). Furthermore, national governments have greatly increased the amount of taxes collected from citizens. From 1960 to 1970, OECD nations on average increased their share of tax revenue as a percentage of Gross Domestic Product from 26 to 32 percent, and in the difficult 1970s from 32 to 37 percent. Given the continued expansion of the national product, in the difficult 1970s the average national government could increase the real value of taxes collected by more than half in constant money terms and more than four times in current money terms (calculated from OECD 1981, Table 1).

Working in the Official Economy is the norm — both statistically and in terms of social values — in every Western nation today. The majority of the population of working age is in work, and expects to be in work. In nearly every OECD country rates of participation in the officially recorded labour forces have remained well above 90 per cent for men of age 25–54, and have risen notably for women (OECD 1979, Tables III–3, III–8). Moreover, opinion surveys show that the great majority of people find their work satisfactory and satisfying (European Community, 1975).

Structural changes in postwar society have strengthened institutions of the Official Economy. Industrialization has brought all adults into the money economy, however remote their residence or whatever their occupation. Urbanization has broken up the family as a farm-based unit producing for the Domestic Economy, and movement to the cities has given women opportunities to take paid employment in offices and factories. Mechanization and mass marketing have meant that consumers now buy goods that cannot be produced outside the Official Economy. Whereas a horse could be reared and shod in the Domestic Economy, an automobile can only be manufactured within the Official Economy. Sliced bread and Corn Flakes are typical products of the Official Economy, substituting for goods formerly produced in the Domestic Economy.

The intensive capitalization of production has concentrated production in factories requiring far more investment than the artisan workshop that they replace. The bureaucratization of production has made it harder for producers to avoid taxes, because large impersonal organizations are more easily scrutinized by government than are individual households. Democratization has increased the legitimacy of governments, making it easier for officials to secure co-operation in reporting economic activities for tax purposes. Social status is derived from an individual's occupation within the Official Economy or, in the case of a housewife, from the occupation of her husband rather than from activities in the Domestic Economy. Except in deviant sub-cultures, working in the Unofficial Economy lowers social status.

The great majority of people participate in the Official Economy because it is an inescapable condition of their occupation, or of the circumstances of their employer. This is most obviously the case in occupations in which the government is the sole or primary employer: teaching, postal work, the police and the civil service. Public employment today covers from one-fifth to one-third of total employment (Rose, 1980a). Occupations concentrated in large bureaucratized firms that must keep accurate records to function and routinely report data about their employees to government are invariably recorded in the Official Economy. Individuals do not have an equal choice between taking a full-time job in the Official or the Unofficial Economy. In Western nations today, the great bulk of the labour force is mobilized into the Official Economy.

Government offers positive cash benefits to participate in the Official Economy. Only by working in the Official Economy can individuals be registered for unemployment benefit; in many countries registration is also required for participation in health insurance programmes. In addition to these immediate benefits, work in the Official Economy is often a condition of an individual qualifying for a pension upon retirement. Moreover, the beneficiaries of social security programmes usually have only a small proportion of the cost deducted from their wages. The bulk of the social security levy is paid by the employer, thus giving the employee a vested interest in enforcing tax payments by others. The extent to which earmarked social security taxes can be used to encourage tax payment is greatest in Italy, where employers pay 83 percent of total social security taxes, and the employers' social security taxes yield 30 percent more money than does income tax. Notwithstanding the historic aversion to paying income tax, taxes on income (that is, social security and income tax together) total 18 percent of the national product in Italy, more than these taxes raise in the United Kingdom (OECD, 1981: Tables 4, 9).

Modern states can and do make use of a wide variety of tax handles to extract the money they need to finance contemporary welfare state benefits. Income tax yields two-fifths of revenue in the average OECD country, and social security taxes another fifth. Consumption taxes — VAT, customs and excise taxes — provide another quarter of tax revenue (OECD, 1981, Tables 6–7). Where income tax is collected on a Pay As You Earn basis via employers, then government has a relatively effective tax handle to limit evasion. This is even more true if social security taxes are collected simultaneously with income taxes. Many important consumption goods, such as tobacco and petrol, are particularly amenable to effective taxation and taxation at high rates. Property taxes are levied on assets that are not easily hidden. So effective are indirect taxes that an individual who worked entirely in the Unofficial Economy would still pay about 15 percent of his income in indirect taxes.

The effect of taxation upon work effort is complex (Brown, 1980). Taxation can encourage individuals to increase work in the Official Economy in order to compensate for the reduction of gross income by taxation. However, because marginal tax rates are high, not least for low-paid workers in the poverty trap, this may discourage additional work in the Official Economy and encourage the devotion of time to leisure or other activities outside the Official Economy (Kay and King, 1980: 111ff.).

The immediate incentive of the Official Economy is to reduce tax paid by reducing the proportion of income liable to tax. Tax avoidance by definition refers to work in the Official Economy; it is an effective as well as legal means of not paying tax on officially reported income. High marginal rates of taxation fall disproportionately upon people who are most likely to understand the complexities of tax laws, to influence the enactment of these laws, and to have professional advisors to assist them in arranging their affairs so as to minimize taxes by maximizing allowable deductions from gross income in the Official Economy. For example, a person with a gross income of 100,000 units could, by reducing income liable to taxation to 60,000 units, pay an average tax of one-third and a marginal rate of 50 percent of taxable income — and yet still only pay one-fifth of total gross income in tax.

The size of the Official Economy today is great, but it is not constant. In the past decade, rising unemployment has made it difficult for some people to enter the Official Economy or to remain securely employed. From 1971 to 1981, unemployment rates doubled in most OECD countries, and are currently running at about 10 percent in European countries. With rising unemployment, economic stagnation and fiscal stress, individuals at the margin may shift to work in the Unofficial or Domestic Economy to maintain consumption. But their first preference is to obtain the benefits of an income in the Official Economy.

III
Constraints upon demand and supply in the Unofficial Economy

Given the spotlight of publicity that has shone upon the Unofficial Economy in recent years, it can hardly be described as an unobserved economy (CENSIS, 1976). But anecdotes tell us nothing about magnitudes. To estimate the magnitude of consumption supported by the Unofficial Economy today, we need to know something about the attitudes of people to buying and selling services outside officially recognized markets. We also need to consider the structural opportunities and incentives for people to act as buyers and sellers in the Unofficial Economy. A desire to buy goods cheaper or to evade tax is not proof of accomplishment, any more than a desire to make money or to be employed is proof of economic success in the Official Economy.

Social surveys are one important source of data about the Unofficial Economy. Transactions in the Unofficial Economy are social relationships between a buyer and a producer-seller. Transactions in the Unofficial Economy are illegal, but a legal norm is not necessarily a social norm. Illegality means that official statistics are not a reliable or valid guide to tax evasion. Social surveys can examine the extent of social acceptance of illegal transactions in the Unofficial Economy.

There is now available a considerable amount of survey data from several Western nations about attitudes toward taxation and tax evasion. The evidence supports the following generalizations about the limits as well as the potential of the Unofficial Economy.

(1) *Attitudes toward taxation are inadequate evidence of acceptance or participation in the Unofficial Economy*. The rationale for asking people what they think of taxes is that a dislike of taxes is supposed to predispose people toward accepting tax evasion. A simple question asking people whether they think taxes are too high or too low will invariably find that many people believe taxes are too high (see, for example, Peretz, 1982: 475). But finding that taxes are considered too high is no more proof that taxation is likely to be evaded than is learning that people think death rates are too high. Both death and taxes remain certain.

(a) Taxes are not an issue of great political concern to voters. If taxation is to lead individuals to actions that challenge government's authority, then it should have a high priority in the opinions of voters. But this is not the case (cf. Lowery and Sigelman, 1981). When voters are asked by the Gallup Poll which are the most urgent problems facing the country at present, taxation usually receives few mentions. The most important problems today are usually unemployment and the cost of living. When voters are asked to choose between a party that would reduce unemployment or reduce income tax, 72 percent favour the reduction of unemployment as against 14 percent the reduction of taxes (*Gallup Political Index* No. 265, 1982: 5).

(b) There is an expectation that taxes will rise. Since 1957 the British Gallup Poll has collected data about popular expectations of taxes rising, falling or staying the same. In 18 of the past 26 years a plurality of respondents say that they believe taxes will rise in the next year, in four years a plurality expect taxes to stay the same, and in four years, fall. On average, for the past ten years 55 percent expect taxes to increase, 15 percent expect taxes to fall and 30 percent expect taxes to stay the same or have no opinion (*Gallup Political Index* No. 268, 1982: 19). Nor does the median voter expect income tax ever to drop substantially (*Gallup Political Index* No. 258, 1982: 7).

(c) Present levels of taxes are accepted as a reasonable exchange for present levels of welfare state benefits. Whereas taxes are unpopular,

TABLE 1
Popular attitudes toward taxes and benefits in Britain, 1978–1983

Preferred option	Oct. 1978 %	May 1979 %	Feb. 1980 %	Mar. 1981 %	Feb. 1982 %	Mar. 1983 %
Taxes being cut, even if it means some reduction in government services, such as health, education and welfare	25	34	22	20	21	23
Things should be left as they are	23	25	20	23	26	22
Government services such as health, education and welfare should be extended, even if it means some increases in taxes	39	34	52	49	49	49
Don't know	13	7	6	8	5	6

Sources: Gallup Political Index No. 219:15 (1978); No. 225:7 (1979); No. 234; 6 (1980); No. 271:12 (1983).

the health, education, and pensions benefits of the contemporary welfare state tend to be popular. In fiscal system terms, the question is whether or not people prefer taxes and spending to remain the same, or be altered by cutting taxes *and* welfare state services, or by increasing both. When the Gallup Poll asks people to choose between these alternatives, there is a consistent majority against cutting taxes; only one-fifth to one-third of the voters would wish to cut taxes if it meant cutting welfare state spending too (Table 1). In four of the five surveys taken in the past five years, more voters favoured increasing taxes in order to increase spending than favoured a cut in both. In May, 1979, when the Conservatives won a general election the proportion favouring cutting taxes was only 34 percent, no more than the proportion favouring an increase in taxes. What is particularly striking is that after a period of Conservative government in which cuts have been promoted by the government's rhetoric (if not by its actions), the proportion of voters favouring higher taxes and spending has risen to nearly half, more than twice as large as the proportion favouring cuts all around.

The readiness of the British public to support present (or higher) levels of taxes in order to finance welfare state benefits is matched by Americans. Surveys undertaken since 1975 for the United States Advisory Commission on Intergovernmental Relations (ACIR, 1982: Table 6, Appendix B) have found that Americans favouring a cut in taxes and public services are consistently in a minority, in 1982 totalling 36 percent, as against 42 percent favouring the status quo, 8 percent favouring increasing taxes and services, and 14 percent with no opinion. American opinion shows less positive support for increasing welfare services than Britain, but is very ready to accept taxation as it is. This finding is supported too by public opinion data from other countries (International Gallup, 1980: 75ff.; 1981: 33ff.).

(2) *Attitudes toward tax evasion are negative*. Survey questions about tax evasion concern issues going well beyond work in the Unofficial Economy. Some familiar forms of tax evasion do *not* involve the production or sale of goods and services, but rather fraudulent over-reporting of tax deductions, theft, or other types of illegal activities that do not alter the size of the national product (Blades, 1982:31). Hence, positive attitudes toward tax evasion must be discounted significantly to allow for the extent to which non-productive forms of tax evasion influence answers.

(a) Tolerance of tax evasion is limited. A majority surveyed do *not* tolerate tax evasion. Vogel's (1974: Table 6) pioneering 1969 Swedish study found that only 22 percent of respondents were prepared to excuse tax fraud on the grounds of economic need induced by fiscal demands (see also Wärneryd and Wålerud, 1982). In the United Kingdom, Keenan and Dean (1980: Table 1) found that the median respondent consistently disagreed with a series of statements justifying different forms of tax evasion. In the United States, 87 percent of respondents in a survey by Song and Yarborough (1978: Table 2) disagreed with the statement, 'Tax dodging is not a serious crime'. The overall pattern of replies is aptly summed up as: 'Most people feel that the tax laws should be respected, but do not feel that violations constitute so serious a crime as to warrant physical imprisonment' (Song and Yarborough, 1978: 433; see also CSR, 1980: chapter 5).

(b) Predisposition to participate in tax evasion is low. Given uncertainties about whether people will admit tax evasion in interviews, answers to predispositional questions about tax evasion can be considered a significant indicator of the likelihood of a person becoming involved in the Unofficial Economy, either as producer or

buyer. Vogel's pioneering Swedish study (1974: Tables 3–4) found that an average of 79 percent of Swedes disagreed with a series of five statements justifying tax evasion. Moreover, less than 30 percent of Swedes stated that they thought there was little or no probability that they would be caught if they did evade taxes (Vogel, 1974: Tables 3–4). In the United States, a similar pattern was found in a nationwide survey; on average 83 percent disagreed with statements justifying tax evasion (e.g., 'the chances of getting caught are so low that it is worthwhile trying to cheat'), as against 12 percent endorsing justifications for tax evasion (CSR, 1980: Table 5.11). Since three-quarters or more of all taxpayers reject the idea that people are justified in evading taxes, there is very limited social encouragement for individuals to engage in tax evasion.

(c) Actual involvement in tax evasion is lower still. Swedish evidence is particularly interesting, for Sweden has the highest level of taxation in the OECD world; in 1980 taxes were equivalent to 50 percent of the national product, a substantial increase from 41 percent in 1970. When a national sample of Swedes was asked whether they had received untaxed cash payments in the past year, 7 percent replied that this had happened once or twice, and 5 percent more often than that. A total of 11 percent said that they sometimes paid for goods or services in the Unofficial Economy, and another 31 percent that they had occasionally done this (Wärneryd and Wålerud, 1982: Table 1). An estimate of 12 percent working in the Unofficial Economy at least once in a year closely corresponds with a Swedish SIFO study, which reported 14 percent thus involved (Zetterberg and Frankel, 1981: 41). The very limited amount of work reported in the Unofficial Economy is an important caution against confusing the incidence of such activity with the volume of production thus generated.

A nationwide American survey using a locked box to collect anonymously the replies of respondents found that 12 percent admitted purposely failing to report some income on their tax returns. Inasmuch as this figure includes individuals whose non-reporting was done without the knowledge of the person or organization purchasing the service, it overestimates exchanges in the Unofficial Economy. Moreover, the average total of money involved in the transactions was low ($529), less than 5 percent of average income. Only one percent of the sample reported that they had ever failed to report more than $1,000 of income in any one year. American survey evidence emphasizes both the low incidence of tax evasion among the population, and implies a low proportion of the national product being sold in the Unofficial Economy.

The predisposition to pay taxes legally does not mean that people maximize tax payments; it suggests that legal tax avoidance by minimizing tax liabilities is far more widespread than tax evasion. In every western society tax laws provide a number of means by which taxable income can be reduced, and careful planning can increase the benefits of tax expenditures to a substantial fraction of tax payers (cf. Treasury, 1982: 94ff.). When Wärneryd and Wålerud (1982: Table 10) analysed their Swedish sample, they found that regular taxpayers were 45 percent of the total, tax planners who arranged affairs to avoid some taxes legally were 38 percent, and persons who sometimes engaged in tax evasion, 17 percent. Tax avoiders are not only several times more numerous than tax evaders, but also by definition are included within the Official Economy.

While survey evidence is not conclusive it is consistent: it shows that the great majority of people in Sweden and America, countries with very different tax levels but a common rhetoric of tax protest, are *against* participation in the Unofficial Economy. Vogel's interpretative conclusion (1974: 511) — 'Tax evasion is quite common in Sweden' — is not borne out by his own evidence. To regard tax evasion in the Unofficial Economy as high only makes sense if one has the unrealistically naive assumption that all laws are always obeyed and that national income accounts ought to measure all economic activity. A methodological bias of social psychologists in favour of correlating attitudes with each other often leads to an emphasis upon the statistical association between tax evasion and attitudes toward taxation. But the relationship is usually weak (cf. Wärneryd and Wålerud, 1982: Table 9; Vogel, 1974; Spicer and Lundstedt, 1976), and should not be allowed to obscure the fundamental finding: tax evasion remains socially unacceptable in Anglo-Saxon countries, and the incidence and frequency of participation in the Unofficial Economy is also low.

Given the limits of survey data about illegal behaviour, it is necessary to compare such estimates with estimates that can be derived from analysing structural opportunities and incentives to participate in the Unofficial Economy. If everyone has lots of opportunity and incentive to evade taxes through unofficial work, then survey evidence may be considered to underestimate greatly the extent of activity in the Unofficial Economy. On the other hand, if structural analysis shows that there are many obstacles to work in the Unofficial Economy, this will confirm survey evidence of its low limits.

The basic economic assumptions of the Unobserved Economy are simple albeit immoral, namely, that both buyers and sellers can be better off exchanging goods and services in the tax-free Unofficial Economy than in the more or less heavily taxed Official Economy. The Official Price (*OP*) of goods and services in the Official Economy can be said to be determined by four summary factors: Wages (*W*), Materials (*M*), Capital goods (*C*), and Taxes (*T*), levied on the preceding factors.

$$OP = W + M + C + T(W+M+C) \qquad (2)$$

For transactions to be agreed in the Unofficial Economy, two conditions must be met: (i) the Unofficial Price (*UP*) must be less than the Official Price for the would-be buyer, and (ii) the Unofficial Wage (*UW*) must be more than the Official Wage for the producer. Unless *both* these conditions are met, there will be insufficient incentive for goods and services to be produced unofficially.

The principal incentive offered customers in the Unofficial Economy is a saving in price resulting from the absence of a tax on wages. The saving to the customer is less than the full tax unpaid, for a worker will usually want a portion to augment earnings; otherwise there is little incentive to enter the Unofficial Economy.[1] The size of the price advantage in the Unofficial Economy depends upon the proportion of the total price determined by wages, and the rate of tax upon factors of production, particularly the marginal rate of tax upon a worker's wage.

The paradigm case of a product suited to the Unofficial Economy is a service that can be produced with virtually no investment in materials or capital goods, say, baby-sitting or window-cleaning. But the scope for such services is limited; even a joiner or an electrician will need some tools, and often a car to get to and from work. Anyone who tries to depend solely upon the Unofficial Economy for a living will have little or no opportunity to acquire materials or capital goods cheaply by legal means. By contrast, a worker who supplements a primary job in the Official Economy with a second job in the Unofficial Economy may borrow equipment for unofficial weekend work with the tacit consent of an employer, or buy goods at a discount from his employer, or obtain them without payment as a perk or by pilferage (see, e.g., South, 1981).

The Unofficial Economy is ill-suited to the production of manufactured goods, for the labour cost is typically a limited fraction of total cost. Capital cost in manufacturing is likely to be so high that only a limited liability company may meet it, and the machinery so complex that it cannot be borrowed for the weekend. Whereas a motor mechanic may borrow equipment to assist in doing repair work on the side, a vehicle builder cannot borrow a production line to assist in building a car. Industrial workers may pilfer goods after they have been manufactured and recorded in the Official Economy, but this does not increase the total product of a nation, it only redistributes it.

The marginal rate of tax upon the worker's wage is also of great importance, for this determines the saving available for division between the producer and buyer of products in the Unofficial Economy. If wages represent 80 percent of the cost, but a worker's marginal rate of tax is only 10 percent, then the potential price discount is at the most only 8 percent. By contrast, if the marginal rate of income and social security tax is 40 percent, then the Official Price can be discounted by up to 32 percent (that is 40 percent of 80 percent). Moreover, if a VAT charge of 15 percent is also waived, then the official price can be discounted by a further 12 percent. In such circumstances, the Unofficial Price need only be 61 percent of the Official Price in order to make a deal in the Unofficial Economy attractive to both buyer and seller. If the difference between the Unofficial and Official level is split between buyer and seller, then the purchaser procures services at almost a 20 percent discount, and the worker receives almost one-third more than would be earned in the Official Economy. Calculations are very sensitive to the wage component of the total price; for example, if the wage component is half the total price, then at a 40 percent marginal rate of tax on earnings plus 15 percent saved on VAT, the maximum potential saving is 24 percent, a sum giving little price incentive to the purchaser, if divided with the seller.

Marginal rates of taxation are likely to be high only under circumstances which restrict the incentives of producers to enter the Unofficial Economy. A worker with ordinary earnings will only pay the standard rate of income tax and social security on every additional unit of earning; much of earnings will be exempt because of tax allowances, or taxed at a below-standard rate. Thus there is no incentive to draw most of one's income from the Unofficial Economy. Moreover, the welfare state offers a positive incentive for an individual to be registered as a taxpayer in the Official Economy in order to be eligible for employment-related benefits.

Once an employee is registered in the Official Economy, then if progressive tax rates apply, the incentive to produce goods in the Unofficial Economy increases at the margin. This can be done by 'moonlighting', that is, taking a second job, or working in the Unofficial Economy to supplement a job in the Official Economy. In Italy, even the government recognizes this practice, setting the hours for many public officials from 8 am to 2 pm in order that they qualify in the Official Economy for social security benefits, and still have time for moonlighting after a mid-day meal. But the number of second jobs in an economy appears limited. Even studies intended to highlight moonlighting as 'a problem of our times' (e.g. de Grazia, 1980: 551ff. and Alden and Saha, 1978) suggest that less than 10 percent of the labour force in the Official Economy is thus employed. Moreover, the increase in total working hours makes the attraction of additional earnings by moonlighting decline rapidly as against leisure time.

Even if working in the Unofficial Economy is worthwhile to the workers, is it worthwhile to the buyer? The cost advantage is real, but limited. There are, of course, a number of non-economic motives for purchasers in the Unofficial Economy. For example, within a face-to-face set of neighbourhood relationships there may be advantages in dealing with a known and convenient person, for instance, a neighbour's son who shovels snow, or an electrician who belongs to the darts team at the local pub. But to employ strangers to do a major house repair runs the risk of fly-by-night workmanship for a relatively small net cash reward.

When the concept of a buyer is extended from an individual household to a firm, the advantages of purchasing goods in the Unofficial Economy decline. A firm that spends money buying goods and services will want to enter the sums paid in its books in order to offset expenditure against revenue, thus reducing its tax liability for profits. Self-employed persons also have an incentive to maximize the number of receipts they collect as proof of expenses, thus increasing deductions from gross income and minimizing their net taxable income. Contini (1981) describes a tendency for vertical integration between the Official and Unofficial economies in Italy, involving hosiery, textiles and toys produced by people working at home, and even components for industrial goods. But such vertical integration not only assumes an unusual degree of social collaboration outside the law, but also a very weak and inefficient public administration incapable of identifying large-scale tax evasion, or enforcing laws. Conditions found in Italy are not to be taken for granted elsewhere (cf. Cragg and Dawson,1981).

Cutting wages by putting out work to individuals who do not pay national taxes can be done more cheaply within the law by substituting imports from countries which can produce them more cheaply. There is no need for a firm to organize the purchase of goods in the Unofficial Economy, if the same goods can be supplied more cheaply and efficiently from Hong Kong, Taiwan or Brazil. Government actions to reduce customs levies further encourages imports, which are rising in most Western nations today.

Everyone who writes about the Unofficial Economy can produce examples of its goods and services, and of occupational groups able to work part-time in the Unofficial Economy. But how typical are the products and occupations suited to the Unofficial Economy? They must be goods and services that do not require complex accounting systems, bureaucracies and technologies extending nationwide or internationally, as do banking, insurance, or the telephone service. Moreover, they must be goods and services that do not require great capital investment, or have their cost determined principally by the cost of materials, as do steel or motor cars. And they must be products that can be produced 'invisibly' rather than in factories that are very visible to tax collectors. The greater the limitations on the goods and services capable of being produced in the Unofficial Economy, the less its aggregate significance.

The records of the Official Economy are a reasonable source of data for estimating the size of the Unobserved Economy. The demand and supply of Unofficial Economy products is for the most part related to the Observed Economy. The more that an individual seeks to work outside the Official Economy, the greater the use of materials and capital goods in the Official Economy. Whereas a youth who mows a neighbour's lawn with a neighbour's lawnmower requires only a cash wage, a youth who wishes to work all summer in the grass-cutting business will need equipment and a car to transport the equipment from job to job, just like a worker in the Official Economy.

The employed population of the United Kingdom can be divided into three broad categories according to the potential for Unofficial production in different industries and services (cf. Blades, 1982: 41). There is a high opportunity to enter the Unofficial Economy in services requiring a moderate amount of capital and materials, and produced by small-scale enterprises or the self-employed; there is a low opportunity in industries that are heterogeneous in terms of capital or materials; and virtually nil opportunity in capital-intensive industries, such as manufacturing and energy, and in public administration.

The most striking feature of the British labour force is the relatively low proportion — an estimated 11 percent — that meets the criteria for high potential participation in the Unofficial

TABLE 2
Employment according to likely opportunities to work in the unobserved economy

	N (000)	Total %
(A) *Relatively high*		
Construction	1,265	5.6
Textiles, leather and clothing	813	3.6
Agricultural, forestry, fishing	370	1.6
Total	2,448	10.9
(B) *Relatively low*		
Professional & scientific services	3,717	16.5
Distributive trades	2,790	12.4
Miscellaneous services	2,519	11.2
Total	9,026	40.1
(C) *Virtually nil*		
Engineering and allied industries	3,121	13.9
Public administration	1,596	7.1
Transport and communication	1,500	6.7
Rest of manufacturing	1,322	5.9
Insurance, banking and finance	1,258	5.6
Food, drink and tobacco manufacturing	681	3.0
Chemicals, coal and petroleum	470	2.1
Metal manufacturing	401	1.8
Mining and quarrying	344	1.5
Gas, electricity and water	347	1.5
Total	11,040	49.0

Source: Compiled from Central Statistical Office, *Social Trends* No. 13 (London: HMSO, 1982), Table 4.7. Data for 1980.

Economy: farmers, construction workers and persons in the clothing trade (Table 2). In addition, another 40 percent have low but still noteworthy opportunities to enter the Unofficial Economy. Within the distributive trades there are possibilities in the supply of services, but a restaurant must show some workers on its books, pay rent and buy food and drink in the Official Economy. In professional and scientific services, some opportunities may arise for moonlighting, taking cash as a fee without a receipt. The fact remains that virtually half of the labour force has almost nil opportunity to engage in the Unofficial Economy. People cannot carry out public administration, mining, chemical manufacturing, or run railways by themselves or unobserved.

Estimates can only be rough and ready. Within the categories of employment where nil opportunities for unofficial work are likely to

TABLE 3
Hours worked in the Unofficial Economy, according to differential employment opportunities

	Low estimate		High estimate	
	N persons (000)	Hours %	N persons (000)	Hours %
(A) *High opportunity* (2,488,000)				
(1) High realization (75% $P \times$ 50% OE)			918	37
(2) Low realization (75% $P \times$ 33% OE)	612	25		
(B) *Low opportunity* (9,026,000)				
(1) High realization (33% $P \times$ 20% OE)			601	6
(2) Low realization (25% $P \times$ 10% OE)	225	2.5		
(C) *Nil opportunity* (11,040,000)				
(1) High realization (10% $P \times$ 10% OE)			110	1
(2) Low realization (10% $P \times$ 5% OE)	55	0.5		
Total added to Unofficial Economy	892	4.0	1,629	7.2

P = Participation in the Unofficial Economy estimated as a % of numbers participating in the Official Economy.
OE = Hours in Unofficial Economy estimated as a % of hours worked in the Official Economy.

Source: Calculated from data in Table 2.

exist, there will be many exceptions. There may be occupations with a high propensity to moonlight in low propensity industries, and vice versa. Therefore, Table 3 presents two estimates, one high and one low, of the scale of unofficial work in Britain today. The high estimate assumes that of those with a high opportunity to participate in the Unofficial Economy three-quarters will do so, and spend half as much again as their normal working time in the Unofficial Economy, that is, about 20 hours a week; of those with a low opportunity, one-third will participate the equivalent of one day a week; and among those with virtually nil opportunity, 10 percent will participate a half day a week.

A relatively generous estimate of participation in the Unofficial Economy adds an additional 7.2 percent of labour to the Official Economy (Table 3). The alternative lower estimate of work in the Unofficial Economy is 4.0 percent. Two features of these estimates are noteworthy: (i) the small distance between the high and low estimates since the group with a high opportunity to participate is a relatively small fraction of the whole, and (ii) the low total size of the Unofficial Economy, whichever assumption is used.

To test the sensitivity of the above employment based estimates comparisons were made with the proportion of the Gross Domestic Product contributed by each industry (Central Statistical Office, 1982; T 1.9–10). The proportion of GDP contributed by industries with a high opportunity for evasion was 10.7 percent, virtually the same as their share of employment. When sectors of the economy were analysed, with the self-employed and employees of unincorporated businesses treated as having a high opportunity for tax evasion (as against employees of industrial and commercial companies, financial institutions, and government institutions), the share of Gross Domestic Product produced in the high opportunity sector rose only slightly to 13.5 percent. Whatever measure of activity in the Official Economy is used, only a small fraction has a high opportunity for substantial work in the Unofficial Economy. Since only a portion of the potential for evasion will be realized, an industry or sector approach confirms the conclusions of the occupational approach set out in Table 3.

Comparing labour force estimates of the Unofficial Economy with estimates derived from other data bases, methods and assumptions of varying degrees of plausibility, shows a very high degree of agreement (Table 4). Of nine estimates of the magnitude of the Unofficial Economy, the lowest estimate is 2 percent of GDP, and

TABLE 4
Alternative estimates of the size of the unobserved economy in the United Kingdom

Type of estimate	**Size/Range as % of GDP**
Income-Expenditure discrepancy in National Accounts (O'Higgins, 1982:5)	2
Expenditure-Income discrepancy in Family Expenditure Survey	
a) Dilnot-Morris (1981:66) assumptions	2–3
b) O'Higgins (1982:17) assumptions	3–8
Hold second job (Macafee, 1980:86)	3
Currency/Deposits (Matthews) 1981	3–11
Labour force (Rose: above Table 3)	4–7
Inland Revenue estimates (1981:27)	7.5
Taxpayers Compliance Measurement Programme (Projection of US IRS figures to UK; O'Higgins, 1982:11)	9–11
Financial transactions (Feige, 1981)	15

Note: The year given is usually 1979; the Matthews and Feige estimates are particularly variable from year to year.

the highest, 15 percent. The median estimate, taking the lower of a pair of figures, is 3 percent; taking the higher of a pair of estimates, the median figure is 8 percent. To speak of the Unofficial Economy as small is to speak in relative terms; the median figures suggest a product equal to several hundred pounds per employed person. But such sums are relatively small when measured against a national product of about £250 billion.

Whether the Unofficial Economy is growing is doubtful. On *a priori* grounds, the case for arguing that people will work additional hours in the Unofficial Economy in order to augment take-home pay is tantamount to saying that higher taxation leads people to work more hours to earn more. But empirical research does not confirm this assumption (Brown, 1980). Given the comparatively high standards of living in OECD nations today, it would be as reasonable to assume a disincentive effect, that at the margin people will prefer more leisure to more work. Moreover, in periods of economic recession demand will fall as buyers lack the cash to enter the cash-only economy (cf. O'Higgins, 1982).

IV
The resources of the Domestic Economy

How much do the resources of the Domestic Economy contribute to current consumption? How elastic is the productive capacity of the Domestic Economy, and under what circumstances can we expect it to grow or contract?

Time is the great resource that constrains all economic activity; everyone has 168 hours to invest each week in a variety of activities. A distinctive feature of the Domestic Economy is the relatively large amount of time that is potentially available for investment. This can be expressed in the abstract, when tT is total Time, tD is discretionary time, tS is sleep, and tPC is personal care:

$$tD = tT - (tS + tPC + tOE + tUE) \tag{3}$$

A clear indication of the magnitude of discretionary time available can be derived from a major British study of the activities of British adults, based upon hour-by-hour time-budget diaries of a week (Gershuny, 1981: Table 1). It found that on average adults spend 45 hours a week sleeping; another 31 hours a week in personal care that individuals must do for themselves, such as eating and washing (cf. Hill, 1979: 34ff.); and 29 hours a week on average in paid employment, with an estimated two hours a week additional (7 percent) participation in the Unofficial Economy. Each adult therefore has on average 61 hours a week in discretionary time.[2]

Any calculation of average discretionary time inevitably obscures very important differences between persons in paid work, and persons not in paid work, principally housewives. The amount of time spent sleeping remains the same for both groups (45 hours a week), and that spent in personal care varies little (30 hours for persons in paid work, as against 35 hours for persons not in work). Since persons in work spend on average 39 hours in the Official Economy and an estimated 3 hours in the Unofficial Economy, this leaves them 51 hours a week discretionary time, as against 88 hours a week of discretionary time for persons not in paid work (Gershuny and Thomas, forthcoming: Table 4.5).

Given so much discretionary time, under what circumstances would we expect individuals to engage in production in the Domestic Economy? In the abstract, the answer is simple: when the Domestic Economy Price (DEP) is less than the Unofficial Economy Price and the Official Economy Price. By definition, in the Domestic Economy, money wages are 0. Therefore, the Domestic Economy Price is determined very differently from the Official Economy Price:

$$DEP = 0 + M + C + T(0 + M + C) \tag{4}$$

Production in the Domestic Economy has a large relative price advantage when the cost of the product is primarily the wage cost, for example, child care, where it is as much as 100 percent, or preparing meals, where it is also very substantial. By contrast, the price advantage is low when the cost of materials is high; for example, when laying a new carpet the principal cost is not the labour for installation but the purchase of the carpet itself. The price advantage is also low when the capital cost is high, for example, developing colour film. Capital cost includes human capital; the skill required for cooking a gourmet meal is greater than that for frying eggs, and caring for a deaf child greater than that of caring for a child with full hearing. The larger the share of the wage element in the production of goods, the greater the real (albeit non-monetized) benefit in producing these goods and services in the Domestic Economy.

The production of goods and services in the Domestic Economy cannot be analysed in terms of a simple trade-off between unpaid work and leisure. Many household goods and services must of necessity be produced domestically. It is no longer possible to employ people to provide all the domestic services required in an ordinary household. Even in an era of rising unemployment, few people come forward to offer labour as servants, as happened a century ago. The alternative to cooking some meals for oneself may be starvation, and the alternative to providing *some* care for one's own children may be child neglect or abandonment. The rise of the welfare state has made the provision of personal services, such as caring for the elderly, the sick and disabled a responsibility of the Official Economy public sector; formerly such work was almost exclusively in the Domestic Economy. Concurrently, there has been a rising price for household services. Women now enter the Official Economy to sell personal services formerly produced at home, and men spend more time working in the Do-It-Yourself Domestic Economy because of the high money price of purchasing home repair services in the Official or Unofficial Economy.

The benefits of domestic production are multiple: the household gains goods and services and the producer may gain an intangible but significant utility from pride in workmanship or a hobby. Moreover, people may prefer home-cooked meals or 'home-made' child care rather than goods and service acquired through the cash nexus. There are intangible benefits for the household as a whole from the altruistic and affectionate exchange of services outside the money economy; in certain circumstances, monetized goods and services are unacceptable (Webley, Lea and Portalska, 1983; Titmuss, 1970).

There is an inverse relation between the incentives for work in the Unofficial Economy as against the Domestic Economy. The higher the wage content of a job, the higher the price will be in the Unofficial Economy. For example if wages are 67 percent of the cost of painting a house in the Official Economy and materials and capital goods 15 percent, then the price in the Unofficial Economy will be at least 82 percent of the Official Price. By contrast, in the Domestic Economy, it will be 15 percent of the Official Price, because no money wage is paid. When production in the Domestic Economy loses its price advantage to the Official Economy because the wage component is small, the Unofficial Economy also loses out.

Given the distinctive characteristics of production in the Domestic Economy, how much individual consumption can be provided by work in the Domestic Economy? Conceptually, we may divide the discretionary time of individuals into three different primary categories; only the third concerns the Domestic Economy.

(1) *Pastimes*. Activities that do not involve the consumption or production of monetized goods and services, for instance talking with friends or going for a walk.

(2) *Leisure consumption*. Activities that require spending money in the Official or Unofficial Economy, for instance talking to a friend at a pub, going to the cinema or taking a drive in a car.

(3) *Housework and productive leisure*. Activities in the Domestic Economy that produce marketable goods and services without money payment, for instance making meals for a family or servicing the family car.

Given the large quantity of adults' discretionary time — an average of 61 hours a week — we would expect a family to invest a substantial amount in pastimes and leisure consumption as well as in unpaid housework and productive leisure. These activities differ greatly in significance for national income accounts. Whereas pastimes have at most a trivial effect upon the Official Economy, leisure consumption is significant because it involves money expenditure. Unpaid housework and productive leisure are more difficult to handle empirically, because they involve non-monetized activities, yet they are important in producing goods and services.

A reasonable estimate of the magnitude of time invested in each of these different discretionary activities can be obtained by re-analysing time-budget data collected by J. I. Gershuny (1981: Table 1), which fits well the three categories defined above. Time-budget analysis shows that housework and productive leisure account for the largest proportion of discretionary time, 23 hours per week for the average adult in 1975 (Table 5). A very substantial amount of time is also spent on other components of discretionary time. A total of 21 hours a week is devoted to costless pastimes, and 17 hours to leisure consumption, allocating half the time spent viewing TV to consumption leisure, in view of the capital cost of equipment, and

TABLE 5
The allocation of discretionary time in the week

	1961		**1975**		**Change 1975–61**	
	Hrs	**%**	**Hrs**	**%**	**Hrs**	**%**
1. *Pastimes* (Walks, visiting friends, relaxing, conversation, etc. half of TV-radio-records time)*	20	34	21	35	+1	+1
2. *Leisure consumption* (Travel, cinema, dances, clubs, pubs, reading newspapers, half of TV-radio-records time)*	12	21	17	28	+5	+7
3. *Unpaid housework and productive leisure* (Cooking, housework, odd jobs, gardening, shopping, child care, study, knitting, sewing, etc.).	26	44	23	38	−3	−6
Totals	59		61		+2.5	

* Time spent in viewing and listening, 17.5 hours, 1961: 16.5 hours 1975.

Source: Calculated from Gershuny, 1981: Table 1.

half to pastimes, since the marginal cost of using the equipment is very low. Whereas leisure consumption is measured in the Official Economy, productive leisure is not entered there, because it is not monetized production.

As might be expected, the total amount of discretionary time increased from 1961 to 1975, because of the shortening of the working week and a rise in the number of part-time women workers in the Official Economy. Moreover, the growth of affluence has permitted the substitution of purchased goods and service for domestic production. Housework and productive leisure time has therefore decreased from 44 percent of total leisure time to 38 percent, a change balanced by an increase in leisure consumption (Table 5). But leisure consumption is still the least important of the three uses of discretionary time. People spend much more time doing nothing or in productive leisure than in leisure activities that enter the national income accounts.

The stability of unpaid housework and productive leisure reflects the fact that the activities classified thus — preparing meals, cleaning the house and making beds, odd jobs, shopping, caring for children, looking after clothes, etc. — are continuous household necessities. The allocation of these tasks may change substantially between sexes within households (cf. Gershuny, 1982); and there are substantial variations in the amount of time spent in different tasks between households. Notwithstanding this, what is striking is the great and persisting importance of productive leisure within the home, whether measured in terms of total hours or as a percentage of total discretionary time.

Moreover, there is very substantial cross-national similarity in the amount of time that people spend in housework and productive leisure. According to a multi-national time-budget study in 12 countries, including America, France, Germany (East and West), Poland, Bulgaria, the Soviet Union and Peru (Szalai et al., 1972), the extremes in productive leisure range from 31 hours a week in Yugoslavia to 17 hours a week reported in Bulgaria. In surveys in Western nations 27 hours a week was devoted to productive leisure in West Germany, 22 hours in American cities, 20 hours a week in French cities, and 17 hours a week in Belgium, and 24 to 27 hours a week reported in contemporaneous British studies (Szalai et al., 1972: 114). The similarities in the Domestic Economy of many different societies should not be surprising. The Domestic Economy is important in every society, for it produces universal necessities.

V
The relative significance of the three economies

Given the existence of three different economies, we must ask: What is the relative significance of each for maintaining individual consumption? The first step is to add together the product of the Official Economy and the Unofficial Economy. Table 3 indicates that the Unofficial Economy adds about 6 percent to labour in the Official Economy. The actual money value of the Unofficial Economy will depend upon whether the value of its workers' output is the same as in the Official Economy, or whether it is less because it does not involve expensive capital goods. The money value is also affected by whether it is reckoned as a proportion of the Gross National Product at market prices (£249bn in 1981), as a proportion of total income from employment and self-employment (£165bn) or as a proportion of total consumer expenditure (£151bn) (Central Statistical Office, 1982: Tables 1:1–2). Whatever base is used, the money value of the Unofficial Economy is large enough to attract press headlines — 'billions spent' — and anecdotes — 'He'll do it for £50 cash in hand'. But the Unofficial Economy remains small as a proportion of total monetized economic activity in Britain today.

By contrast, the Domestic Economy is large in absolute and relative terms. One reason is the participation rate. Whereas there are about 23 million people in work in Britain today, there are 40 million people between the ages of 16 and 74 producing goods and services in the Domestic Economy. If we multiply the average time spent in productive leisure (23 hours a week) by this population, we have a total of 920 million hours a week spent in productive leisure compared with a total of 840 million hours of work in the Official Economy each week, and an additional 50 million hours in the Unofficial Economy. As many hours are invested each week in producing goods and services in the Domestic Economy as in the Official Economy, and when allowance is made for the fact that there is little or no holiday time in the Domestic Economy, its role is further enhanced. If 1961 figures are used, when there was a larger work force and a slightly longer working week, the number of hours worked weekly in the Official Economy then was about 935 million and an additional 55 million in the Unofficial Economy, totalling 990 million hours worked weekly for money, as against 978 million hours in the Domestic Economy.

Time, like money, is easily measured, and it is also scarce. Unlike the measuring rod of money, time can be used to measure activities in the Domestic Economy. Activity in three economies can thus be added together using labour input in each as the unit of account. This is reasonable, for the production of goods and services always involves a labour input. On this basis, two of the economies — the Official and Domestic economies — are almost equal in size; the Unofficial Economy is of little significance (Table 6). Moreover, the share of total labour that each economy contributes in society has remained very stable from 1961 to 1975, notwithstanding changes in the number of hours worked, and in the Official Economy and the Domestic Economy. The net effect has been to reduce hours worked in the three economies altogether by an estimated 8 percent, thanks to productivity increases. If the money output of the Domestic Economy were valued differently from the labour input, the overall conclusion would remain the same: the Official Economy and the Domestic Economy are each of great importance in maintaining individual consumption.

The estimates of the relative importance of the Official and Domestic economies in Britain are very consistent with estimates produced by a variety of methods for other countries. For example in the United States, Eisner et al. (1981: Table 22) calculate that the contribution of household production to total income (that is, monetized and non-monetized production together) has ranged between 35 and 39 percent from 1946 to 1976. Since the American estimate is based upon dollar values not labour input, it is comparable to that in Table 6. Nordhaus and Tobin (1973: 509ff.)

TABLE 6
Estimated total labour hours in the three economies

	1961		1975	
	N hrs (mn per week)	%	N hrs (mn per week)	%
Official Economy	935	47	840	46
Unofficial Economy	55	3	50	3
Domestic Economy	978	50	920	51
Totals	1,968	100	1,810	100

Source: Calculated from Tables 3 and 5; see also footnotes 5 and 6.

similarly calculate that in 1929 non-market work produced 39 percent of national output in the market and non-market sectors together, rising to 50 percent in the depression year 1935, and returning to 39 percent by 1965 (see also Sametz, 1968: 84ff.). Estimates for Canada (Adler and Hawrylyshyn, 1978) and for France are also broadly consistent (Barthelemy, 1981: 171). In Scandinavian societies with very high rates of female participation in the labour force, the Official Economy might be relatively more important vis à vis the Domestic Economy than in Britain. In Italy, the Unofficial Economy should be relatively more important than in most OECD countries, given the importance of the peasantry, of anti-state attitudes, and the exceptional social predisposition to condone and to organize tax evasion (cf. Contini, 1981; Martino, 1981).

To understand how individuals maintain consumption in times of fiscal stress, we must ask: To what extent can goods and services produced in the Official Economy be substituted by goods and services produced in the Domestic Economy? Insofar as this is possible, then individuals can get by with consumption increasing in the Domestic Economy as consumption falls in the Official Economy. Whereas the Unofficial Economy is not well suited to maintain consumption in times of recession because of a shortage of buyers, the Domestic Economy can produce more goods and services. In a recession, people have more time to work at home and there is today an increasing use of capital equipment within the home, thus extending the productive capacity of the ordinary household.

The objects of household expenditure in the Official Economy can be grouped into three categories: those with a relatively high potential for substitution from the Domestic Economy; those with a medium to low potential; and those with nil potential for substitution. On this basis, there is the potential to substitute goods and services in the Domestic Economy for a substantial portion of total consumer expenditure (Table 7).

(1) *High potential substitutability* (23 percent). Ironically, the most significant substitution — unpaid housework for domestic service — was realized in the first half of the twentieth century with the virtual disappearance of paid domestic servants. Because middle-class families no longer paid servants to do things for them did not mean that cooking, making beds, cleaning, gardening and driving a car were left undone. These services are now provided in the Domestic

TABLE 7
The distribution of household expenditure in the Official Economy by likely opportunity to substitute in the Domestic Economy

	£bn	%
(A) *High substitutability*		
Alcoholic drink	11.4	
Catering and accommodation	7.6	
Household maintenance	5.0	
Miscellaneous recreational goods	4.3	
Other services	5.3	
Domestic service	0.5	
Total	34.1	(23)
(B) *Medium to low substitutability*		
Food	24.1	
Clothing	10.1	
Travel	5.2	
Maintaining cars	3.7	
Entertainment services (TV purchase; admissions, etc.)	3.0	
Other miscellaneous goods	2.6	
Expenditure abroad	3.0	
Total	51.7	(34)
(C) *Nil substitutability*		
Housing rent, rates	19.2	
Durable goods	12.2	
Fuel and light	7.8	
Tobacco	5.5	
Running a car (petrol, licence)	6.5	
Other household goods	3.9	
Chemists' goods	2.3	
Post, telephone	2.5	
Insurance	2.2	
Books, newspapers	2.2	
Betting and gaming	1.3	
Total	65.4	(43)

Source: Compiled from Central Statistical Office *National Income and Expenditure* (1982) Table 4.6, consumers' expenditure at current prices.

Economy, often in ways that involve capital-intensive equipment, for instance washing machines, vacuum cleaners, power lawnmowers, etc. Today, a high potential for substituting domestic production is found in expenditure on meals and holiday accommodation, household maintenance and recreation. The largest substitutable expenditure item — alcoholic drink — still remains important in the Official Economy, even though it is in principle easy to substitute home-brew beer for drink purchased in the Official Economy.

(2) *Medium-to-low substitutability* (34 percent). Food is the largest entry in this category: a small amount of food can be grown, more time can be invested in preparing food at home rather than buying frozen or prepared foods, and meals made with cheaper foods can provide the same nutritional value. Expenditure on clothing can be substituted by making some clothes at home, by repairing clothes to give them longer life, and buying and altering second-hand clothes. Expenditure on travel can be reduced through pooled use of travel facilities, bicycling, or walking, and costless pastimes can to some extent be substituted for leisure consumption.

(3) *Nil substitutability* (43 percent). Families can economize, in the sense of spending less money on goods and services in this category, but they cannot substitute equivalent home-made goods and services for many products of the Official Economy. A car can be driven slowly to economize on petrol, but it cannot be driven without petrol, nor can petrol be produced at home. A letter may be substituted for a long-distance telephone call, but individuals cannot communicate simply by shouting from city to city. Nor is self-insurance the same as pooling risks across many households.

The capacity of a household to get by through production in the Domestic Economy or by simply foregoing the purchase of particular goods and services will vary greatly with the composition of the household. Young workers living with their parents will not need to spend money to duplicate household equipment that their parents provide, and they may not be asked to pay the economic cost of their food, lodging and other necessities. Pensioners have had a lifetime of work in which to accumulate many goods, and may live rent-free by owning their own house. An unemployed person does not need to maintain expenditure on a weekly basis for consumer durable goods or a car. Capital invested in durable household goods can be stretched for a number of years before replacement is absolutely necessary.

The composition of a household affects the impact of unemployment upon consumption. If an unemployed person is young and unmarried (50 percent of the total of male unemployed), he or she can draw upon the resources of other members of their family of origin by living at home. If a man is made unemployed, there is a prospect that a wife will be bringing home an income, the position of one-sixth of unemployed males, and an unemployed wife can have an employed husband. The unemployed spouse may turn to increased domestic production, while the other partner continues to provide a money income to purchase goods of the Official Economy that cannot be foregone. The families where unemployment is likely to bear hardest — the husband out of work, the wife not working and with small children at home — constitutes only one-sixth of the unemployed, or two percent of the labour force (*Social Trends*, 1981; Tables 4. 25–26).

The possibility of substituting domestic production for that of the Official Economy is most important for unemployed people, who gain an extra 40 hours of unobligated time each week, as well as suffering a reduction in money income. A study of unemployed male workers in Belfast (Kilpatrick and Trew, 1982: Table 2) has found that unemployed males are likely to increase the amount of time spent in domestic work by upwards of 16 hours a week. Of the additional time, a portion is devoted to do-it-yourself activities, and another portion to child care. By contrast, the amount of additional time devoted to personal care increases by only a few hours each week. A Finnish survey (Salmi, 1981: Table 4) similarly found that unemployed persons spend 12 hours a week more in domestic work than do employed persons. Production in the Domestic Economy is a significant resource for unemployed people; it can help them get by in the face of a decline in their Official Economy income.

The resources of households today are such that most families have the domestic capital and the cash flow to provide a significant number of goods and services for themselves, whether in work or out of work. In December, 1982, after years of persisting economic difficulties only 4 percent of a British Gallup Poll sample reported that they were running into debt, and another 9 percent that they were having to draw on their savings to meet household needs. Fifty percent said that they were making ends meet, and 33 percent that they were saving money (*Gallup Political Index* 272, 1983:10).

As macro-economic conditions change, there is ample scope at the margin for substitution between the Official and Domestic

Economies. In a booming economy, people use increased earnings to spend more money on leisure consumption and to buy durable goods (refrigerators, freezers and dishwashers) in the Official Economy to shorten time spent on laborious tasks in the Domestic Economy. When demand for labour in the Official Economy slackens, individuals will spend less time in work, and marginal workers will be counted out of its labour force. But this gives more time and more incentive for individuals to produce goods and services in the Domestic Economy to substitute for products formerly purchased in the Official Economy. Activities recorded in the national income accounts will increase in the former circumstances, and decrease in the latter. *From the viewpoint of the individual, total consumption remains the same*.

Movement in and out of the Official Economy reduces the value of national income accounts as a measure of individual consumption. If macro-economic attention is concentrated exclusively upon national accounts, this will intensify the *appearance* of cyclical changes. The substitution of official for domestic production in boom times makes the height of the boom higher, just as the substitution of domestic for official production in recession makes the depth of the recession appear greater. Misperception based upon misleading statistics can lead to policies that are misdirected (cf. McGee and Feige, 1982).

But from the viewpoint of the ordinary individual, *counter-cyclical* movement back and forth between the Official and the Domestic Economies has positive advantages. It is a strategy for getting by in an economy that is full of ups and downs. When the Official Economy is booming, a family has more money coming in, and can use that money to buy freedom from what are considered household chores, as well as to finance leisure consumption. When the Official Economy is slack, individuals can use their domestic resources to maintain consumption. Fiscal stress undoubtedly creates economic difficulties, but the extent of these difficulties should not be exaggerated by assuming that statistics of the Official Economy—or anecdotes about the Unofficial Economy — represent the only alternatives open to people. The resourcefulness of individuals and households is of primary importance in getting by.

NOTES

1. Where prices are controlled and goods are rationed, there may be incentives for buyers to pay more than the artificially low Official Price. Likewise, when wage rates

are set at prices well above what market pressures recommend, there are incentives for marginal workers to reduce wages below the artificially high Official Price.

2. That is, 168 hours of weekly time less 45 hours for sleep, 31 for personal care, 29 hours on average for work in the Official Economy, and 2 hours on average for work in the Unofficial Economy.

REFERENCES

ACIR (1982) *Changing Public Attitudes on Governments and Taxes*. Washington DC: Advisory Commission on Intergovernmental Relations.

Adler, H.J. and Hawrylshyn, Oli (1978) 'Estimates of the Value of Household Work, Canada, 1961 and 1971', *Review of Income and Wealth*, 24, 4.

Alden, J.D. and Saha, S.K. (1978) 'An analysis of Second Jobholding in the EEC', *Regional Studies*, 12.

Alt, James (1979) *The Politics of Economic Decline*. Cambridge: Cambridge University Press.

Barthelemy, Phillippe (1981) *L'economie Souterraine: Concepts et Mesures*. Aix-en-Provence: Centre d'Analyse Economique, Faculté d'Economique Appliquée d'Aix-Marseille.

Blades, Derek (1982) 'The Hidden Economy and the National Accounts', *Economic Outlook Occasional Studies*. Paris: Organization for Economic Co-operation and Development, June, 1982.

Brown, C.V. (1980) *Taxation and Labour Supply*. London: Allen and Unwin.

CENSIS (1976) *L'Occupazione Occulta: caratteristiche della partecipazione al lavoro in Italia*. Rome: CENSIS Ricerca 2.

Central Statistical Office (1982) *National Income and Expenditure*. London: Her Majesty's Stationery Office.

Charles, Prince, 1981. 'Sayings of the Week'. *The Observer*, 22 November.

Contini, Bruno (1981) 'Dropping Out; Notes on the Italian Economy'. *Journal of Contemporary Studies*, 4, 3: 79–89.

Cragg, A. and Dawson, T., 1981. *Qualitative Research Among Home Workers*. London: Department of Employment Research Paper No. 21.

CSR (1980) *A General Taxpayer Opinion Survey*. Washington, DC: Prepared for the Internal Revenue Service.

Dilnot, A. and Morris, N. (1981) 'What Do We Know About the Black Economy?', *Fiscal Studies*, 2, 1: 58–73.

Eisner, Robert et al. (1981) 'Total Incomes in the United States: 1946 to 1976'. Gouvieux, France: 17th Annual Conference, International Association for Research in Income and Wealth.

European Community (1975) *European Men and Women: A Comparison of their Attitudes to Some of the Problems Facing Society*. Brussels: Survey Report for the Commission of the European Community.

Feige, Edgar, 1981. 'The United Kingdom's Unobserved Economy: A Preliminary Assessment'. *Journal of Economic Affairs*, 1, 4: 205–12.

Franklin, S.H. (1969) *The European Peasantry*. London: Methuen.

Gallup Political Index (monthly) London: Social Surveys Gallup Poll Ltd.

Gershuny, J. I. 1978. *After Industrial Society: The Emerging Self-Service Economy*. London: Macmillan.

Gershuny, J.I. (1981) 'Changement des Modeles de Loisir, Royaume Uni. 1961–1974/5'. *Temps Libres*, 4: 115–34.

Gershuny, J.I. (1982) 'Household Work Strategies: Sexual Segregation and Inequality', Mexico City: World Congress of the International Sociological Association.

Gershuny, J.I. and Pahl, R.E. (1979) 'Work Outside Employment: Some Preliminary Speculations'. *New Universities Quarterly*, 34, 1: 120–5.

Gershuny, J.I. and Thomas, G.S. (forthcoming) *Changing Times*. London: Oxford University Press.

Grazia, Raffaele de (1980) 'Clandestine Employment: A Problem of Our Times'. *International Labour Review*, 119,5: 549–63.

Grossman, Gregory (1977) 'The Second Economy of the USSR'. *Problems of Communism* (September–October): 25–40.

Hawrylyshyn, Oli (1974) *A Review of Recent Proposals for Modifying and Extending the Measure of GNP*. Ottawa: Statistics Canada Number 13–558 Occasional.

Hill, T.P. (1979) 'Do-It-Yourself and GDP'. *The Review of Income and Wealth*, 25,1: 31–40.

Inland Revenue (1981) *Annual Report*. London: HMSO, No. 123.

International Gallup (1980, 1981) *The International Gallup Polls, 1978 (1980); The International Gallup Polls, 1979 (1981)*. Wilmington, Del.: Scholarly Resources.

Katsenelinboigen, A. (1977) 'Coloured Markets in the Soviet Union'. *Soviet Studies*, 291: 62–85.

Kay, John and King, M.A. (1980) *The British Tax System*. London: Oxford University Press, 2nd ed.

Keenan, A. and Dean, P.N. (1980) 'Moral Evaluations of Tax Evasion'. Edinburgh: Heriot-Watt University, unpublished paper.

Kilpatrick, Rosemary and Trew, Karen (1982) 'What Unemployed Men Do: A Belfast Sample', Belfast: Psychology Department, Queen's University, unpublished paper.

Lowery, David and Sigelman, Lee (1981) 'Understanding the Tax Revolt: Eight Explanations'. *American Political Science Review*, 75,4: 963–74.

Macafee, Kerrick (1980) 'A Glimpse of the Hidden Economy in the National Accounts'. *Economic Trends*, 316: 81–7.

McGee, R.T. and Feige, E.L., (1982) 'Policy Illusion, Macroeconomic Instability and the Unobserved Economy'. Wassenaar: Netherlands Institute for Advanced Study, unpublished paper.

Martino, Antonio, 1981. 'Measuring Italy's Underground Economy'. *Policy Review*, 16 (Spring): 87–106.

Matthews, K. (1981) 'The Demand for Currency and the Rise of the Black Economy, 1973–79'. *Liverpool Research Group Economic Bulletin*, 2.

Nordhaus, W. and Tobin, J. (1973) 'Is Growth Obsolete?' in Moss, Milton (ed.) *The Measurement of Economic and Social Performance*. New York: 509–32.

OECD (1979) *Demographic Trends, 1950–1990*. Paris: Organisation for Economic Co-operation and Development.

OECD (1981) *Economic Outlook*, No. 30 (December). Paris: Organisation for Economic Co-operation and Development.

OECD (1982) *Historical Statistics, 1960–1980*. Paris: Organisation for Economic Co-operation and Development.

O'Higgins, Michael (1982) 'Assessing the Underground Economy in the United

Kingdom', Wassenaar: Netherlands Institute for Advanced Study Conference, unpublished paper.

Peretz, Paul (1982) 'There was no Tax Revolt!' *Politics and Society*, 11, 2: 231–49.

Rose, Richard (1980) 'Ordinary People in Extraordinary Economic Circumstances' in Rose, R. (ed.), *Challenge to Governance*. London and Beverly Hills: Sage Publications, 151–74.

Rose, Richard (1980a) *Changes in Public Employment: A Multi-Dimensional Comparative Analysis*. Glasgow: University of Strathclyde Studies in Public Policy No. 61.

Rose, Richard, 1980b. 'Misperceiving Public Expenditure: Feelings about "Cuts"', in Levine, C.H. and Rubin, Irene (eds.) *Fiscal Stress and Public Policy*. London and Beverly Hills: Sage Publications, 203–30.

Rose, Richard, 1980c. *Do Parties Make a Difference*? London: Macmillan.

Rose, Richard (1982) 'National Employment, Public Employment and Social Security: Implications for Public Income Maintenance in the 1980s', Glasgow: Centre for the Study of Public Policy, unpublished paper.

Rose, Richard, and Peters, B. Guy (1978) *Can Government Go Bankrupt?* New York: Basic Books.

Salmi, H. (1981) 'Experience in the Estimation of Hours Worked in the Time use Survey in Finland'. Paris: OECD MAS/WP7(81)2, Annex 7.

Sametz, A.W. (1968) 'Production of Goods and Services: The Measurement of Economic Growth' in Sheldon, E.B. and Moore, W.E. (eds.) *Indicators of Social Change*. New York: Russell Sage Foundation, 77–96.

Smith, Adrian (1981) 'The Informal Economy'. *Lloyds Bank Review* (July): 45–61.

Social Trends (1982) London: HMSO, No. 13.

Song, Young-dahl and Yarborough, T.E. (1978) 'Tax Ethics and Taxpayer Attitudes: a Survey'. *Public Administration Review*, 38,5: 442–52.

South, N. (1981) 'The Informal Economy and Local Labour Markets' in Laite, Julian (ed.) *Bibliographies on Local Labour Markets and the Informal Economy*. London: Social Science Research Council.

Spicer, M.W. and Lundstedt, S.B. (1976) 'Understanding Tax Evasion'. *Public Finance* 31,2: 295–304.

Szalai, Alexander et al., (1972) *The Use of Time*. The Hague and Paris: Mouton.

Titmuss, R.M. (1970) *The Gift Relationship*. London: Allen and Unwin.

Treasury (1982) *The Government's Expenditure Policy, 1982–83 to 1984–85*. London: HMSO, Cmnd. 8494–I, II.

Vogel, Joachim (1974) 'Taxation and Public Opinion in Sweden'. *National Tax Journal*, 27,4: 499–513.

Wärneryd, K.E. and Wålerud, Bengt (1982) 'Taxes and Economic Behavior: Some Interview Data on Tax Evasion in Sweden'. *Journal of Economic Psychology*, 2, 3, 182–212.

Webley, P., Lea, S.E.G. and Portalska, R. (1983) 'The Unacceptability of Money as a Gift'. *Journal of Economic Psychology* (in press).

Zetterberg, Hans and Frankel, Greta (1981) 'Working Less and Enjoying It More in Sweden'. *Public Opinion*, 4,4: 41–45.

6

Governmental Intervention into Local Economies under Market Conditions: The Case of Urban Renewal

Oliver P. Williams
University of Pennsylvania

Debate over public or private approaches to urban redevelopment is structured not only by philosophical differences, but also by the particular experiences of specific cities and nations. There is a general predisposition to react against recent programmes when the overall urban situation worsens. The resulting public-private programmatic oscillation often reflects unwarranted generalization based on insufficient experience. A number of nations, especially the United States, seems to be currently shifting to private approaches in urban renewal after a period of intense public intervention. In this paper we examine some of the events which underly this shift and then endeavour to establish some general propositions about public and private approaches to urban renewal. Finally, we look at the politics of urban renewal and suggest a practical course of action for the short term.

The central reality of urban renewal in capitalist nations is that market forces are more powerful than government regulation in shaping national systems of cities. This is taken as a given. The analysis here does not provide a critique of markets as shapers of urban systems, but identifies what markets cannot do, which in turn implies proper roles for positive government action in revitalizing older cities. While urban renewal policies have differed significantly between the United States and many European nations since the Second World War, those differences may well lessen in the future. There are common parameters of urban change which influence urban systems in all advanced industrial societies. If cities are to have a different future this will result from varied national political responses.

Beginnings of modern urban renewal

Differences between European and American urban renewal policies in recent decades have resulted from a number of factors including contrasting ages of cities and ideological differences of national political parties. However, the single event which made the greatest difference was the war. The wartime destruction legitimized large-scale, national governmental intervention in Europe. The rush to rebuild in the late 1940s and early 1950s took a variety of forms. Some cities were rebuilt along pre-war lines despite new transportation and communication technologies; some, such as Rotterdam, represented substantial departures from the past; and a new town thrust found favour in England. Regardless of the content of the plans, the legitimacy of government-directed, financed and implemented city building efforts was well established.

While Europe was launching its rebuilding programme, America was debating what to do. In a long and bitter domestic controversy three groups fought for the soul of the proposed national urban renewal programme. These were the housers, the planners and the developers (Gelfand, 1975). The decade-long fight culminated in the Housing Act of 1949 and its 'compromise' essentially gave the housers the meaningless preamble, the developers the operational part of the legislation and the planners very little at all. The planning professionals did make something of a mark on the legislative revisions to the Act during the 1950s, but the major thrust of urban redevelopment was very much a tool for aiding and abetting the private developers in their effort to find a role in the old built-up areas of cities.

While there were sharp debates among the professional and academic urbanists who participated in designing and promoting the national redevelopment programmes, viewed from a thirty-year perspective one is struck by the common themes that run through their discussions. It was agreed that: (1) a principal problem of existing cities was that they were unplanned, (2) cities were the culminating expression of our civilization, and (3) their continued central place in our society was assured. As cities were the centres of our society, it was essential to make them right—efficient, habitable and rational.[1]

This faith was substantial, continued to be expressed and eventually gained a place in the language of urban renewal legislation. The 'workable programmes' of the 1950s envisioned a process which would gradually renew entire cities. This optimism was fed and encouraged by the European experience where planning had an important place in ambitious urban renewal processes. In Europe new towns had been built, old cities such as Stockholm were substantially altered, and plans were being made sufficiently comprehensive to envision the reshaping of entire national systems of cities. Indeed most nations in the north and east of Europe had a national system of cities planned at one time or another which stated where growth was to occur and where not.

Two factors have lead to a change of perspective on both sides of the Atlantic. The first was the emergence of complicated redistributive issues associated with urban renewal. The battle of 1949 in the United States between the housers and developers suggests the general pattern. Was urban renewal to be used as a means of creating a better living environment for lower-income urban dwellers or was it to enhance the economic base of the city? In nation after nation programmes which received initial broad support became embroiled in controversy concerning just who was benefiting from the renewal process.

The second development was the growing uncertainty about the future direction for cities. The term 'post-industrial cities' came into general usage but there was no longer a blueprint for what a city should be. Doubt strengthened the case for using the market rather than government planning in guiding urban renewal.

The withering of urban development programmes

Urban redevelopment not only lost its conceptual underpinnings but its difficulties cost it political support. In the United States the original urban renewal programme of 1949 disappeared as it became submerged into the Community Development Block Grant created in 1974. Its political history is one of the more fascinating episodes in American politics. A programme identified with the conservatives in conception, it became attached to the liberals in operation and its mounting political problems finally enabled a conservative administration to bury it. No sooner was it destroyed than it was recreated in a new form by the Democrats in a guise which is now approved by the Republicans.

The 1949 Act provided a mechanism through which blighted land could be cleared and consigned to private developers at market prices who would then redevelop it in the private sector. The initial clearance efforts were performed with a ruthless disregard for the inhabitants, especially the poor, in the targeted area. These efforts were also performed with little regard for the private market which was supposed to use this cleared land, but which proved not to want it about 90 percent of the time. The result was often purposeless clearance which only induced greater hardships. The political reaction added regulations to provide safeguards. By the time the programme was a decade old it was one of the most bureaucratized. Planners and the professionals presided over layers of regulations at all levels. The complexity of rebuilding a city was clearly beyond the grasp of those who first envisioned the programme.

At the operational level, urban renewal of blighted residential areas has proved to be difficult under any circumstances. Not only in the United States but in every European nation, the sticky political problems became well known. However it is done, a neighbourhood is likely to be dismembered. Renewal nearly always means a reduction in population, because part of the problem in slums is overuse of dwellings. Government standards always make for more expensive, and usually very expensive, replacement housing. These standards often make housing for low-income people more expensive than that built by the market for the middle class. The disruption, relocations, and costs spell a loss of political support.

In a federal system such as the United States, substantive policy debates become transposed into constitutional ones involving federalism. Critics argue that a programme is implemented at the wrong level. Reagan's New Federalism has many antecedents. Urban renewal was successfully 'returned' to the localities by President Ford and merged with a variety of other programmes in the Community Development Block Grant (CDBG) legislation of 1974. The results of this shift have been much monitored; one general conclusion is clear. The political dynamics of local communities caused federal CDBG funds to be divided up among many different claimants, that is, if there was anything to be divided. Federal grants are seen by local officials as 'free' in the sense that they are provided by national rather than local taxpayers. One option is to simply use these funds to offset local taxes, a short-term political benefit. Another is to satisfy as many political claimants as possible. This alternative means that it is difficult to use CDBG funds for large and lumpy capital expenditures in one place. This, of course, is what urban renewal in the Act of 1949 did. The result of CDBG has been the near stoppage of large-scale urban renewal projects.

The one urban initiative of any significance by the Carter Administration was the Urban Development Action Grant (UDAG) programme. While a small programme (variously from $400,000,000 to $765,000,000 annually, thus far), it does provide under different conditions the very big lump sums of money earmarked for particular cities which disappeared under CDBG. The new problem is that federal grants to cities are tied to matching private investments. The federal money need not be used for clearance or any of the classic urban renewal purposes, but it can be. In fact, UDAG money can now be used to construct local infrastructure, which was a *local* responsibility of the urban renewal 1949 Act provisions. The central UDAG feature is that the federal contribution gives leverage to private investment. Since private investment is frequently job creating, UDAG becomes a tool to convert the economic base of old cities through a process which requires physical changes, that is urban renewal.

Thus far the programme is politically popular and it has withstood assaults from the Reagan budget knife. It fits the public-private partnership format which is currently approved. But on the other hand it is a federal, conditional grant with the critical decisions being made by Washington bureaucrats, a set of circumstances which has been ideologically disquieting to the administration.

While the programme is small and it is unlikely to have a major impact on urban America at the present rate, the difference in its political fortune is worthy of reflection. This will be considered after turning to the conceptual task of analysing public and private roles in urban renewal.

Urban renewal as a response to market failure

In capitalist societies discussions of urban renewal as a form of governmental intervention into urban processes must begin with the issue of market failure. Cities in market societies are largely built by private investment, thus, the legitimacy of government intervention rests on recognized shortcomings of market: its inability to redistribute, its failure to incorporate the costs of negative externalities in pricing products, and its inappropriateness for providing public goods.

The redistributive rationale of urban renewal usually centres on housing. The case for social housing rests on the fact that the private sector cannot provide adequate numbers of units for low-income populations. Because of this failing in private supplies, substandard, privately owned units are occupied by the poor, or more commonly overoccupied. This is the classic slum situation. There is no economic incentive for private rebuilding of obsolete structures unless accompanied by price increases which place them far out of the reach of existing occupants.

Urban renewal not focused directly on improving the physical condition of housing for low-income populations is usually greeted with suspicion by those who see urban renewal as a welfare measure. Efforts to use physical renewal as an instrument of economic recovery must always take the form of a direct or indirect subsidy to private entrepreneurs. Since entrepreneurs and their investors are rarely poor, it appears that such use of urban renewal is diverting government funds from the poor to the rich. This is the argument which often blocks city use of CDBG funds for economic development. However, if the result of economic development projects is an enhancement of economic opportunity for the poor and unemployed, then the redistributive goal may be met, or at least benefits are general across income levels.

The second rationale for legitimizing urban renewal is to socialize negative externalities which accumulate from obsolete employment areas. Commercial and industrial sites are exploited by their users until they are no longer profitable and are left either abandoned or under-utilized. At this point the land/building has little value. The reason it has little value is that the cost of restoring it to a useful state was never incorporated in the price of products made or sold at the site. The analogy is the empty beer can thrown on the highway. The cost of disposing of the empty is socially born, for not to do so means living in an increasingly junk-filled environment. Similarly, not cleaning up the old industrial site and restoring it to social use is the functional equivalent of leaving beer cans along the highway. Non-highway-users might advocate this. Those who have left cities or do not use older parts of cities may as well.

It certainly can be argued that the beneficiaries of the use-and-abandon policy include not only owners, but also former workers and customers. It might even be argued that the city as a corporate entity gained in the past by its generosity to its space users and now is stuck with the delayed costs. While this may be the case, the negative externality effects of abandonment actually affect many who were never a party to the earlier cosy arrangement. Thus, urban renewal is a belated way of socializing the cost of those negative externalities.

The third, public goods argument conceives cities as being built on a public infrastructure foundation of public works and social policies. Cities have a kind of physical and social constitution as well as a legal-political one. Just as legal constitutions must occasionally be amended, so too with the physical. When a city shifts from one orientation to another, then a substantial public reinvestment must take place. Again, urban renewal becomes a major facilitating instrument.

Any one of these three justifications provides sufficient grounds for government intervention, though this cannot settle the policy issues. These general arguments can legitimize renewal, but they cannot determine whether or not particular proposals are wise actions, because there is no way to calculate opportunity costs. Furthermore, these arguments are rarely politically sufficient because proposals are seldom matters of righting past wrongs, but rather prophecies for the future. When physical alterations are made to the city, existing access relations based on physical arrangements are altered. When changes are made by government, all these consequences are thrown into the public arena. The stresses which result from market-based changes facilitated by urban renewal are politicized. Future gains and losses are likely to loom larger in the political scale than past rights and wrongs. Urban renewal politics is about whose access needs are to be served in the future.

Physical or functional obsolescence?

Physical obsolescence is a very simple and understandable proposition. A city is a physical thing. Buildings do get old and wear out. The notion of replacing worn-out parts is easily comprehensible. If physical obsolescence was the problem being addressed by urban renewal, the political problems would be relatively modest. The fact is that disuse of urban structures is more likely to come from functional rather than physical obsolescence.

Functional obsolescence, if substantial, foretells a political power shift in the community; a new elite is going to take over. Historically, the great urban renewal waves have resulted from adaptation of cities to the requirements of new elites. When the Hellenist empire-builders took over the citizen-controlled city states of Greece, a grand urban renewal project ensued. Big governments need big bureaucracies and hence big buildings. The modest acropolis had to be ripped apart and enlarged; big boulevards suitable for military wheeled vehicles had to be constructed where once the foot path prevailed. A similar urban renewal flurry followed the territorial princes when they moved their capitals into the walled mediaeval towns. Haussman's boulevards of Paris had more than aesthetic meaning.

Today's urban renewal is very unlike most historical examples which usually occurred when old elites fell and new ones took over. Modern urban renewal in both the United States and Europe arrived at the time when the industrial elites had largely abandoned the city. They no longer needed it. But what is taking place is really not the analogue of Hellenistic Greece, because there is not an elite change in the society generally but only at the urban level. It is not a matter of the newly emergent elite wresting power from the old. It is more a matter of who will fill the vacuum, if anyone, and dominate cities for the next generation.

The urban renewal issue of the 1950s and the 1960s was whether the functional adaptation was going to be planned by the state or left to the market. There were substantial differences in practice on either side of the Atlantic. There was never any real doubt in the United States that the market was going to guide urban renewal. But the early clearance efforts proved a great disappointment to the designers of the initial legislation. Often a market offering was made of cleared urban land, but nobody bid. Investors did not want the old slum sites. The error was conceiving urban renewal as physical not functional obsolescence. While it is true that the legislation specifically divorced the new use of urban renewal land from the old use, the assumption was that the old-time customers were still around and if one could only increase the supply of urban land suitable for development (after all there were no inner area vacant sites) at a reasonable price, then the market would be rejuvenated.

The result of the urban land market failure was that the city (with federal help) had to bail out the programme. Sites were filled with public facilities, often public housing. After this initial failure the programme veered towards clearing marketable sites. This meant a shift from a physical to a functional definition of obsolescence. Blight standards were altered, or even fabricated. Blighted housing criteria were diluted. New service industry and major institutional directors began to move forward to assume the role of the new urban elite.

The European experience was different to the extent that governmental intervention meant more social housing and a greater emphasis on social transportation. But when the public sector assumed that it could guide a national system of cities its plans faltered. Whether it was containing London, redirecting the urban pattern of France, industrializing backward areas in various nations or designating growth areas in the Netherlands, the power of public regulation and direction proved less effective than was hoped. In market societies, there are strict limits to the possibilities of publicly directed urban development.

Urban redevelopment in market societies

Job opportunities in a market economy are largely a result of private sector actions. Because capital is supposed to be more mobile than labour, most democratic nations have attempted to steer capital. Claims for regional parity during times of underemployment create public pressures to bring jobs to labour-surplus areas. There are a number of public decisions which in fact have profound affects on where jobs will be created. The routing of roads, railroads and canals, the construction of ports and airports, defence decisions, energy policies, tax legislation, and a variety of other measures affect location decisions of private firms. To this list can be added urban redevelopment. The problem of government-financed urban renewal is not a matter of legitimacy but one of predictability. Specified programmes have foundered, not because of the ideological basis of urban renewal, but because they failed to accept subordination to the market.

In the more direct approaches to guiding job locations (which includes some urban renewal programmes) there are essentially two types of strategies. Subsidies can be given to alter the locational decisions of firms. Or one can entice firms to locate at a site by making desired goods more accessible to that site through public actions. Both are efforts to create a more attractive profit environment for the firm. Both introduce changes in the structure of cities through government intervention and consequently they have implications beyond the immediate parties involved. Is it possible to lay out any general guidelines for these kinds of market intervention?

As in all subsidy programmes, one of the issues is how deep should the subsidy be. Though urban renewal programmes may disguise subsidies, the actual techniques include the classical land value write-down, specially designed and publicly furnished infrastructure features (parking lots, access roads, sewer and water hook-ups), and low-cost loans. In the latter case the amount of the subsidy is easier to calculate, because there is a market price for money. In the other cases the subsidy is more hidden. The current three United States federal programme sources of urban redevelopment funds (CBDG, UDAG and Economic Development), allow any of the above. The issue is how far should subsidies go? How much is too much? Two answers can be given which establish limiting principles. They address the matter of when to subsidize and when not to.

The best answer of when to subsidize is when the market is likely to achieve the objective anyway without the subsidy. This sounds like silly advice, but private investors are always looking for extra margins of safety. As I have argued elsewhere, there is good reason to believe some economic development programmes expend money to achieve purposes which are likely to be achieved anyway through the market (Clark and Williams, 1983). For example, the United States is still subsidizing the industrialization of the non-metropolitan hinterland even though market forces have discovered these areas, served as they now are by the federally financed interstate highway network.

At the other extreme there must be a recognition that we cannot rebuild the system of cities entirely through subsidies and public action. In brief, urban renewal must go with the market, not against it. When private firms are willing to locate in existing cities, but something is standing in the way, urban renewal can make a contribution. The old cities which are divesting their industrial base, but show signs of conversion to service centres, can be aided by government renewal programmes. On the other hand, if one raises the subsidy high enough, almost any firm can be bribed into altering its location strategy. However, if the private entrepreneur must engage in a risk, there is some assurance that the subsidized firm looks upon the location as one which can be successfully used for a profitable operation.

If the obstacle to private investment is the residue of negative externalities left over from past practices, then the socialization of these costs is appropriate. Or if the subsidy is for conversion of the infrastructure to begin a new ‘physical constitution’, that too can be rationalized. However, there must be private capital at risk before urban redevelopment can be used for economic redevelopment. The market must give a signal before government can play a role or else we are back to where we were in the 1950s.

The politics of urban uncertainty

Perhaps the most pervasive urban trend both in the United States and throughout Europe is the decentralization of urban areas. Declining populations and jobs in central areas is pervasive with only a few exceptions (Hall and Hay, 1980). The technological basis for the decentralization is not a mystery. The list of factors includes greater mobility and technology which makes information available on terms nearly independent of its place of origin. The core areas of cities, once the prime locations for accessing and exchanging information, are needed less and less for these purposes.

As the term 'post industrial' implies the decentralizing process is in part a shift from making products to providing services or processing information. The new urban system is not only decentralized, but the nature of that decentralization is in the process of being created. The political problem is that while the old centralizing urban form was predictable, the new decentralizing one is not. In a multinucleated urban form the substitutability of places is greatly expanded. From the standpoint of local government, there is much greater uncertainty as to what functions and firms are likely to be attracted to a particular place. Competition among places becomes more intense as locational substitutions become easier.

Can the problem be solved by shifting controls to the national level? In Europe the attempts to design and then actually guide the national system of cities have not been overly successful. Such national designs often begin from environmental, communal or defence premises. They have not been ignorant of entrepreneurial interests, but, after all, planning is supposed to guide such interests, not simply acquiesce to them. The early new-towns policies were an attempt to reconcile community values and industrial interests. There were some successes. However, more recently, industrial growth, particularly in the 'hi-tec' areas, does not seem to have been attracted to the new towns. Instead, they follow a locational logic which is not anticipated in existing plans. Efforts to industrialize the hinterland or remote areas have been more successful. Here it would appear that entrepreneurial searches for lower wage forces is compatible with national policies (Ashcroft, 1980).

One of the constraints of politically directed locational policy is the effects of international competition. While many firms are strictly nation-bound, an increasing percentage are international shoppers. The last decades have witnessed many cases of firms opting for the national environment which least interfered with its preferences. Similarly, in the United States a nationally directed urban policy with reference to the location of capital investment is greatly inhibited by the federal system. The degree to which the federal government may favour particular urban areas in particular states is politically constrained. It is impossible for the United States to have a New York policy in the same way that there has been a London and a Paris policy.

Decentralization, indeterminacy, and international competition all reinforce the market in urban redevelopment. Government action almost needs to be preceded by market indication of interest. This is not a normative plea for urbanism based on free market principles. It is a statement of the political reality of contemporary urban change.

There are obvious exceptions to these decentralizing trends. The office towers burgeoning in New York and London point to the other, but smaller, current world urban trend. There is a tier of world cities emerging in which are located corporate and political decision centres. These cities conform to the traditional centralized urban form. They exist to service face-to-face contacts and they specialize in the nonstandardized communication exchanges peculiar to control centres and certain urban based development process (Williams, 1983).

It is highly doubtful that this *world city* model will ever reach the scale of industrial urbanism. There are some echoes in core areas of second- and third-tier cities where regional headquarters are centred. However, many corporate headquarters, even of very large firms do not necessarily require classical central locations. This is a truth that the Renaissance Center in Detroit is now confronting. One cannot successfully ape New York by building New York-like structures.

But what of redistribution?

One of the justifications for urban renewal is to correct for the inability of markets to bring about redistribution. To Harry Truman, urban renewal was legitimized as welfare policy. It was to be part of the Fair Deal. It was certainly viewed by the housing planners as a plan for removing substandard housing and replacing it with standard homes at affordable prices for low-income families. Because in the Housing Act of 1949 the planners only received the preamble, the ideology of redistribution was often enshrined more in the rhetoric of urban renewal than in the effects. However, if urban renewal does not have broad benefits across income groups, it is difficult to defend.

The battle enjoined in the great debate of the 1940s is a real one, that often takes on errant forms. The debate is often housing versus economic-base politics, city centre renewal versus the neighbourhoods, displacement or replacement of low-income housing. The same tension found its way into the recent UDAG legislation even though it was ostensibly an economic development programme. The legislation as passed called for a suitable balance between projects designed to reclaim under-utilized property for industrial purposes, renew commercial employment centres and restore seriously deteriorated neighbourhoods. This was administratively coded into industrial, commercial and neighbourhood projects. There was substantial pressure during the Carter administration from the lineal descendants of the 1949 planners to define neighbourhood projects as housing rehabilitation. However, the legislative requirement for private investment content made it an awkward programme for housing the very poor. If UDAG and similar programmes have any beneficial effect for low-income populations, it must be through employment generated by industrial and commercial projects. However, this strategy has gained little support among those interested in redistribution.

Those who seek redistributive goals in urban renewal have often described economic development projects as subsidies to the well-off. How can one justify subsidies to Hyatt Regency hotels or Libby Owens Glass when there are so many poor people underhoused? However, if income problems are a function of unemployment, jobs would seem to have priority over housing. Since jobs are largely generated in the private sector, short of public works, urban renewal subsidies have to go to corporate investors. If it is the intention to transfer capital to labour through urban renewal, it must take the form of a corporate bribe. However, the rationale of urban renewal is that by keying the bribe to a physical alteration of the urban structure, a base may be constructed for subsequent non-subsidized job-creating investment. That is what distinguishes urban renewal from other types of producer pay-offs such as farm price supports, shipping aids and the scores of other industrial subsidies in the United States and other countries. If the 'bribe' is a carefully calculated form of urban renewal it should not create profits for inefficient firms.

However, it is likely that urban-renewal-based economic development must go beyond the classic approaches of free land and infrastructure supports. Whether we are talking of free enterprise zones, low interest loans, or traditional physical renewal, for these high bribes to be worthwhile there has to be some beneficial social product in the form of positive externalities. This may be the anchoring of sunk investments in existing homes and businesses or the initiation of some kind of sustaining developmental process. There are success stories which document that this can happen including revitalized central business districts, industrial parks and commercial complexes that do 'work' as businesses. These have created broad employment and helped labour remain in the cities. There are also any number of failures.

The redistributive case is a tenuous one and more difficult to document than either that of socializing the cost of negative externalities, or replacing public infrastructure which take the form of public goods. However, to many low income people with limited mobility, capital-to-labour schemes make sense. Where marginal subsidies can bring this about, it seems preferable to welfare checks and a higher priority than subsidized housing.

A political footnote

One of the practical problems with urban renewal schemes which are directed at declining urban areas is that their national political appeal is insufficiently broad. Characteristically in the United States, remedial programmes targeted at specific areas can rarely be focused narrowly on the most needy places. In order to get congressional support the potential beneficiaries have to be many. This has lead to the ludicrous situation in which to obtain funds for specific needy areas the funds must be made generally available. European capital-to-labour programmes have at times experienced the same political history.

There is a possible political solution if the nation has both a declining and a growing region, such as in the United States today. Rapid growth also creates problems for the poor which take a very different form. In a growing city, there may be jobs, but there is inevitably a serious housing problem for low-income families. Growth stimulates the private housing sector into production, but it only services the middle and upper income range. The fixed stock of low-rent housing comes under increasing pressure. This drives rents up faster than wage rates for low-income workers. Rents become disproportionately inflated in relation to other consumer goods which do not have localized supply problems.

Thus, it would appear politically sensible and feasible to have a national urban renewal programme that tilted towards economic development and jobs projects in declining cities and towards subsidized social housing supply in impacted growing areas. While there are housing problems in declining areas, these are most severe for the unemployable. For the employable, jobs are the key to improved living conditions. Such a scheme would appear to have the necessary formula for political support.

On the face of it this situation appears to be a case for local option or decentralization of decision making. Where conditions differ so much regionally, it suggests that project selection is best left to the local city governments. Paradoxically, this probably cannot work. If the CDBG experience is a guide, cities with declining employment have so many needs that local political pressure prevents the making of either long-term or large-scale investments. Whether growing cities would of their own choice use unrestricted federal money for low-income housing is also problematical, though the evidence here is less well developed. The federal strings greatly strengthen the hand of local supporters when it comes to targeting benefits.

Summary

This paper has looked at the role of urban redevelopment programmes in nations with market economies. The power of private markets in shaping cities is too great to be ignored by publicly financed intervention schemes. This lesson is documented by experiences of the postwar years. Redevelopment has a legitimate role in the areas of market failure, including redistribution, externality problems and public goods provision. However, as a subsidy, it must steer a course away from ineffectual outlays which have little impact and on the other hand not give outright support to inefficient operations. In brief, the intervention must steer a course of prudent, market-sensitive intervention. It should facilitate market trends and try to guide private investments to serve public needs. The result will not be a gleaming city but some results may be achieved in buffering the ill effects of decline, easing the pain of transition for the less well off, and socializing costs so that they will be more fairly born.

NOTE

1. A major study at the time was under the direction of Coleman Woodbury and its report included expressions by Catherine Bauer, Henry S. Churchill, Arthur B. Gallion, Victor Jones, G. Holmes Perkins, William Slayton and others.

REFERENCES

Ashcroft, Brian (1980) 'The Evaluation of Regional Policy in Europe: A Survey and Critique' (unpublished paper).

Clark, Richard and Williams, Oliver P. (1983) 'National Urban Policy and Economic Development Programs' (forthcoming).

Gelfand, Mark I. (1975) *A Nation of Cities*. New York, Oxford University Press.

Hall, Peter and Hay, D. (1980) *Growth Centers in the European Urban System*. London: Heinemann.

Williams, Oliver P. (1983) 'Decline of Cities as Centers of Development: Political Implications' (unpublished paper).

Woodbury C. (ed.), (1953) *The Future of Cities and Urban Redevelopment*. Chicago: Chicago University Press.

7

Corporatism and the Public-Private Distinction

Wyn Grant
University of Warwick

Introduction

This chapter is particularly concerned with institutional arrangements that attempt to combine elements of governmental choice and private choice so as to transcend the conflict between public and private modes of allocation. Lane (page 9) poses the 'allocation problem' in terms of the questions: 'How much of the total resources of society should be left to government choice concerning consumption and investment? And how much should be turned over for private choice?' The inherent instability of agricultural markets has led to the development of solutions which do not rely on a clear distinction between goods allocated by government and goods which are to be allocated by the market. Rather, a market continues to exist, but it is one that is structured by the setting of certain key prices by government (including the EEC). The setting of key prices does not, of itself, reconcile conflicts of interest; indeed, it may exacerbate them as parties with different interests seeking to influence the price-setting authority. Hence, the need arises for mediating institutions on the borderline between public and private domains which can promote cooperative relationships without eliminating market competition.

The mention of conflicting interests, and of intermediary institutions as a mean of reconciling such interests, directs our attention to neocorporatist theory. Corporatist theorists have long been interested in the interpenetration of the public and the private, although Schmitter points out that the 'interpenetration of public and private decision arenas' (Schmitter, 1979: 15) is a shared basic assumption of pluralism and corporatism. However, in a corporatist arrangement affected interests are made co-responsible 'for the implementation of policy decisions, which then take on a characteristically semi-public or para-state quality' (Schmitter, 1982: 263).

In this chapter, corporatism is understood as 'a mode of policy formation, in which formally designated interest associations are incorporated within the process of authoritative decision making and implementation' (Schmitter, 1981: 295). Attempting to find such arrangements in the United Kingdom, a country which has often seemed prone to an almost anarchic form of liberalism, might seem to be a forlorn task. However, 'deep inhibitions about exercising "public power"' and the absence of 'approving or neutral uses of the term "state"' (Dyson, 1980: 247–48) in a sense do create an opportunity for arrangements that bridge the public and the private, that simultaneously combine self-help, mutual cooperation and the protection and the assistance of government. In a country where there are few corporatist arrangements, those neocorporatist arrangements that do exist are of particular importance. This chapter uses the example of the milk marketing system in Britain, and of other agricultural marketing arrangements, to contribute to the debate on the relationship between the public and the private. Its relevance to discussion of the allocation problem has already been pointed out, but it also contributes to the discussion about the proper place of governmental authority in society and to the debate about how much of the means of production should be owned by government. Marketing boards offer a corporative solution to these problems through a combination of public authority, private choice and democratic legitimating mechanisms. Just as 'the public-private distinction is not *one* distinction but several' (Lane, page 8) so there is a range of possible solutions to the problem of reconciling public and private allocation mechanisms of which marketing boards are one.

The milk marketing system in Britain

The milk marketing scheme was established in 1933 in an attempt to cope with the depressed condition of the dairy sector. The scheme was set up as a result of a mixture of government initiative, interest organization involvement and consent by the individual farmer in the form of a poll of producers. There are actually five boards, one in

England and Wales, three in Scotland and one in Northern Ireland, but this discussion will concentrate on the English and Welsh board, with some reference to significant differences in the main Scottish scheme.

The milk marketing boards were placed under government control during the second world war and until 1954, and the scheme has been modified on a number of occasions, most recently to cope with European Community objections in 1979. However, the guiding principles remain those established in 1933. Moreover, a poll ordered by the European Community shows that the scheme retains the support of the overwhelming support of producers, with 99.48 percent of all producers voting for the Board's continuance.

The Milk Marketing Board likes to describe itself as 'one of the largest agricultural cooperatives in the world, owned and run by the dairy farmers of England and Wales', 'a huge marketing and manufacturing organization, aggressively pursuing the interests of dairy farmers' (promotional literature). The Board employs around 13,500 staff, but places considerable emphasis on the fact that it is a democratically controlled organization. The Board, which generally meets for two days a month, has fifteen elected members (farmers) and three members appointed by the Minister of Agriculture. The three appointed members are not government officials, nor are they appointed as representatives of the Minister or any special interest. They might best be described as non-executive directors, individuals with special knowledge or experience in fields other than farming (e.g. marketing) who can, when needed, bring a wider viewpoint to the Board's discussions. Once appointed, they act in their own right and are not required to report back to the Minister.

Twelve of the elected members are elected on a regional basis and three are elected nationally (there is also a system of regional committees). Electoral contests are not unusual. Sometimes there are rivalries between different parts of a region (so one candidate is described, to quote a recent example, as 'the Warwickshire candidate' in the local press) or contests have occurred 'over the merits of different breeds of dairy cattle' (Self and Storing, 1962: 104). The franchise is slightly unusual in that each producer has one vote, plus one vote for every ten milch cows in his possession, so larger producers have more votes. The Board takes great care to ensure that the bovine equivalent of impersonation does not take place. For a sample of producers, the number of milch cows claimed is checked against their recorded production; if there is a discrepancy, a Board official will literally go 'into the field' and count the cows. The Board distributes election addresses for a fee of £500. The scrupulous care that the Board takes over the election process may have a deeper significance than a simple wish to adhere to democratic norms. In an organization which mixes the public and the private, and whose members (who ultimately have the right to dissolve the Board) are generally individualistic in outlook, it is important to give farmers more than an economic incentive for continuing to support the Board. The Board therefore stresses its democratic character, although it tempers the emphasis on farmer involvement by pointing out that: 'The modern farmer has little time to do much more than concentrate on the job he knows best — getting the best quality milk from his cows.'

How the scheme works

The influence of the Milk Marketing Board rests on the fact that it purchases almost all the milk produced by farmers (there is a small group of producer processors and producer retailers who will be discussed separately later). (See Figure 1.) A farmer intending to produce milk for sale (but not a farmer intending solely to produce cheese or butter) must first obtain government authority to do so and then apply to the Milk Marketing Board to be registered as a producer. The Board undertakes to market all the milk the farmer wishes to sell; to arrange for its collection and transport; to maximize returns by giving priority in the allocation of supplies to the most remunerative markets; to negotiate centrally with the dairy trade to obtain the best possible prices for manufacturing milk.

Different prices are obtained, and different pricing systems operate, for liquid milk and manufacturing milk. Taking liquid milk first, the maximum retail price for liquid milk in England and Wales is fixed by the Minister of Agriculture. So, too, is the maximum wholesale price — the price at which the Board sells to the liquid milk processor and distributor (the price fixed by the Minister has usually been accepted by the Board and buyers as the selling price, but in November 1979 the Dairy Trade Federation initially refused to accept the higher price set by the Minister). The difference between these two prices is the distributive margin, made up of handling and processing costs and the dairy's profit margin. The way in which this margin is calculated is described below.

FIGURE 1
The milk marketing system in England and Wales: A simplified version

Farmers
— elect the majority of Board members
— consign their milk for sale to the Board (or operate by arrangement with the Board as producer retailers or producer processors)

The Board
— buys all milk offered to it by farmers
— sells milk to the dairy trade for liquid sale and manufacturing
— itself produces a wide range of dairy products through its commercial arm, Dairy Crest

The Dairy Trade Federation
— represents milk processors and retailers
— negotiates with the Board in the Joint Committee over manufacturing prices, the allocation of supplies etc.
— represents the Board in Europe

The Government
— provides the legislative framework for the operations of the Board and Joint Committee
— appoints three members of the Board
— fixes the maximum wholesale price
— fixes the maximum retail price
— maintains a system for monitoring handling and processing costs involving a target rate of profit
— influences community intervention prices and largely determines the level of the Green Pound

This figure is intended to assist understanding of the text — its reading in isolation from the text would not permit a full understanding of the scheme.

Different arrangements have applied in Scotland since 1981. The Government still retains control over the price at which milk is sold to the trade but control of retail milk prices has ended in the sense that price control has been moved from the retail price payable by consumers to the point of dispatch from the dairy or depot, a maximum 'ex dairy' price. It was stated that a principal reason for this change was the almost equal split in Scottish milk sales between shops and doorstep delivery. Control of the retail price leads to an element of cross subsidization of doorstep deliveries from purchasers from shops. However, these changes in Scotland could be more than a response to special local market conditions. They could also be interpreted as a political experiment in decontrol, supported from the highest political level, which may have important long-run implications for the whole milk marketing system in Britain.

There is significant government intervention in dairy profit margins. The government maintains a system for monitoring handling and processing costs for liquid milk through a costings sample. New participants are selected by agreement between the Minister and the Dairy Trade Federations. The Dairy Trade Federations have agreed to use their 'best endeavours' to persuade selected costees to take part, but the Minister can compel them as a last resort. 'Best endeavours' is a characteristically British notion, involving the use of a mixture of persuasion and obligation instead of compulsion. A target rate of profit for milk processing and wholesale sales is determined by reference to a selected group of food-manufacturing companies; the target rate of profit for milk retailing is determined by reference to a selected group of food-retailing companies. The agreed target range of profit is in the lower end of a possible range suggested by a firm of accountants who reviewed the system because it is considered that the dairy industry runs a lower degree of risk compared to the more general food industry in the reference groups. Costees who persistently make a loss will be eliminated from the sample and retrospective adjustments will be made only if the target rate of profit deviates by more than 5 percent. The costing system therefore operates very much as an 'automatic pilot' and does not generally require discretionary ministerial decisions. Nevertheless, it does represent a significant form of public intervention in what is generally regarded as one of the most crucial areas of autonomy for a private firm: its ability to influence its own level of profit, although clearly an individual firm can still do better than the average by higher capital investment, more efficient working methods, etc.

Before considering the system by which prices for manufacturing milk are arrived at, one important consideration needs to be discussed: the Milk Marketing Board is itself a manufacturer of dairy products. It only has about 5 percent of the total retail trade in liquid milk, but it is 'the largest manufacturer of butter and skimmed milk powder in the country and the major producer of hard cheeses' (Consumers' Committee, 1981: 3). The Board built and purchased a number of plants over the years, so that it had sixty-seven by 1980 compared with the thirteen it had in the 1930s, but the biggest development was the purchase of sixteen creameries from the major private dairy company, Unigate, in 1979. The Board seems to have been influenced by a concern that some or all of these plants might go out of production; rather than allow that to happen, a better course of action would be to acquire the plants and modernize them. This transfer of assets from a private concern to a quasi-governmental agency was achieved without any of the political controversy that would normally attend any transfer of assets away from the private sector in Britain, indicating that the marketing board format represents a politically acceptable solution to the ownership problem in the case of plants in need of rejuvenation.

The fact that the average price for milk for manufacturing is significantly lower than that for liquid milk is a potentially awkward issue, particularly given the increasing proportion of milk that is used for manufacture. The Board has been criticized because its manufacturing prices are a comparatively low proportion of the target price compared with cooperatives in the rest of Europe. The price of milk for manufacture is negotiated product by product in a Joint Committee with the Dairy Trade Federation (the Joint Committee is discussed more fully below). There is a separate price for each use to which the milk is put, with, for example, a relatively high price for use for fresh cream and a relatively low price for use for butter. The floor price for milk for manufacture is derived from the EEC intervention prices for butter and milk powder, but the prices ultimately arrived at depend on market forces of supply and demand and the skill of the negotiators. The Government exerts an indirect influence on the negotiation process in two ways. First, the EEC intervention (and target) prices are converted into sterling at the artificial 'Green Pound' rate. From 1973 to 1979, manufacturing prices were consistently lower than they would otherwise have been because of the Green Pound system. Government exerts a degree of control over the Green Pound rate (Grant, 1981) and hence over manufacturing returns. Furthermore, although manufacturing prices are dealt with in a different way from prices for liquid milk, the price for retail milk (determined by the Government) clearly has some influence on the price for manufacturing milk.

Although they account for only 2 percent of the milk produced in Britain, producer retailers and producer processors — farmers processing their own milk for sale on a retail round or to shops — are a controversial group. They do not have to pay the European

Community's co-responsibility levy, since they are not seen as contributing to the Community's milk surplus, and some large dairy groups are afraid of being undercut by what they see as unfair competition. These farmer processors do represent a departure, albeit a minor one, from the concept of the Board as a monopoly supplier. Moreover, the issue is capable of being politicized in terms of a clash between big business and small-scale entrepreneurs.

The Dairy Trade Federation

Before considering the work of the Joint Committee, it is necessary to discuss the other party to the Joint Committee apart from the Board, the Dairy Trade Federation. However, in order to understand the Dairy Trade Federation, it is necessary to outline briefly the structure of the dairy industry in England and Wales (the Scottish dairy industry is less concentrated). By 1980 the Milk Marketing Board was the largest buyer of milk in England (about 27 percent). The three largest dairy companies — Unigate, Express (Grand Metropolitan group) and Northern — accounted for around 30 to 35 percent. The Cooperatives (retail cooperatives) took another quarter, leaving the remaining 15 percent or so for smaller companies (Agricultural Committee, 1980: 99). In other words, the industry is relatively highly concentrated, although plant sizes have been relatively small (although they are becoming significantly larger), and retailing is often in the hands of small-scale independent dairymen who buy their milk wholesale from the larger companies.

The Dairy Trade Federation is an association of associations with four constituent members representing the large private firms, the cooperatives and the bottle milk buyers organized in two associations. The Federation of Milk Marketing Boards and the Dairy Trade Federations in Scotland and Northern Ireland are affiliated for the purposes of European representation. The DTF's funds are raised largely from a levy collected by the MMB. In their supply contracts with the MMB, almost all first hand buyers have undertaken to pay a levy, on quantity of milk purchased, to the DTF. It should be noted that this is obligatory rather than compulsory; the appropriate clause can be struck out of the contract. In practice, this is a very effective way of raising the DTF's funds, much more effective than the usual subscription method. The arrangement is generally justified in terms of administrative convenience by the

DTF and MMB, but it is another illustration of the partnership relationship between the two organizations.

The Joint Committee

The Joint Committee is a unique arrangement for Britain: it represents a statutory framework for negotiation between an interest organization representing an industry (the DTF) and a quasi-governmental organization (the MMB). In the neutral, academic sense of that term, it is a corporatist arrangement. The nearest comparison in Britain is the relationship established between the National Farmers' Union and the Ministry of Agriculture under the terms of the 1947 Agricultural Act, but that has never involved a formal negotiating body, even though it has led to a very extensive and intensive network of contacts between the Ministry and the NFU. The Joint Committee was set up as a consultative committee when the scheme was revived in 1954, although it should be noted that the DTF was not founded until British accession to the Community in 1973, the manufacturing side being represented before 1973 by the Central Milk Distributive Committee. A 1979 amendment established the Joint Committee as a negotiating body in response to pressure from the trade and to comply with EEC regulations. The relevant statutory instrument has strong corporatist undertones in so far as it designates a named organization as being representative of a particular interest and delegates specific powers to the Joint Committee. The statutory instrument further provides that 'All questions to be decided by the Joint Committee shall be decided by resolution upon which the members appointed by the Board and the members appointed by the Dairy Trade Federation or other body or bodies aforesaid shall each collectively have one vote. The Committee shall not be taken to have agreed unless both such votes have been cast in the same direction.' This is not, however, a recipe for decision making by exhaustion, as there is provision for an arbitration procedure if the Joint Committee is unable to agree.

Apart from its ability to negotiate prices for milk for use in the manufacture of thirteen categories of product the Joint Committee has the power to allocate milk supplies and is involved in training and education, product quality and research. It has eleven specialized committees, panels and working parties dealing with matters ranging from marketing and nutrition to the allocation of milk for cheese making. Thus, one has a publicly established body carrying out functions which would normally be regarded as the prerogative of individual enterprises. The Joint Committee is undoubtedly a more acceptable interventionist mechanism from the viewpoint of the firms in the industry than the state. It is also important to note that the range of activities referred to could not be carried out simply through manipulation of the price mechanism, but require some form of institutional arrangement.

The changing milk marketing system

As should be apparent from the discussion so far, the milk marketing system has changed in a number of ways over the years. However, the basic objective remains unchanged. As described by the Ministry of Agriculture, 'the purpose of the boards has been to strengthen the relative position of producers in the market place' (Agriculture Committee, 1980: 14). Nevertheless, this apparently stable system has had to deal with a number of challenges and problems in recent years which could undermine the framework of cooperative action.

European membership has obviously had an impact on the UK dairy industry, and there may be further impacts in the future if, for example, there are significant imports of UHT milk from Community countries. It should be stressed that not all the impacts have been negative; membership of the Community has opened up a new market for British dairy products, and renewed efforts are now being made by the Government to stimulate exports of British food products through the Food From Britain organization, set up in imitation of the so-called German 'green export miracle'.

The milk marketing boards successfully fought off a threat from the Community to declare their activities incompatible with the Rome Treaty. The Community was persuaded that the boards performed a useful function in relation to the consumption of milk in the UK and Reg. 804/68 was amended to allow for the existence anywhere in the Community of marketing organizations of a particular kind under rules set out in Article 25. A number of detailed changes had to be made in the scheme, for instance producers may withhold milk for the purpose of exporting it, either as liquid or after manufacture into milk products or for the purpose of converting it into butter and skimmed milk powder and selling these products below the price that could be obtained in that way. Certain small producers who wish to sell milk to the final consumer are entitled to obtain exemption to do so under the revised regulations.

However, perhaps the most important consequences of Community membership was the termination of the system of government support through guaranteed prices and standard quantities at the end of the UK's transitional period of entry on 31st December 1977. Until the end of 1977, the Board was guaranteed a price fixed annually by the Minister of Agriculture. From 1974 to 1977, the guarantee applied to all milk produced and thus effectively determined the Board's income (before 1974 it has applied to only part of production, the so-called 'standard quantity'). When the market returns produced less than the guaranteed sum, the Government made up the difference to the Board. Thus, in 1975, admittedly a peak year for such subsidies, market receipts were 3.8p per litre, the government adjustment was 2.7p per litre, giving a total of 6.5p per litre, and making possible a net payment to producers of just under 6.2p per litre. The simultaneous end to consumer subsidies affected sales adversely. Looking at the industry as a whole, there can be little doubt that the end of the guaranteed price had far-reaching implications which have still not been fully worked through. They have made negotiations between the boards and the trade tougher and there have been quite serious tensions in some of the negotiations, particularly in Scotland.

In February 1983, the European Court of Justice ruled that Britain must allow imports of ready-packed UHT (Ultra Heat Treated) milk. One packaging firm inserted an advertisement in the *Financial Times* which asked: 'Is Britain's fresh milk industry about to be engulfed by a tidal wave of cheap imported UHT milk?' Although the advertisement went on to assert that consumers would prefer fresh milk, there were good reasons for disquiet in the trade. The DTF's liquid milk director has estimated that the retail price in shops for overseas milk could be 5p a pint cheaper than the current maximum price at present charged in the UK. More generally, the tensions arising from Community membership were illustrated by disagreements between the milk marketing boards and the farmers' unions at the end of 1983 about the steps that should be taken to deal with the Community's growing milk surplus. Domestic management of this problem is bound to lead to decisions which adversely affect the incomes of at least some farmers and hence may undermine their loyalty to the marketing board system.

The public and the private and the MMB

The question of whether the MMB is part of 'the state' is a difficult one to pursue in the British context. Although the concept has attracted increasing attention from British academics in recent years, terms such as 'corporate state' are almost exclusively used to denote loss of freedom. As Dyson points out: 'In the absence of the idea of the state as a cultural symbol the emphasis falls on the Crown as the focus of shared rituals and ceremony, pomp and theatricality' (Dyson, 1980: 248). However, Dyson emphasises: 'The temptation to label Crown-in-Parliament the state institution is avoided once it is recognized that this institution does not embody, or represent a part of, the more extensive idea of the state' (Dyson, 1980: 43).

Much of the discussion of the blurring of the public and the private in Britain has concentrated on the proliferation of quasi-governmental and quasi-non-governmental organizations. The creators of this terminology admit that it 'turns out to be lacking in rigour' (Hague, Mackenzie and Barker, 1975: 13). For a start: 'The distinction between governmental and quasi-governmental bodies is far from being a precise one' (Hood and Mackenzie, 1975: 411). The distinction between quasi-governmental and quasi-non-governmental is, if anything, less clear. However, according to a table set out by Hood and Mackenzie (1975: 422-23), a sufficient condition of qualifying as a quasi-governmental organization is 'special chartered or statutory powers to punish offenders or to raise licences or levies for specified purposes'. The Milk Marketing Scheme does make provision for penalties to be imposed on registered producers for specified offences and these matters are dealt with by a Disciplinary Committee of the Board.

The spread of quasi-governmental organizations has become a political issue in Britain and determined attempts at 'quango hunting' have been made by the Thatcher Government, although 'quangocide' has been less common than some of the opponents of such organizations had hoped (Hood, 1980). However, the milk marketing boards have not been a target of the quango hunters (Wilding, 1982: 36).

Wilding stressed the high degree of independence of the boards from government and certainly the MMB would not see itself as part of the state. However, John Cherrington, an experienced if sometimes controversial farmer and agricultural journalist, takes a less charitable view of the MMB: 'The Milk Marketing Board was used as a means of securing Government control of the milk market, a task which would have been impossible without it. Again I doubt if farmers really suffered from this policy, but I do not think that they realised how what they thought was their Board was being used' (Cherrington, 1979: 138).

Clearly, the boards do have a special relationship with government. The Board operates within a carefully defined statutory scheme which, for example, prohibits it from producing margarine. The Minister of Agriculture has the power to override any Board decision if he thinks it harmful to other interests, although that power is hedged with qualifications and has never been used. The Minister appoints a Consumer Committee which reports to him on the working of the scheme and which could be seen as analogous to the consumer committees which exist in the nationalized industries. Above all, the Ministry very much controls the economic context for the Board both through the CAP mechanisms and through direct control of the distributive margins and the retail price: it also has a considerable influence on manufacturing milk prices. However, within these constraints, the Board has considerable freedom to use its general power to regulate marketing.

Corporatist theories stress the importance of an historical process through which 'the distinction between private and public action' weakens (Schmitter, 1981: 291). Marketing boards could be presented as an example of the working out of this historical process in a particular issue arena. However, the development of the marketing boards seems to have been little affected by any fluctuations in the popularity of corporatist arrangements in the wider society. This is probably a reflection of the extent to which agricultural politics is conducted in a 'closed world' by producers and experts, an issue arena which is to some extent insulated from wider political pressures. Certainly, corporatist theorists have stressed that: 'Practices resembling the corporatist model are quite unevenly distributed across issue arenas' (Schmitter, 1982: 265).

The Milk Marketing Board is an interesting example of market regulation through means which combine elements of the private and the public. Are there any broader lessons that can be drawn from its experience, and from its relationship with the Dairy Trade Federation, in terms of the economic and political dilemmas posed by the growing size of the public sector in Western countries? For example, does the Board and its relationship with the DTF offer an example of how quasi-governmental organizations and business interest associations acting as effective intermediaries can develop a working partnership which creates an increasing capacity for public action without actually increasing the size of the public sector? In order to attempt to answer these questions, two tasks must be tackled. First, other marketing board arrangements in Britain will be briefly examined, to see whether the marketing board concept is applicable to areas other than milk. Secondly, the operation of the marketing board system will be related to the more general issues which arise from an examination of the relationship between the public and the private.

Other marketing boards in Britain

The milk marketing boards constitute the most important statutorily based agricultural marketing system in Britain. There is a Wool Marketing Board, which operates on a smaller scale, as well as a Potato Marketing Board, which is beset with problems. The Hops Marketing Board has been dissolved as a statutory arrangement. Schemes which did exist for bacon pigs, tomatoes and cucumbers, and eggs have been dissolved. A proposal for a cereals board was opposed by the millers and dropped. Why has the Milk Marketing Board been so successful when other boards have failed? Supporters of the scheme would point to the skill, dedication and accumulated expertise of the Board's staffs, and there certainly is a sense in which success breeds success. Sceptics such as Cherrington argue that the MMB has 'successfully kept farmers in ignorance of the milk market for the last forty years' (Cherrington, 1979: 130). Of course, farmers are willing to cooperate in arrangements which provide them with an assured outlet and satisfactory return for their produce, but are sometimes less willing to adapt their production to market requirements or to accept restraints on their level of production.

Are there any general factors which can account for the success of the milk boards and the failure of other boards? Perishability of the product is one important consideration. Unless milk is transported speedily to the processing plant, it becomes worthless. Farmers can gain the benefit of significant economies of scale through collective marketing and this is best done on a national rather than a regional basis. Regional discrepancies in prices paid by the Board are much smaller than they once were; before the war, Cherrington gained enough to pay a cowman's wages by moving his herd from one MMB region to another (Cherrington, 1979: 130).

However, milk is not the only perishable product. Tomatoes, for example, are perishable, admittedly over a longer period than milk, but the tomato board was dissolved by its members. The problem with horticultural products is that 'mass standardization is difficult' (Self and Storing, 1962: 94) and this leads to endless disputes over such matters as grading. Milk needs a less complex grading system: most milk sold in Britain is pasteurized, although there are four other designations (homogenized/EHT; sterilized; untreated farm bottled or 'green top'; Channel Islands and South Devon or 'gold top') and a discretion to charge a slightly higher price for 'Kosher' milk. Similarly, Cherrington makes the point that 'Livestock are so infinitely variable that a complete board would be difficult to run and administer' (Cherrington, 1979: 131).

A third, if somewhat intangible, factor is the nature of the producers themselves. If a scheme is to succeed, producers need to have sufficient responsibility to offset any immediate problems against the balance of the long run advantage. In areas such as tomatoes, potatoes and eggs, one is often dealing with small-scale, economically marginal producers who may blame their vulnerability on the marketing arrangement rather than on their own position in the market. These producers then cause a great deal of trouble for the board, often out of all proportion to their numbers. For example, in the case of the Tomato and Cucumber Board 'it quickly fell foul of a group of abolitionists. This group secured representation on the Board itself, whose annual general meeting became the scene of unruly disputations over its continued existence' (Self and Storing, 1962: 95). After a campaign of disruption, the abolitionists succeeded in securing a majority in a poll for revocation of the scheme at the fourth attempt (Giddings, 1974: 26). These difficulties with abolitionists will be examined below in more detail in relation to eggs.

The Egg Board which was dissolved and replaced by an independent Eggs Authority under the 1970 Agriculture Act, faced a 'basic problem . . . of continuing and growing over-supply which . . . persistently depressed producer prices in spite of the Board's attempts to support them' (Giddings, 1974: 27). Eggs sold through the Board received a lion stamp which was the focus of a considerable advertising campaign, but 'consumers regarded stamped eggs with considerable suspicion (as they had clearly been through packing stations) and were quite prepared to pay a premium for unstamped eggs in the belief that they were fresher' (Giddings, 1974: 28). Consumers turned in increasing numbers to small-scale producer retailers. Many of these smaller producers were organized in the Poultry Association of Great Britain, but the Minister ruled that this organization 'did not substantially represent egg producers' (Self and Storing, 1974: 101). This was, of course, a very different situation from the dairy industry where the MMB had effective interest intermediaries in the form of the NFU and the DTF to deal with; it suggests that such effective intermediaries representing producers and, where appropriate, manufacturing purchasers may be important to the success of an agricultural marketing scheme.

Objectors to the egg scheme formed themselves into a group called SOCEM (Society of Objectors to Compulsory Egg Marketing). There were a number of incidents at the Board's headquarters involving the smashing of eggs, which provided very suitable missiles for this kind of activity, offering the possibility of humiliating one's opponents without harming them. In 1960 police had to be called to the first meeting of the disciplinary committee of the Egg Marketing Board after disturbances had occurred. As soon as the meeting began, one protestor stood up and shouted: 'Ladies and Gentlemen, Germany 1939. The German Reich. Heil Hitler.' The campaign also received quite a lot of support from the more populist right-wing newspapers such as the *Daily Express*. The eventual replacement of the Board was more than a consequence of the abolitionist campaign, being related to such factors as 'the rapid technological development in the industry that rendered a marketing board inappropriate and its marketing powers virtually irrelevant' and 'the perverse consumer preference for unstamped eggs' (Giddings, 1974: 202). However, 'the decline in producer support weakened the Board's political position to such an extent that it was unable to maintain attitudes of principle either on marketing arrangements or its own constitution' (Giddings, 1974: 203).

The Egg Board may not have failed if, like the Milk Marketing Board in its earlier days, it had succeeded in gaining control over the marketing of all eggs sold off farms. In the early days of the Milk Marketing Scheme producer-retailers were a severe problem, and gaining control at that stage over this section of the industry, which was much larger than it is now, was one of the major achievements of the Board. Had the Egg Board achieved that, all the difficulties it got into with the 'Little Lion' campaign might never have come about.

The success of the Milk Marketing Board is due to a considerable extent to the nature of the scheme itself which represents a set of checks and balances, giving the Board the right to sole purchase of all milk sold off farms, but seeking to protect all other interests in the industry from any possible abuse of such enormous power. So far as producers are concerned, it imposes on the Board the statutory obligation to accept all their milk. So far as the trade is concerned, there is a statutory obligation to negotiate prices and all other marketing matters with them in Joint Committee. In addition, there are significant control mechanisms — the provision for a committee of investigation to consider complaints about the scheme and its operation referred by the Minister, and the existence of a consumer's committee which from time to time reviews the operation of the scheme (and any other complaints about agricultural marketing schemes) and considers complaints about the effect of the scheme (or other schemes) on domestic consumers. It is also worth mentioning the complex procedure for approval of a marketing scheme — submission; public enquiry, ministerial and parliamentary approval; referendum of producers — not many regulatory bodies could succeed in passing all these tests. The particular success of the milk marketing scheme rests to a considerable extent on the fact that it gives enormous marketing powers to the Board, whilst at the same time giving rights to all the other interests in the dairy business.

Even the successful milk marketing board system has been affected by changes in the financial relationship with government and the economic structure of the industry since Britain became a member of the Community. The question of UHT milk imports is the latest problem to arise in a Community context. It is also vulnerable in the long run to changes in the wider political environment. The Conservative Government in its second term of office has a 'drier' Minister of Agriculture and might look less favourably on attempts to externally regulate the working of the market mechanism.

Who benefits?

The question of who gains and who benefits from the milk marketing board system is a difficult one to resolve. Dairy farmers undoubtedly benefited in so far as they have obtained what an outside observer can only regard as a fair return for their product and, perhaps what is more important from their point of view, a steady, assured income in the form of the 'milk cheque'. It is true that they have to work hard, 365 days a year, and that, whereas there are quite a lot of rich arable farmers, there are very few rich dairy farmers. Nevertheless, their position has to be compared with what it would be in the absence of a milk marketing system. Individual farmers, particularly those able to mount their own delivery system in an urban area, might benefit, but most dairy farmers would be worse off. Liquid sales of milk in the UK are nearly three times the Community average in terms of percentage of total utilization by dairies and it would be difficult to sustain this level of consumption in the absence of a comprehensive doorstep delivery system. Any deregulation of milk would so depress prices that the expensive doorstep delivery system could not be maintained in its present form; liquid sales would fall sharply; and many farmers would be forced out of milk production and perhaps out of farming altogether.

The benefits and costs of the system for consumers are more difficult to assess. In the absence of the present system of regulation, the price paid by consumers might well fall in the short run. However, as farms and dairies went out of production because they could not survive at lower prices, so prices would be forced up again. Indeed, it is probable that the industry as a whole would become more oligopolistic than it is already. The doorstep delivery system would also probably disappear or be severely restricted in scope. In earlier presentations of this paper abroad, the British attachment to the doorstep delivery system has been seen by foreign commentators as perverse and irrational. Whether or not the belief that milk should be delivered to the home early in the morning is a cultural quirk, there is little doubt that consumers do have a strong attachment to the doorstep delivery system. That attachment might, of course, become weaker if they realised its true cost or were offered the alternative between cheaper milk in the shops which they could carry home or a more expensive doorstep delivery service. The real losers from a collapse of the doorstep delivery system would, of course, be the milkmen who would lose their jobs. In a buoyant economy, they would be redeployed into more productive employment, but that is unlikely to happen to a group of workers with few transferable skills in the present state of the British economy. It could also be argued that the milk marketing board system has inhibited product development. The validity of this argument, which has some support among agricultural economists, is difficult to assess, but it could be that the stability of the milk marketing system has an opportunity cost in terms of innovative capacity, although the MMB would doubtless point to the new products they have developed in recent years.

The dairy companies have paid a lower price for milk for manufacture than for milk for liquid sale and could be said to have benefited from the existence of a cooperative and stable framework for the conduct of relationships with their raw material suppliers. On the other hand, returns from the dairy trade have generally been low. This could well continue to be the case in the absence of a marketing arrangement and it may not disturb companies whose main base is in dairying and have become accustomed to a fairly low rate of return. However, it may disturb conglomerates who can compare the profits obtained from dairying with the returns from their other activities. Grand Metropolitan has interests which range from hotels through holidays to health-care, but its food division — effectively Express Dairies — was the only major area of activity to report lower trading profits in 1982. 18.3 percent of the company's capital was tied up in the dairy business, but it contributed less than 10 percent of its trading profit. Grand Metropolitan noted in its 1982 report: 'A system more responsive to the needs of the marketplace would benefit everyone in the long term.'

Neocorporatist arrangements may generate additional capacity to solve pressing economic and political problems in a way which enhances, rather than detracts from, the status of both public and private sectors. As the example of the Milk Marketing Board shows, such devices are compatible with highly democratic representative arrangements. Nevertheless, fear and suspicion of such arrangements runs deep, particularly if the label 'corporatist' is attached to them. The marketing boards would simply see themselves as cooperatives, albeit state-sponsored ones. The MMB's relationship with the DTF is corporatist in an analytic neutral sense, but the participants would probably prefer to refer to it as a working partnership in which differences are resolved through painstaking negotiation in an atmosphere of mutual respect.

Conclusions

The interpenetration of the public and the private is, almost by definition an untidy matter and it is not possible to see in the case presented here the workings of an unseen corporatist hand. Rather, a solution has evolved to the problems of a particular agricultural market which suits those concerned and which also appears to serve the public interest. That this has produced arrangements which may be termed corporatist does not represent the working out of some grand historical design, but simply shows that the course of history has led to a set of arrangements which happen to coincide with the analytical definition of corporatism. This does not mean that this case study can tell us nothing about the relationship between the growth of neocorporatism and the interpenetration of the public and the private. What is interesting is the way in which this case study conforms to the general picture drawn by Wolfgang Streeck in a preliminary (and therefore tentative) appraisal of the research findings of the German team working in the IIM project (Streeck, 1982: 28).

This case study may also help to make clear the distinction between corporatism and étatisme which are often confused with one another. Corporatist institutions are not mere creatures of the state, the fifth columnists of creeping socialism; indeed, to survive, they have to justify themselves to a number of audiences in different ways. The Milk Marketing Board has to satisfy the state that it is operating in the public interest, but it also has to convince its producer members that it is protecting their interests and the dairy trade that it is safeguarding their interests. The emphasis placed in the scheme on democratic principles as the basis for its creation, operation and review in part reflects the needs to satisfy the values of the libertarian British environment. It represents a working example of what Cawson has identified as 'self-government' for 'individuals in groups' (Cawson, 1982: 112). However, all corporatist intermediaries, whatever the political environment in which they operate, must have adequate mechanisms for mobilizing the support of their members and retaining the confidence of the state and other bodies with which they interact.

What is particularly interesting about the Milk Marketing Board is that it is not just an attempt to reconcile public and private interests, but that it is also directly involved in commercial operations. Corporatist arrangements have generally been seen as devices to mediate between the state and key social interests. However, in this case there is a third element in the sense of a potential problem of market failure. The Board operates not just as an intermediary between its members and the state, or even between its members and the dairy trade, but also engages directly in market operations. The significance of this market intervention goes beyond the Board's ability to strengthen the industry by launching successful new products such as Lymeswold cheese. It also raises questions about the general character of corporatist arrangements and their intermediary position, not just between public and private interests, but between market and state.

The Milk Marketing Board combines elements of both the public and the private: its commercial marketing arm, Dairy Crest, differs little from any other dairy company: but its functions as a board embrace a more ambivalent combination of the public and the private. For example, its producer members elect the board and could ultimately dissolve it, but they can be disciplined by the board utilizing powers specified in a statutory scheme. The Board is not part of the machinery of government, but the prices at which it buys and sells are greatly influenced by government decisions. The Dairy Trade Federation represents private commercial enterprises, but much of its work is conducted in a Joint Committee whose powers are specified in a statutory instrument.

It must be stressed that the dairy trade as a whole, whatever disagreements it may have with the Board or the Government over particular issues, does not feel threatened by this unusual arrangement: on the contrary, it feels more threatened by the possibility of de-control. Businessmen in the industry are well aware of the unusual and ambivalent character of the arrangements within which they work, but they are also prepared to defend them.

The problem of defining bodies like the MMB in terms of some categorization of the public and the private is a very difficult one. It may not even be very helpful to attempt it. The Board is not part of the public sector, as such, but neither is it an ordinary commercial enterprise or even a conventional producers' cooperative. One general lesson that can be drawn is that the increasing use of quasi-governmental organizations to solve collective problems increases the difficulty of measuring the size of the public sector.

There has been a growing disillusionment with conventional forms of nationalization (Tivey, 1982), but 'privatization' often brings new problems in its train. One should not be too optimistic about the possibility of a way out of the conflict between public and private methods of allocation. The mechanisms developed in the British dairy industry offer an acceptable means of taking economic decisions within a framework of public accountability, but it has proved difficult to establish similar arrangements in other areas of agricultural production, let alone to generalize the idea of a state-sponsored producer's cooperative to other areas of the economy. Moreover, even the milk marketing system itself may be undermined in the long run by the present fashion for 'privatization' and by the obligations that result from British participation in a wider economic market in the form of the European Economic Community.

NOTE

This chapter is based on research funded by the Nuffield Foundation. I am grateful for comments by Wolfgang Streeck of the International Institute of Management in West Berlin; and by Jim Burns, Philip Giddings, Don Mills and Alan Swinbank of the University of Reading. I would also like to thank the Dairy Trade Federation and the Milk Marketing Board for their willingness to assist with the research on which this chapter is based.

REFERENCES

Agricultural Committee (1980) 'First Report from the House of Commons Select Committee on Agriculture, 1979–80'. *Economic, Social and Health Implications on the CAP on Milk and Dairy Products*. London: HMSO.

Cawson, A. (1982) *Corporatism and Welfare*. London: Heinemann.

Cherrington, J. (1979) *On the Smell of an Oily Rag: My 50 Years of Farming*. London: Northwood.

Consumer's Committee (1981). Consumer's Committee for England and Wales (as established under the Agricultural Marketing Act, 1958), 'Report on the Effect of the Milk Marketing Scheme on Consumers' (typescript). London: the Consumers' Committee.

Dyson, K. (1980) *The State Tradition in Western Europe*. Oxford: Martin Robertson.

Giddings, P. (1974) *Marketing Boards and Ministers*. Farnborough: Saxon House.

Grant, W. (1981) 'The Politics of the Green Pound'. *Journal of Common Market Studies*, 19: 313–29.

Hague, D. C., Mackenzie, W. J. M., and Barker, A. (eds.) (1975) *Public Policy and Private Interests: The Institutions of Compromise*. London: Macmillan.

Hood, C. (1980) 'The Politics of Quangocide'. *Policy and Politics*, 8, 3: 247–66.

Hood, C. and Mackenzie, W. J. M. 'The Problem of Classifying Institutions' in Hague, D. C., Mackenzie W. J. M. and Barker, A. (eds.) op. cit., 409–23.

Lane, J. E. (1985) 'Public Policy or Markets? The Demarcation Problem', ch. 1 in this volume.

Schmitter, P. C. (1979) 'Still the Century of Corporatism?' (pp. 7–52) in Schmitter, P. C. and Lehmbruch, G. (eds.), *Trends Towards Corporatist Intermediation*. London: Sage.

Schmitter, P. C. (1981) 'Interest Intermediation and Regime Governability in Contemporary Western Europe and North America' (pp. 287–327) in Berger, S. (ed.), *Organizing Interests in Western Europe*. Cambridge: the University Press.

Schmitter, P. C. (1982) 'Reflections on Where the Theory of Neo-Corporatism has Gone and Where the Praxis of Neo-Corporatism may be Going' (pp. 249–79) in Lehmbruch, G. and Schmitter, P. (eds.), *Patterns of Corporatist Policy-Making*. London: Sage.

Schmitter, P. C. and Streeck, W. (1981) 'A Research Design to Study the Associative Action of Business in the Advanced Industrial Societies of Western Europe' (mimeo.). Berlin: International Institute of Management.

Self, P. and Storing, H. J. (1962) *The State and the Farmer*. London: Allen and Unwin.

Streeck, W. (1982) 'Between Pluralism and Corporatism. German Business Associations and the State'. Paper presented at the IPSA World Congress, Rio de Janeiro and the ISA World Congress, Mexico City, August 1982.

Tivey, L. (1982) 'Nationalized Industries as Organized Interests'. *Public Administration*, 60: 42–55.

Wilding, R. (1982) 'A Triangular Affair: Quangos, Ministers and MPs', (pp. 34–43) in Barker, A. (ed.) *Quangos in Britain*. London: Macmillan.

8

Taming the Housing Market

Manfred Konukiewitz
Freie Universität, Berlin

Public, private and 'hybrid' sectors

The literature on the growth of the welfare state and the role of governments in a 'mixed economy' has for long used a two-sector model which represents distinct modes for the provision of goods and services. The model contrasts:

— a private sector in which goods and services are provided by private suppliers on the basis of value exchange in response to effective demand, and

— a public sector in which goods and services are provided 'free' (i.e. with a tax price), on the basis of the user fees or some other principle which is not related to the supply-and-demand mechanism of the market place.

This dichotomy is no doubt conceptually stimulating because it allows to contrast in ideal-type clarity the constitutive elements of distinct institutional principles, as they are represented in Table 1.

Theoretical analysis in welfare economics and public finance has assumed that, while the private sector represents a basically efficient

TABLE 1

	Public sector	Private sector
Principal actor roles	Government, citizen	Entrepreneur, consumer
Motivational source	'Common good'	Self-interest
Source of income	Taxes, fees	Value exchange
Dominating mode of interaction	Hierarchy	Contract
Symbolic institution	Bureau	Market place

mode for the provision of goods and services, it also exhibits structural weaknesses ('market failures') which can be satisfactorily corrected only through public institutions, that is government at various organizational levels (Weisbrod, 1978: 17).

Recently, however, social scientists and economists have turned attention and analytic efforts to another sector which has been variably associated with terms like 'third sector' (Levitt, 1973), 'voluntary' or 'not-for-profit sector' (Weisbrod, 1977), 'public interest organizations' (Weisbrod, 1978), 'quasi-non-governmental organizations' (Pifer, 1975), as well as the 'contract state' (Hague et al., 1975).

Primarily empirical analysis showed that many economic activities are carried out in a context which can neither be termed purely private nor purely governmental but which represents an interpenetration of both. While private sector activities have been the subject of theoretical study at least since the days of Ricardo, Smith and Marx, and the economic analysis of the public sector has made significant progress in the recent past, the existence of yet another mode for the provision of goods and services 'confronts us with a gap in our theories' (Weisbrod, 1977: 52).

Theoretical efforts to analyse these 'hybrid' organizations have come from two main sources. Economists have developed an interest chiefly in private organizations which are operated on a not-for-profit basis and are satisfying functions which are predominantly 'public' or 'collective' in nature. These organizations, like churches, charity funds, foundations, or educational institutions, are quite often supported by voluntary membership and receive a significant share of their revenues from voluntary donations, membership dues and similar kinds of non-exchange-related contributions. In an attempt to build a theory of these organizations, Weisbrod (1978: 30) has hypothesized that these organizations perform substitute functions for government whenever 'government failures' (an analogue to market failures) prevent a satisfactory delivery of public goods and services.

Political scientists and administrative sociologists have pursued the study of 'hybrid' organizations from a different starting point: they have observed growth on the 'margins of the state' (Sharkansky, 1979) through the proliferation of 'fringe bodies' outside the institutional government proper. These organizations perform public tasks, authorized by contract or legal acts, and are mainly financed through tax money, yet their structure differs significantly from that of governmental organizations. Examples of these organizations include independent commissions, boards of inquiry, public enterprises like development banks, etc. In a constitutional perspective, the growth of these 'fringe bodies' poses problems for traditional democratic norms like accountability and legislative control.

Particularly British scientists have done empirical and analytical work in this area, coining the term 'quangos' (quasi-non-governmental organizations) for governmental institutions outside the traditional boundaries and 'quangocide' for deliberate policies to abolish these institutions as what some regard as a cancerous outgrowth from proper government (Hague et al., 1975; Chester, 1979; Johnson, 1979; Schuppert, 1981).

Once the importance of this hybrid sector is recognized, it should be clear that the two-sector model of a mixed economy is a heroic simplification, which nevertheless may be of good use for improving our conceptual understanding. A more accurate reflection of reality would, however, be a three-sector model, comprising a public sector, a private sector and an intermediate 'hybrid' sector. The conceptual clarity of our initial dichotomy has to be sacrificed: neither does the hybrid sector possess the internal cohesion that we find in the other two sectors, nor does it have specific features and institutions similar to the others. But, after all, that is why it is appropriately being called 'hybrid'.

The purpose of this chapter is to contribute to the analysis of this sector, providing bits of empirical evidence by presenting the case of Germany's public-interest housing companies (PIHC). These companies cover an important share of the housing service market, but they are not without competition: an even larger share of the rental housing services is provided by private landlords who may be either individuals or incorporated enterprises. Thus the rental housing market offers an opportunity to study and compare the simultaneous operation of the sectors in the provision of a service. For lack of empirical material (the Federal Republic does not, unlike the UK or the US, have any public housing sector), public sector services cannot be included in the comparison.

It should be noted that this situation is quite unusual. For most goods and services, there is one dominant mode of provision while the others may at best fill out a residual role. Not so in the market for housing services. Most countries with mixed economies have, besides a private market, also special markets in the public or the hybrid sectors which are under public influence in varying degrees. Access to these special markets is usually limited by legal and administrative criteria linked to some conception of individual need: households which satisfy these criteria qualify for entry into the special market. Competition between the private and the other sectors, is, therefore, incomplete: households which qualify for the special markets can also enter the private market (whatever their prospects for success may be), but not all households entering the private market will be eligible for the other sectors.

Public involvement in the provision of housing

To gain a better understanding of the competing sectors and their respective roles, it will be useful to discuss the reasons and motives for public involvement in the provision of housing. By drawing on economic analysis, we can conclude that housing is a private good. None of the criteria for public goods apply (Head, 1974; Lane, p. 17):

Non-excludability: 'free riders' can be excluded from consumption, and in fact they are most effectively excluded with the aid of door-locks and other devices designed to ensure individual consumption.

Jointness: usage of housing is highly individual, even though in tenement houses and particularly in high rise buildings there are some features (halls, stairways, elevators, parking garages) which have to be used jointly.

Non-rejectability: if housing is supplied to one consumer, it can very well be rejected by others, notwithstanding the obvious fact that at least in the northern and moderate climatic regions, some kind of housing is needed by everybody.

If this analysis is correct, it can be concluded that inefficient allocation is not a reason for public intervention; we must look for other reasons. Here we can point to some traits of the housing service market which strongly suggest that there are 'structural' inadequacies which call for corrective action by government and lie at the root of the numerous housing policies.

Non-substitutability: housing is a basic need and cannot be substituted by other goods or services. Thus consumers are deprived of a basic option in response to unfavourable market conditions: they cannot cease consumption.

Limited elasticity: there are limits as to how much a consumer can adjust his housing consumption to his available funds. This is particularly true for families whose housing needs are rising in proportion to family size but whose disposable income is shrinking.

Long adjustment periods: because it takes several years for a housing unit to progress from the planning stage to the marketing stage, the supply of housing services reacts very slowly to increases in demand. Housing shortages are thus a recurrent, if not regular, experience in the housing market.

Extended durability: from a technical viewpoint, housing units can survive hundred or more years. Investment decisions thus involve very long time periods and, in combination with the characteristic long-term credit financing, also long-term risks with regard to future marketability. Housing investors are usually extremely cautious and will not invest if in doubt.

All these characteristics will make it more likely than not that housing markets are in a state of imbalance or at least experience recurring periods of supply deficits. Market power is tilted towards the suppliers of housing services; disadvantaged are those consumers with small resources (relative to their consumption needs) or with socially stigmatized traits (minorities, immigrants, etc.). These outcomes of a purely private housing service system conflict with basic societal norms about minimum standards of housing for everybody; housing policies seek to correct these equity deficits by giving the disadvantaged consumer groups a 'second chance' through special markets with a subsidized supply, through income supplements designed to improve individual purchasing power, or through other policy instruments. These policies are designed to correct the equity outcomes of private market transactions and serve a redistributive purpose.

Clearly there are also other motives for housing policy measures. These are, however, of less relevance to the non-private sectors. Most tax abatements, for instance, are aimed at inducing housing investment by actors who are hardly in need of redistributive benefits. An economic rationale for these policies can only be found if housing is considered a meritory good which is being undervalued by the individual actors. In recent times, tax abatements have been extensively used to stimulate housing construction as a 'trigger' for economic growth, implying that the utility of housing construction for the general public is not being accurately reflected by the decisions of the individual housing investors.[1]

Although these distinct motives for public involvement are

frequently intertwined (and even more often confused in the public debate), it seems important to keep them apart for analytical reasons. For an analysis of public-interest housing companies, emphasis will clearly be on the redistributional purpose, since, as a brief look at their history and their structural features will show, they were intended as instruments of social action.

Public-interest housing corporations as 'hybrid' organizations

The first public-interest housing enterprises were founded in Germany in the second half of the nineteenth century, when — in the wake of the industrial revolution — housing for the working-class population flocking into the booming cities was offered almost exclusively by private developers. Miserable housing conditions — overcrowded, unhealthy and expensive dwellings in quickly built-up quarters — were regarded as being at the root of the 'social question' by many critics of social conditions. Reform-minded citizens of 'bourgeois' background (like Damaschke and Huber) joined together with leading industrialists (like Krupp) and enlightened members of the ruling houses to provide an alternative to the private developers who were scarcely restrained by public planning or other kinds of public control (cf. Konukiewitz and Wollmann, 1982). This alternative was very much influenced by the ideas of the housing reform movement and aimed to provide small family homes with a vegetable garden at a price which working-class families could afford. The enterprises which were founded to build these homes were called 'public-interest' to dissociate them from the 'housing speculators' of the private sector and to reflect their 'not-for-profit' business conduct. The first direct governmental involvement with these enterprises were legal measures granting tax privileges directly linked to the objective of building working-class family homes (Flender, 1967: 44). Until the first world war, the public-interest enterprises did not win more than a minor share of the housing market. After the war, however, the housing misery triggered a wave of new public-interest enterprises, supported by funds from churches, trade unions, municipalities, pension funds and also industrial enterprises. By now, tax privileges had been written into national law, but it was not until 1930 that a law was enacted, inspired by a growing misuse of the term 'public-interest', which defined the responsibilities and a code of conduct for public-interest housing enterprises.

The basic features of this law are still in effect today. As they have evolved, the public-interest housing companies are basically private institutions with some important public elements. They are *private* in the following aspects:

— They are private-law companies, either as limited liability companies (mostly), stock companies or foundations.
— They conduct business as any other corporation, with some important limitations which will be outlined below.
— In accordance with corporation law, management enjoys relative independence in day-to-day decision making from supervising bodies.
— Decision-making and accounting procedures are similar to those in private business.
— Employment practices are identical with those in private business. Employees are not civil servants.

In contrast, there are other ways in which the public-interest housing corporations are *public*:

— They are exempt from corporation and wealth tax. This tax privilege is contingent upon observance of the rules laid down in the Public Interest Act and subsequent judicial interpretation. These rules mainly concern limitations on the business behaviour. The most important limitations are:
— Business is limited to the housing market. Enterprises must re-invest earnings into new housing or modernization within a certain reference period.
— Housing construction is limited to 'small homes', that is dwellings not larger than 120 square metres. This limitation is observed to guarantee that public-interest enterprises cater to the 'broad strata of the population' (as the legal term goes) and do not branch out into upper-class housing. There are, however, no general eligibility criteria for access to housing owned by public-interest corporations, unless the buildings were constructed and financed within the general social housing subsidy programme (which holds true for a majority of housing units).
— All pricing procedures are bound to the cost compensation principle, that is, a public-interest enterprise cannot charge more (for rent, in a sale, etc.) than it needs to compensate for its own cost (cost also including a reasonable return on the invested capital). Since the principle as such leaves plenty of room for

judgement, an elaborate set of rules has been devised to regulate pricing decisions in detail.

— Corporations cannot give an annual return of more than 4 percent on the capital provided by share-holders.

— In the case of withdrawal from the corporation, a share-holder cannot take out more than the nominal amount he has invested in the company. Thus, the companies with their accumulated property form a kind of trust fund under the supervision of the share-holders.

Compliance with these rules is primarily controlled by the compulsory associations of public-interest enterprises, in the last resort, however, by the governmental authority responsible for licensing public-interest enterprises. Theoretically, the public-interest status can be withdrawn on the grounds of violation of these rules, but there are no practical experiences with that sanction.

Today, public-interest housing companies occupy a fairly important segment of the rental housing market. Table 2 does not

TABLE 2
Ownership of housing units in the Federal Republic (1978)

Total no. of housing units	21,399,200
Rental units	13,518,800
Owner-occupied units	7,880,400
Rental units owned by:	
Public-interest housing companies	2,339,600
Housing cooperatives[a]	986,800
Private housing companies	328,100
Governmental bodies[b]	638,700
Misc. corporations	688,900
Private (individual) landlords	8,536,700

[a] Housing cooperatives are, as a rule, also subject to public-interest law. They will be disregarded in the paper, however, because they pose a special set of definitional problems. In Weisbrod's (1978, 20) definition of public-interest organizations, for instance, cooperatives would not be included because they serve the interests of their members and do not aim to produce external benefits.

[b] Housing units in the direct ownership of governmental bodies are usually intended for use by members of the civil service or of the armed forces and thus do not represent a 'public sector'.

Source: Federal housing survey 1978, Wohnungswirtschaftliches Jahrbuch 1977/78 and own computations.

TABLE 3
Size structure of public-interest housing companies (1980)

Size range (in no. of housing) units	No. of PIHC's	Housing units
	29	—
1- 100	49	2,412
101- 500	110	29,371
501- 1.000	99	72,805
1.001- 2.000	107	158,640
2.001- 3.000	54	134,752
3.001- 4.000	35	120,322
4.001- 5.000	19	97,886
5.001- 7.000	35	201,888
7.001-10.000	41	337,112
10.001-15.000	15	182,037
15.001-25.000	26	487,845
25.001-50.000	7	261,818
50.001 and above	3	252,931
Total	629	2,339,819

Source: Wohnungswirtschaftliches Jahrbuch 1980/81.

fully reflect their relative importance because these companies are primarily active in the critical urban housing markets.

The size of public-interest housing companies varies over a wide range. A notable share is held by companies with 10,000 housing units or more which must be considered very large enterprises. The largest companies are:

— Neue Heimat, an enterprise owned jointly by the German trade unions:
— VEBA, a subsidiary of the large, federally owned coal and energy conglomerate;
— SAGA, a company owned by the city of Hamburg.

Most companies are dominated by one share-holding institution. Table 4 shows this affiliation of the companies and reveals some important information about their institutional context.

It will be interesting to note that local governments and the other governmental levels together are dominant in more than 50 percent of the companies. These companies hold 46.7 percent of the total PIHC-owned housing stock. There is some room for the argument

TABLE 4
Dominant share-holders of public-interest housing companies

Dominant institutions	**% of PIHC's**	**% of PIHC-owned housing stock**
Churches	3.3	2.0
Trade unions	4.8	13.8
Housing Corporations	7.7	5.4
Industrial enterprises	10.9	12.5
Pension funds, public insurance funds	2.2	3.4
Federal railway and mail	3.5	4.6
Federal and state governments	3.2	14.6
Local governments	49.9	32.1
Private insurance companies, banks	2.3	1.6
Private persons	3.7	1.2
Miscellaneous	8.5	8.8
Total	100	100

Source: Wohnungswirtschaftliches Jahrbuch 1980/81.

that this share represents a public sector in the 'disguise' of public interest companies.

Performance of public-interest housing companies and the private sector

We now come back to the comparative purpose of this paper in an evaluation perspective that seeks to compare distinct modes of housing service provision. It would be most interesting to analyse the full performance of the competing sectors and to draw conclusions on their relative strengths and weaknesses. For such a sweeping approach we do not have sufficient empirical data, however. Instead this paper will focus on the redistributive function of the public-interest sector and, in a comparison with the private sector, will ask in what respects and to what extent this redistributive function is being executed. This endeavour requires not only an operational definition of 'redistribution', but also a summary of the evidence in the various areas of housing services which are of relevance for possible redistributive effects. For these areas separate 'performance profiles' will be condensed for public-interest companies, as well as for private sector housing operators, summarizing available empirical evidence about the behaviour of the respective actor types in a brief fashion that allows comparison. This approach is a compromise between the need to avoid premature sweeping generalizations and the need to be concise enough to contribute to theoretical discussion.

Redistributional effects in the provision of housing services can be achieved in a number of ways. There is certainly no one particular indicator of redistribution. It may mean lower cost for equal housing, but also better housing for equal costs. It may mean better tenant security, but it may also mean easier access to adequate housing.

A combination of purposefully selected indicators will be presented which represents those aspects of housing operators' behaviour with most relevance to the redistributional aspect. The selection distinguishes between *direct* redistributional aspects which affect the individual tenant, and *indirect* aspects which affect the prospects of future tenants.

Indicators of direct redistributional effects

Rent levels: lower rent levels for a given type of housing (lower relative to other sector or average) indicate that revenues are not being maximized at the advantage of the consumer.

Housing standards: high housing standards at a given rent level indicate redistributive effects.

Housing maintenance: housing maintenance is an important aspect influencing the price-service-ratio. Better maintenance at a given rent level is advantageous to the consumer.

Tenant security: rental law legislation gives all tenants a high degree of tenant security, but remaining discretion could be used to the advantage or disadvantage of the tenant.

Tenant selection: policies for tenant selection determine the chances for underprivileged consumers to gain access to decent housing.

Tenant eviction: landlords' reactions to failure to pay rents regularly can vary widely. For underprivileged consumers, it is important whether landlords will seek an eviction order immediately or prefer to find a mutual agreement.

TABLE 5
Performance profile

Direct effects	**Public interest housing companies**	**Private landlords**
Rent levels	PIHC's charge lower rents in most of their housing stock. However, in recently constructed projects rents may be equal to or higher than those in the private sector, due to the cost-compensation principle and the reduction of public subsidies.	Private landlords generally charge at upper market levels unless they have a long and personal relationship with tenant.
Housing standards	Standards are generally high, also in social housing units.	Standards are high, except in parts of pre-first world war stock.
Housing standards	PIHC's generally take care to keep their housing stock in good condition. Existing problems are primarily due to unfavourable social environment.	Absentee landlords have a poor record in housing maintenance Institutional investors and resident landlords take good care or very good care.
Tenant security	Tenant security is very high.	Tenant security may be lower, particularly in cases of condominium conversion, gentrification or personal needs of resident landlords.
Tenant selection	PIHC's are limited in tenant selection for most of their housing stock. They are either bound to eligibility criteria or to local government nominations. Within these limits, they try to select 'respectable' tenants by 'creaming the poor' to avoid deterioration of social environment	Absentee landlords do not screen prospective tenants as long as they are willing to pay high rents. Resident landlords are likely to discriminate against socially deviant stigmatized groups (immigrants, alcoholics, female headed households, etc.)
Tenant eviction	Reaction to financial problems differ, but generally arrangements are sought, possibly in cooperation with the local welfare department.	In case of financial problems, private landlords are likely to seek an eviction order quickly.
Social work	Is not generally practised, but some PIHC's employ social workers in projects with social problems.	Unknown in the private sector.

TABLE 5 (continued)
Performance profile

Indirect effects	**Public interest housing companies**	**Private landlords**
New housing investment	PIHC's maintain a minimum of new housing investment even under adverse market conditions (with the assistance of social housing subsidies).	Private investors cease to invest in new housing under adverse market conditions unless they can take advantage of tax breaks (with a net loss in taxes exceeding the amount of comparable social housing subsidies).
Cost sensitivity	Because of the cost compensation scheme, PIHC's have no incentives to limit the costs of new housing. They are not aggressive bargainers with either construction contractors or banks.	Private investors are more cost-sensitive.
Condominium conversion	PIHC's do not practice condo conversion. (One exeption: Neue Heimat is selling off flats because it is desperately in need of liquid funds.)	Condo conversion is rapidly increasing within the private housing stock with negative effects for tenant security.
Disinvestment	PIHC's do not practice strategies of deliberate disinvestment.	Disinvestment strategies are found with (few) landlords who seek maximum return within a short time period (however not with landlords who view their stock as long-term investment).
Gentrification	PIHC's use moderate gentrification as a strategy to limit the risk of future vacancies and to improve the quality of their tenant clientele.	Gentrification is used excessively by landlords motivated by short-term gains. Private landlords with a long-term perspective modernize 'gently' and seek to limit rent hikes.

Social work: needs for advice and social help often surface in tenant-landlord as well as tenant-tenant conflicts. Attitudes of landlords can vary widely.

Indicators of indirect redistributional effects

New housing investment: new housing investment is influenced by many factors other than housing demand, for instance level of interest rates, rate of inflation, long-term economic forecasts. A continuous housing production will help to avoid gross market imbalances which hurt consumers with low purchasing power.

Cost sensitivity: in a period of spiralling construction costs, cost-conscious behaviour and innovative use of cost-cutting devices influence rent levels and long-term prospects for housing supply particularly in the low-cost market segments.

Condominium conversion: the conversion of rental units to owner-occupant units and the subsequent sale to owner-occupants has a high potential for profits, but reduces the long-term chances of low-income households for decent housing at reasonable cost.

Gentrification: the upgrading of older housing stock through excessive modernization is designed to drive low-income renters out and to replace them with tenants who can afford higher rents.

Disinvestment: disinvestment is a strategy designed to cut housing maintenance costs while extracting high profits through excessive rents from discriminated consumers with no access to decent housing.

In Table 5, the performance of public-interest housing companies and of private-sector landlords in these selected areas will be sketched briefly. The evidence concerning the public-interest corporations is taken from an on-going research project in which the author is involved[2]; evidence on private sector actors is taken from the growing body of other empirical research in housing policy, partly commissioned and published by the Federal Ministry responsible for housing policy.

Conclusions

After this review of performance profiles, it is possible to give a tentative answer to the initial question about the role of the public-interest housing sector in a mixed economy. How effective is the public-interest sector in the pursuit of redistributional objectives? Do public-interest housing companies offer advantages to lower-income or selected clientele groups that the private sector does not offer?

The answer cannot be definite, as this glimpse into the complexities of a comparative evaluation should have made clear, but on the whole, it should be a 'qualified yes'. Public-interest housing companies:

— house more than their share of households who have difficulty finding decent housing because of low purchasing power or discrimination;
— are often the only housing operators in urban regions to cooperate with municipal authorities in satisfying urgent housing needs:
— have a large share of the low-rent market segment with decent housing quality (but, ironically, have some housing with very high rents, due to the cost compensation principle in rent calculation);
— offer better tenant security than most private housing operators;
— abstain generally from business practices (condominium conversion, disinvestment) which adversely affect market chances of low-income households.

However, the affirmative answer requires some qualification, mainly for two reasons:

(1) 'Performance scores' vary over the total set of indicators. Public-interest companies score well in most areas, but poorly in some others. A more detailed study would show that particularly large public-interest companies develop traits which are usually ascribed to large bureaucracies: lack of innovative ideas, incoherence of actions, lack of responsiveness toward clientele. Apart from organizational size, bureaucratic behaviour is also encouraged by those elements of public control which are designed to prevent excessive profit-taking: the cost-compensation principle will on one hand keep prices and charges at a reasonable level, but on the other

hand it reduces incentives for cost-cutting, because costs can be turned over to the tenants or, in the social housing programmes, to the tax payer. This may point to a dilemma of the public-interest sector: to the extent that public accountability is increased, it may experience a loss in flexibility and innovative power.

(2) There is considerable variance of behaviour within the two sectors which is not sufficiently expressed in the performance profiles. In the private sector, the behaviour of absentee landlords who want to make a 'quick buck' is worlds apart from that of the resident landlord with a long-term stake in his property. In the public-interest sector, companies which are owned by municipalities or churches tend to be more aware of their social responsibilities and their 'public' purpose than those owned by trade unions or banks. Most public-interest housing companies develop strong organizational interests which may cause them to minimize their public responsibilities as much as the legal framework will allow. A very good indicator for their orientation is their willingness to cooperate with municipal authorities in the area of tenant selection. This is an area of high potential for conflict, and the exhibited behaviour differs widely.

This points to the need to recognize other factors influencing the behaviour of public-interest housing companies. One important factor is certainly the influence of the mother institutions, not only through the supervisory boards, but perhaps even more through the recruitment of top management and through the general philosophy they impress on their 'satellite' organization. Local politicians or church officials could be embarrassed by the conduct of 'their' company if it engages in questionable practices. Yet the degree of control which these mother institutions exercise again varies considerably, quite often depending on the personalities involved.

Another factor to be taken into account is that most of the housing stock in the possession of public-interest companies was built with public subsidies within the general social housing programme and thus carries strings which, especially in the area of tenant selection, impose tighter limits on management's discretion than the general legal rules for public-interest enterprises.

This comparison of public and private sector housing enterprises did not have the purpose of establishing which sector performs 'better', even in a very general way. Given the diversity within these sectors (which is undoubtedly greater in the private than in the public-interest sector), it is very doubtful whether such a broadly framed question can be gainfully explored at all. The comparison was limited to the respective potential for redistributive effects, albeit with a very broad interpretation. Even within these limits, empirical evidence shows that the internal dynamics of each sector result in specific strengths and weaknesses. While it is hard to see how equity concerns could be adequately represented in a purely private system of housing service provision and without public involvement, housing services would in the long run probably not improve if the public-interest sector had a monopoly. Thus the two sectors should not be viewed as antagonistic and mutually exclusive. They can and apparently do operate in 'peaceful co-existence'.

Today in Germany, not even the most ardent advocates of deregulation and free enterprise doubt that government must intervene to correct the equity outcome that an entirely free housing service market would produce. The welfare state has been here long enough to generate a consensus that government has a responsibility to ensure everybody's access to decent housing. Public debate is now turning to the question whether the traditional instruments of housing policy (and that includes the public-interest enterprises as well as the social housing subsidy system, elements of rental law and features of the tax system) form the most effective way of providing benefits in the right amount to the people who need them most. The problems associated with the public-interest companies certainly give cause to ask whether alternative forms of public involvement and different policies can be conceived which avoid these problems. Proposals range from the establishment of a purely public (municipal) sector to a strengthening of the private sector with sole reliance on income supplements for the support of target-group housing consumption.

NOTES

1. The Advisory Council to the Federal Minister of Economics has, in a recent report, argued against all public involvement in the housing market (except income supplements) on the grounds that the classification of housing as a meritory good is incorrect. The Council has implied that all these policies are based on the meritory good argument, a view which is not shared in this paper (Advisory Council 1982).

2. The project studies local housing policies and the role of public-interest companies in their implementation. It is directed by Hellmut Wollmann and the author, both at Freie Universität Berlin, and supported by a grant from Deutsche Forschungsgemeinschaft.

REFERENCES

Advisory Council (1982) Wissenschaftlicher Beirat beim Bundesministerium für Wirtschaft: Probleme der Wohnungswirtschaft, Bonn.

Chester, N. (1979) 'Fringe Bodies, Quangos, and all That'. *Public Administration*: 51–5.

Flender, A. (1967) 'Aufgaben und Stellung der gemeinnützigen Wohnungswirtschaft', (pp. 35–75) in *Beiträge zu den Grundlagen eines Wohnungswirtschaftsgesetzes*. Hamburg: Hammonia.

Hague, D. C., Mackenzie, W. J. M., and Barker, A. (1975) *Public Policy and Private Interests: The Institutions of Compromise*. London: Macmillan.

Head, J. G. (1974) *Public Goods and Public Welfare*. Durham: Duke University Press.

Johnson, N. (1979) 'Quangos and the Structure of British Government'. *Public Administration*: 379–97.

Konukiewitz, M. and Wollmann, H. (1982) 'Physical Planning in a Federal System: The Case of West Germany', pp. 71–110 in McKay, D. H. (ed.), *Planning and Politics in Western Europe*. London: Macmillan.

Lane, E. (1985) 'Public Policy or Market? The Demarcation Problem' (in this volume).

Levitt, Th. (1973) *The Third Sector*. New York: Amacom.

Pifer, A. (1975) 'The Quasi-Non-Governmental Organization', pp. 380–94 in Hague, D. C. et al., *Public Policy and Private Interests*. London: Macmillan.

Schuppert, G. F. (1981) 'Quangos als Trabanten des Verwaltungssystems'. *Die Öffentliche Verwalt-ng*: 153–60.

Sharkansky, I. (1979) *Whither the State?* Chatham: Chatham House.

Weisbrod, B. A. (1977) *The Voluntary Nonprofit Sector*. Lexington: Lexington Books.

Weisbrod, B. A. (1978) *Public Interest Law: An Economic and Institutional Analysis*. Berkeley: University of California Press.

III

THE LOGIC OF PUBLIC DECISION MAKING

9

From Order to Chaos: Recent Trends in the Study of Public Administration

Lennart Lundquist
Copenhagen University

Introduction

The aim of this chapter is to present some revelatory features of the analysis of public administration during the last decade. When looking for tendencies traceable to different schools of analysis, we are unlikely to find *one* school of public administration. 'Nothing so clearly characterizes the new public administration as disagreement about even central issues, a general imprecision about even major features' (Golembiewski, 1977/1: 121). My thesis is that there is an orientation away from the traditional Weberian model with its rationality, hierarchy etc. The discussion is structured into three sections. For analyses of the administration of the public sector, American, British and West German studies are most important (though the study of public administration in Scandinavia has resulted in some noteworthy contributions). American studies dominate: 'it is thus to America that we must look if we are to consider the study of Public Administration' (Ridley, 1975: 158). References to West German works are unfortunately still rather rare. The same goes for French administrative science. There have already been reviews of the American debate (cf. Charlesworth, 1968; Ostrom, 1973; Dunsire, 1973; Ridley, 1975; Henry, 1975; Golembiewski, 1977: vols 1 and 2; Frederickson, 1980), and the following distinction from the American discussion might be useful: within the study of public administration, there are two main trends; one stresses *public* (political science) whereas the other trend emphasizes *administration* (organization studies). The political science branch has worked on problems such as power and legitimacy, and the organizational branch has studied management and efficiency (Wamsley and Zald, 1973: 62f.; Fesler, 1980). In addition to these two trends there are scholars who contend that public administration should be studied as a special discipline.

A considerable part of modern administrative research is oriented towards political science (for instance Beck Jørgensen, 1981). If we consider political science, it is possible to find some characteristics that occur in the study of public administration. One fundamental and general development in the social sciences is post-behaviouralism. Wollmann mentions three characteristic movements of this trend, which also seem to be relevant in administrative research (Wollmann, 1980: 10ff.):

— from input analysis to output analysis
— from science for knowledge to science for action (from empirical to prescriptive studies)
— from politics (form, power, process, conflict) to policy (content).

Golembiewski offers some further characteristics: post-behaviouralism is macro-oriented, it discusses the problem of values (a normative tendency), and it does not belong to a specific philosophical school (Golembiewski, 1977/1: 25f.). Frederickson, a prominent member of 'New Public Administration' summarizes: 'the post behaviouralist is less "generic" and more "public" than his forebear, less "descriptive" and more "prescriptive", less "institution oriented" and more "client-impact oriented", less "neutral" and more "normative"' (Frederickson, 1980: 12). Underlining all those points is the demand for *relevance*. The idea is that social science research must be able to contribute to the solution of social problems (cf. Premfors, 1979: 281). Political science's answer to this demand is *public policy* or *policy analysis*. One of the most prominent representatives of this genre, Thomas R. Dye, describes policy analysis as 'the thinking man's response to demands for relevance' (Dye in Spadoro, 1975: 53, cf. Dye, 1976). He also maintains that 'policy analysis *is* political science'. Whether Dye will find general support for this standpoint among political scientists is uncertain. However, his declaration may stand as a proclamation for his colleagues, who want to identify policy analysis and administrative research.

The genre of policy analysis has gradually become increasingly difficult to survey, but policy analysis has something to do with 'the stuff of politics' (Simeon, 1976: 548). A policy is broader than single decisions, but narrower than general social movements (Heclo, 1972: 84): it is 'a long line of intention of government' (Golembiewski,

1977/1: 26). Within this vague framework a number of different approaches occur. One discusses whether it is in fact possible to govern modern capitalist society and often the point of departure is pessimistic. In Western democratic studies this question has been discussed in terms of 'government overload' and 'ungovernability' (Rose, 1979; 1980). Marxists have examined the same problem in analyses of structural restrictions (Ronge and Schmieg, 1973) or fiscal crisis (cf. O'Connor 1973, Grauhan and Hickel, 1978). Another approach studies the output and impact of political decisions and their dependence on social, economic and political conditions.

Public policy is a very broad genre: 'Policy analysis is finding out what government do, why they do it, and what difference it makes' (Dye in Spadoro et al., 1975: 31). Is public policy identical with the study of public administration? Sometimes the question is answered in the affirmative (cf. Simeon, 1976: 549). However, there is another development in political science which answers in the negative, namely *implementation analysis*. Hargrove (1975) describes it as 'the missing link' in the policy chain, and Hood asserts that 'the gap which needs to be filled in policy studies is the neglect of the administrative element' (Hood, 1976: v) — a gap to be filled by implementation analysis. Thus, the public policy approach is broader than the public administration one. Is implementation analysis identical with the study of public administration? At present implementation research is probably the most rapidly expanding subdiscipline of political science. Since Pressman and Wildavsky wrote the first work using this approach in 1973, a stream of implementation studies has been published (cf. Nakamura and Smallwood, 1980).

Some important trends

Ten years ago *comparative administration* and *planning* were prominent in the discussion, but for the last five to six years their importance has been declining. It is not easy to explain why. Perhaps comparative administration has met with theoretical problems that are too difficult (cf. Waldo, 1976). There seems to be a new theoretical development in planning research. Besides, its problem area has partly been taken over by 'ungovernability' and 'cut-back management'. In looking for trends we have to explore:

— broader approaches
— policy (content) orientation
— emphasis on later stages of the policy process
— a broader view of rationality
— a dynamic perspective
— stress on participation
— a normative consciousness
— a prescriptive ambition

Broader approaches

A political science analysis of administration must necessarily use general theories of politics: for instance theories of the state, of democracy, of power, of classes, of corporatism and of political economy. Some of these theories offer a perspective on the administration without really widening the analysis. From our point of view, it is important to use theories that include more of the environment of public administration. What is needed is some kind of systems theory. Naturally, the administrative aspect must not be lost. That was sometimes the case in policy analysis: 'Many books on public administration have become so involved in describing public policy that the management of public affairs has been overlooked' (Gortner, 1977: viii). Two well-known comprehensive theories in modern administrative research are interorganizational theory and political economy.

Interorganizational analysis deals with relations between organizations and examines the internal relations of an organization only in so far as they affect its external relations. This analysis has played an important role in organization theory for at least a decade (cf. Beck Jørgensen, 1977), while the study of public administration has turned its attention to it mainly during the last five years. This is somewhat surprising as public administration is often related to an environment of large organizations such as governments, parliaments and interest organizations. As a matter of fact, there has always been an interorganizational aspect to political science, but it has not been formalized in a theory. Interorganizational analysis is used to examine networks of organizations on the same or different levels of administration. The later variant has been particularly espoused by German scholars (Politikverflechtung) (Hanf and Scharpf, 1978). It is not enough to include public organizations in the networks, because private organizations are closely integrated with the public organizations. In an apt phrase, Hernes talks about the negotiated economy and mixed administration (Hernes, 1978: cf. Olsen, 1978). This view has brought forth a distinct unit of analysis with a variety of designations in the literature. Milward works with 'the interorganizational policy system', which 'consists of a more or less closed system of public and private organizations and individuals who are dependent upon each other for resources and linked by a social network which sustains a rough policy consensus. A policy system is a collectivity at the interorganizational field level of analysis; as such it can be used like any other collective unit of analysis — groups, organizations, societies' (Milward, 1982: 475). With Swedish regional policy as the object of analysis, Hjern and Lundmark discuss the inadequacy of the traditional Weberian categories with an hierarchical view of organizations and a clear distinction between the public and the private. They describe a corporatist 'twilight' area, where interest organizations and corporations are involved in the constitutional processes in a way that was never anticipated and where market economy is fettered in an institutional network of public organizations and regulations. As a new unit of analysis they propose 'implementation structure', which consists of a number of people who belong to different organizations and are involved in the implementation of a public policy (Hjern and Lundmark, 1979; cf. Hjern and Porter, 1981). There is a general reaction against older institutional and rational approaches. However, so far, interorganizational (intergovernmental) analysis, while it does not constitute a theory, offers some fundamental insights.

Political economy is an approach that embraces a great number of different schools (Schmied and Treiber, 1975: 48). It should be mentioned that organization theory has begun to apply this approach (Benson, 1975, 1977). One school, the *non-market economy* or *public choice*, builds models on the basis of simple assumptions common in economics, of which self-interest or egoism is a very important one: politicians want to maximize votes and bureaucrats aspire to expansion. Some restrictions are added concerning lack of information and cost of transaction, which makes it possible to discuss behaviour (cf. Simeon, 1976: 577). The method is analogous to that used in economics and other social science disciplines. No doubt it is of great heuristic value: Anthony Downs's book, *An Economic Theory of Democracy* (1957), has had a fundamental influence on the study of political parties. There are also interesting works on public administration (Tullock, 1965; Downs, 1967). Another illustration is Niskanen's theory of the output of a bureau, which is based on a model of the 'purposive behaviour of the manager of a single bureau' (Niskanen, 1971). However, though public choice does not broaden the analysis, it gives it a distinct perspective. More interesting from our point of view are theories which, like the classical study of political economy, examine the relationship between political and economic power in a society: both Western democratic and Marxist studies. An interesting representative of the first type is a work by Wamsley and Zald, which aims at an analysis of the 'interrelation between a political system (a structure of rules) and an economy (a system for producing and exchanging goods and services)' (Wamsley and Zald, 1973: 17). The reason for the authors' choice of the model is that its variables are fundamental determinants of the formation of structures and the bringing about of change. They work with internal and external as well as political and economic variables.

As to the Marxist analysis of public administration, quantitatively it is modest and we have reason to ask why. Wollmann is possibly right when he maintains that Marxism — or at least some of its prominent schools — argues in a base-superstructure-model. From such a perspective the state is determined by the economic structure. A change in the public administration system would imply a preceding, fundamental socio-economic change. Therefore, the restrictions emanating from the economy and the means of affecting these are of major interest for Marxist analysis (cf. Wollmann, 1980: 19f.). A statement from Volker Ronge, a Marxist analyst oriented towards public administration and planning, supports Wollmann's view. According to Ronge, administration is not the theme of an administrative theory, nor planning of a planning theory in a politico-economic perspective. Both administration and planning are themes of a theory that relates the state with its administration and planning to the sphere of production. Changes in the activity of the state may be explained by changes in the process of production (Ronge in Schmied and Treiber, 1975: 56). Cockburn's study of local governments is one example of this approach. She tries to find analogies between state and local government, both of which have the task of reproducing capitalism. Her method does not produce interesting results, She is, however, able to specify — theoretically — the limits of local government activity (Cockburn, 1977). Marxist administrative analysis is often abstract and carried out on a general 'state-level'. However, there are attempts to achieve a 'closer' administrative analysis. Häussermann studies the state as a network of organizations, cooperating or in conflict. From this perspective, the fundamental governmental problem of the bourgeois state is to prevent the class contradictions from developing in a way that is impossible to control (Häussermann, 1977: 12f.). Some very interesting but preliminary attempts to develop a Marxist theory of public administration are presented in an anthology edited by Grottian and Murswieck (1973). The particular value of this approach is that it introduces levels of analysis ranging from social structures to the properties and activities of actors. Another interesting discussion concerns the possibilities of connecting Marxism and policy analysis.

Policy orientation

In administrative theory it is often maintained that the content of politics (policy) are important not only in themselves, but also because content affects the formation and the activities of the administration. Instead of the question: 'Who governs?' the policy approach asks: 'What difference will different governors make?' The second question introduces content into the administrative study (Wollmann, 1980: 12f.). As has already been put forward in this study, content is the fundamental object of analysis in policy studies: 'our main concern is with understanding the *substance* of what governments produce rather than the processes by which they produce it' (Hofferbert, 1974: 5). However, public policy concerns substance in general, not substance particularly connected with public administration. The approach that examines the outputs and impact of the political process is fundamentally devoted to the substance of politics. Analyses of outputs and impact have developed into a technically advanced specialty that has met with great interest, because it was relatively simple to transfer the techniques used in aggregate data analysis to the input side of the political process. A basic question concerns whether socio-economic or political factors shape policy output. Earlier, results pointed to socio-economic factors, but later — with more refined methods — it was possible to demonstrate the influence of politics. To some degree, interest has moved from the question: 'What causes policy?' to,'What policy causes' (Wollmann, 1980: 13). Although output and impact analysis are well established approaches (cf. a report on the early development in Damgaard, 1972), there is still scope for further differentiations, explanations and interpretations (cf. Anckar and Ståhlberg, 1980). Intuitively, it is easy to grasp the importance of the substance of politics. Authorities work in different subject areas which are more or less integrated and which demand separate considerations. It is not difficult to imagine conflicts between authorities in different subject areas in the same geographical area (cf. Mayntz, 1979: 641). However, examinations are usually carried out on the macro-level. It is essential to relate substance and form: substance is important to administrative forms, but the opposite is also true — forms affect substance.

Emphasis on later stages of the policy process

The shift from input to output in political science implies that research focuses on later stages in the political process. This is valid for many approaches, for instance implementation analysis, the perspective of which 'redirects concern to that crucial spot where social programmes and projects get put in place and operate in the field' (Williams, 1980: ix). Two approaches will be discussed below: (1) the relationship between administration and the public and (2) evaluation research.

Relationships between public administration and the public can be differentiated as regards special problems:

— democratic control of bureaucrats
— information from administration to citizens
— citizen participation in preparation and implementation processes
— the relationship between bureaucracy and individual clients.

The first relationship is fundamental more than topical, in public administrative theory. The second is often analysed in disciplines that do not have public administration as their main object of analysis, for instance educational psychology, social psychology and the theory of communication (cf. Katz and Danet, 1973). It is possible to approach the information problem from different points of view: knowledge (cf. Abrahamsson and Strömblom, 1979), power (cf. Ekecrantz, 1975) and communication (cf. Abrahamsson, 1972). The third relationship, citizen participation in administrative processes, will be discussed, together with other forms of participation, below.

This section focuses on the fourth relationship, between bureaucrats and clients. It should be a fundamental political science problem, owing to its quantitative and qualitative importance: 'For ordinary people, political life is more and more characterized by a request for a check, not a trip to the polls.' But, the client relation is often lost in the typologies of participation (Nelson, 1980: 175f.). In West German political science and sociology the problem is discussed under the term 'Bürgernahe'. Important questions posed in this approach are: 'What is a "Bürgernahe" social environment?' and 'How does it change with the general socio-economic development?' Models sketch various citizen roles as well as examining the structural effects of the political system on different categories of citizens (cf. Kaufmann, 1976, 1977; Offe, 1972; Hoffmann-Riem, 1979). American public administration study has developed an approach that examines 'street-level bureaucracy'. It studies the problems of those public servants who have an immediate, personal relationship with the client. These civil servants — at least from the point of view of the clients — have considerable freedom of action, make their decisions under great stress, and have to handle the clients' spontaneous reactions to these decisions. Compared to traditional research on public employees, which focuses mainly on higher civil servants, 'street-level bureaucracy' includes new categories of employees in the administrative analysis, that is social workers, personnel in health services, policemen, teachers and so on (cf. Lipsky, 1980; Prottas, 1979; Yin and Yates, 1975). Street-level bureaucrats are involved in the major part of all the public services. Consequently, they spend a big share of the public budget. They are frequently the ordinary citizen's only contact with the authorities. Therefore, the behaviour of street-level bureaucrats fundamentally affects citizen attitudes towards the state. While social science earlier neglected these bureaucrats, they constituted a classic motif in fiction (cf. Katz and Danet, 1973; Thompson, 1975).

Evaluation research has strong links with output and impact analyses which have already been discussed above. This kind of analysis is not instrinsically related to public administration. Nonetheless, its classifications of policies may make a valuable contribution to administrative research. During the last few decades, politicians have become increasingly discontented with mere information on the activities of the bureaucracy. They also want to know about the impact of these activities (cf. Olsen, 1978: 41).

This demand led to extensive evaluation research. Strictly speaking, this approach should be discussed together with the management sciences. One of the instruments of evaluation research is use of social indicators. Their task is to deepen and extend the analysis by providing continuous information about social conditions and needs information that is valuable not only for social science research but also for practical administration. A lot of resources are invested in evaluation research, and its instruments are becoming more and more refined (cf. Shonfield and Shaw, 1972; Klages, 1973; Werner, 1975; Wollmann and Hellstern, 1977; Rossi et al. 1979). Public measures may be evaluated from various points of view. In terms of impact, we have economic (impact on GNP, balance of trade, price-levels), social (impact on migration, family structure), and political effects (impact on local government, the administration, legal rights) (Olsen, 1978: 41). The total area of evaluation is too extensive to be handled exclusively by social science expertise. It may demand engineering, scientific and medical expertise, etc. (Grumm, 1975: 458).

There is impact at different levels. Golembiewski proposes three points of evaluation: (1) Do measures result in desired and expected effects? (2) Do organizations carry out their tasks effectively? (3) Do individuals function optimally within their organizations? (Golembiewski, 1977, vol. 1: 87). When political measures are directed towards institutional changes, political science expertise is pivotal. What are the effects of constitutional change? What is the effect of a transfer of power between different parts of the state, for instance a weakening of parliamentary control over the administration? What is the impact of a change of electoral arrangements or a change in the relations between central and local government? King, who has developed this argument, maintains that the substance of politics may affect fundamental political conditions such as the linking of political forces, the political structure, the prerequisites of political parties and interest groups, the substance and distribution of political attitudes, the future of a policy and social stability (King, 1975: 309ff.).

A broader view of rationality

Means-end-rationality is a basic element of administrative analysis with its roots in Weber's theory of organization. If rationality is called into question, it probably implies profound changes in current administrative research. We have already discussed approaches that question the organizational rationality that is manifested in hierarchy. Similar tendencies appear in steering theory and decision theory.

Decision theory is traditionally an important approach in the study of organization, and is fundamental to the actor-oriented models that have predominated since the Second World War. Since Herbert Simon's *Administrative Behaviour* (1945), a whole theory of organization has developed with decision as its basic unit of analysis. There are several kinds of decision theory. Here, the focus is on behaviour-oriented models.

For some decades, there was a debate between supporters of bounded rationality ('administrative man', as formulated by Simon) and supporters of incrementalism, ('the science of muddling through', presented by Lindblom). The two models can be said to be exponents of different kinds of rationality. Bounded rationality implies a substantive rationality: means are used to satisfy goals. Incrementalism uses a political rationality: such means are chosen as are politically acceptable. Later, attempts were made to combine the two models, for instance Etzioni's 'mixed scanning' in which policy decisions are made rationally and routine decisions incrementally (Etzioni, 1973). (Supporters of Parkinson's law would perhaps argue the opposite.) The debate on decision theory in administrative studies can be summarized in three main points:

— it was directed towards predetermined goals and rationality in the choice of means,
— it was reductionist, using the individual instead of the organization as point of departure,
— it was not specified in relation to level and scope of application.

The advantage of the rationality assumption is that it makes the spontaneous and accidental understandable. The disadvantage is that the accidental appears planned and the spontaneous, mechanical. Rationality analysis focuses on 'the consistent, programmable, organized, thinking activities of man; to give primacy to behaviour that is related to goals; to assume purpose without asking how it has developed' (Argyris, 1973: 261). Models 'shape' reality, that is determine what we are able to observe, as Allison demonstrates splendidly in his *Essence of Decision* (1971). Different models ask different questions and sometimes discuss different levels of decision.

The individual-collectivity problem has generated a lot of heat in the decision theory debate. Argyris maintains that if we 'are to describe more fully the essence of a decision, we would need to develop a model of the human personality, of interpersonal relations, and group dynamics that relates these variables to actual decision-making processes' (Argyris, 1973: 259). Models of collective decision making are not very frequent. In his excellent analysis of decision theory, Enderud presents a number of models that proceed from the idea that several actors — individuals or groups — participate in the decision-making process. Those models have a perspective of negotiation: the participants partly disagree on objectives (which are given and clearly defined) and are able to negotiate a compromise (Enderud, 1976).

The most promising development in the area of collective decision making is the 'garbage-can model'. The model is characterized by a situation with problematic preferences, muddled technology and part-time participants. It is possible to introduce a number of types of situations, for example (1) anarchy, (2) a situation with some feed-back from previous events and (3) a predicament involving an actor who tries to control the development by means of administrative measures (cf. Olsen, 1972; March and Olsen, 1976; Enderud, 1976, 1977). The garbage-can model takes into consideration all the above-mentioned problematic points, as it supersedes the deadlock that characterizes the discussion between rationalists and incrementalists. However, the model is far from complete. Till now it has been used in its anarchic version which is not very useful in the study of public bureaucracy. It will be necessary to define the model carefully with a view to more structured situations.

Steering theory in an administrative perspective is concerned, primarily, with two relationships: one between politicians and bureaucrats and the other between units at different administrative levels (e.g. central, regional, local). The general discussion on steering (or control) concerns the relationship between the state and citizens, which is not uninteresting from an administrative point of view. The problem is to make explicit the public administration aspect. Furthermore, the macro-level of steering theory is useful as a heuristic instrument in constructing theories for other levels of steering. There are some similarities between steering theory and decision theory. The steering theory school has a rationalist faction which believes in the possibility of central coordination of social activities. This was a basic idea in the earlier theory of planning of which Mannheim was a leading representative. There are other scholars who do not believe in comprehensive planning. They consider its demands on knowledge unrealistic and they mistrust central concentrations of power. Well-known names in this connection are Popper and Hayek.

Models of rationality dominate administrative theory. An important exception is Lindblom's brilliant work, *The Intelligence of Democracy* (1965), that contains a theory of spontaneous and automatic mechanisms of coordination. This work was published during a period in which administrative theory was strongly influenced by rational models, and the book did not get the response it deserved. Studies on macro-steering in recent years differentiate between a number of steering systems. Hernes discusses three such systems; market, democracy and bureaucracy, in order to emphasize systemic interrelationships (Hernes, 1978; cf. Olsen, 1978; Lindblom, 1977). There are models of steering aimed at the administrative level that combine 'substantive' steering (of the kind maintained in planning theory) and 'form' steering (such as system design models preferred by supporters of the market). One possible combination is substantive steering with a low degree of precision and form steering that carefully prescribes organization, processes, personnel and economic resources (Lundquist, 1971, 1972).

We are now able to note the strong links between some of the newer approaches. Decision theory, in its garbage-can version, opens up the analysis of collective decisions, uncertainty, muddled preferences and lack of rationality. Steering theory works with a multitude of steering systems in which substantive rationality is only one possibility. From the point of view of interorganizational analysis these approaches offer new paths in the study of public administration. They belong to the same intellectual tradition.

A dynamic perspective

In times of rapid social change social scientists must look for models capable of describing and explaining change. In this context 'public organizations have always faced a basic dilemma. They are customarily organized to accomplish a given task or to deliver a particular service, and they are expected to be stable, ordered, predictable, anchored to a permanent funding source, and occupying a particular niche in the public sector. The organization has a staff, records, procedures, and policies, all of which result in order and stability. But the public organization is situated in a dynamic and rapidly changing environment to which it must respond' (Frederickson, 1980: 49). This conflict raises a number of fundamental questions. How is administrative change indicated? What causes administrative change? What is its impact? What are the connections between social and administrative change? Two approaches in the literature to these issues will be discussed below. The first is organizational change and the second — a variant of the first — is cutback management or policy termination.

Organizational change is very difficult to master theoretically because change has so many conceivable sources. It seems to be natural to analyse changes in public administration in connection with public sector transformation in general. The public sector has changed quantitatively as there has been tremendous growth. It has also changed qualitatively, from reactive to active measures, from supremacy to service, from liberal intervention to state monopoly capitalism, to choose one enumeration (cf. Schmied and Treiber, 1975: 15ff.).

In studies of change attempts have been made to define indicators on organizational change. In his analysis of the State Department, Warwick asks a number of questions: What is changing (top-level, middle-level or rank-and-file personnel)? How is change brought about (what methods and strategies are used)? (Warwick, 1975: 195). Meyer uses several indicators to describe his object of analysis, namely 'size, divisions, levels of supervision, sections, span of control, formalization, responsibilities, competition' (Meyer, 1979: 39f.). The sociological literature on change sometimes works with a number of interrelated levels, for instance individual, organization and society level (Garner, 1977) or organization, community and society level (Warren, 1977). Different time perspectives may require different models. In the short run it is possible that determinants in the organization or its immediate environment are most important. In the long run we need to examine the more fundamental determinants in the environment (Meyer, 1979: 34f.).

Administrative analyses sometimes extend over longer periods of time. This method has a number of advantages. One of them is that the method permits rough correlations between administrative and social change. Inversely, administrative theory offers an instrument of analysis for studies of history. A masterpiece in this genre is Armstrong's *The European Administrative Elites* (1973). An interesting Scandinavian work is Tarschys's discussion of the 'public revolution' extending over several centuries (Tarschys, 1978). Shorter periods of time may also be useful as a basis for administrative theory (cf. Kaufman, 1976; Ståhlberg, 1976). The study of organizational change demands a broad analytical perspective and this gives rise to methodological considerations: 'If behaviour in organizations is shaped by combinations of individual, interpersonal, structural, environmental, and historical forces, then there is little likelihood of uncovering causal patterns of high generality in a single empirical research study' (Meyer 1979: 38f.). One alternative is, no doubt, long-trend analysis. Anyhow, it is not wise to restrict the study of administrative change to the public organization.

Cut-back management is a variant of change analysis which studies the effects of the declining economy on public administration and public activities. A major problem in this approach is: 'How is a policy terminated and what effect does this termination have?' (de Leon, 1978: 364f., cf. Behn, 1978). It is easy to find out that we know very little about the problems of abolishing an organization. The reason is obvious: it is a quite new experience to modern Western governments (cf. Levine, 1978: 316). Public organizations have seldom been abolished, and if it has happened the process has been very protracted. An empirical examination made by Kaufman confirms this. During the period 1924–1973 only 27 of the organizations under study were abolished. Simultaneously there was a total increase in the number of organizations from 175 to 394 (Kaufman 1976: 44f.). But since 1973, the situation has been radically transformed. Scarcity of resources on all administrative levels will force governments to cut their programmes, abolish public organizations, and fire public employees. The basic dilemma is how to reconstruct a system that has been built for eternal growth (Levine, 1978: 316).

A special approach designated as 'policy termination', 'cut-back management' or 'organizational decline' has started to attack this problem. It offers many useful distinctions. One is the separation between functional and structural termination. In the first case, those activities connected with a certain programme disappear. In the second, the structural arrangements disappear, that is the organization is abolished (de Leon, 1978; Behn, 1978). In order to be able to discuss the problem of termination, a dynamic analytical model is required. Beck Joergensen has outlined a phase model in an interesting work on cutbacks in Danish central administration. He concludes that savings are still in an introductory phase in which the organization and the employees are not seriously threatened (Beck Joergensen, 1981). Levine points out that there is a fundamental methodological problem in the analysis of policy termination. It is caused by the lack of communication between social scientists and students of management. Because of this, there is no link between the 'big' questions about political economy and the more administrative problems of steering in the organizations — a communication that is necessary if these problems are to be solved (Levine, 1978: 316).

Stress on participation

Participation in public administration may profitably be seen from the point of view of democratic theory. In fact, this is often done which is why approaches under this heading are not confined to administrative research. In America 'New Public Administration', 'citizen participation, neighbourhood control, decentralization, and democratic work environment' are standard themes (Frederickson, 1980: 12). As a starting point an enumeration of Waldo will be used. He discusses two forms of participation (Waldo, 1972: 225):

— internal bureaucratic participation (that is the rights of the employees to affect their working conditions)

— citizen participation in administrative processes.

An interesting phenomenon in this connection is the unionization of public employees, a recent occurrence internationally, which has caught the attention of analysis. In this section Waldo's two forms of participation will be discussed. Together with citizen participation, special reference will be made to one of its manifestations, namely corporatism. From the point of view of democratic theory, corporatism is regarded as the negative side of participation.

Internal bureaucratic participation is an important object of analysis in organization theory (cf., for example, Jaques, 1976, and *Administration and Society*, 1975: vol. 1). There are many versions of industrial democracy. One of them, Yugoslavian self-management, is often presented as an ideal (cf. Abrahamsson, 1977). As a consequence of the increased interest in democratic theory, different disciplines have approached each other. Analysts of organizations have studied democracy on the macro-level (cf.

Agersnap and Fivesdal, 1978), and political scientists have taken an interest in organizational theory (Pateman, 1975). Pateman mentions that radical liberal democrats want a theory of organization focusing not on efficiency but on equity, freedom, equality and citizen's rights.

'Industrial democracy' in public administration offers some particular problems. Are there contradictions between macro-democracy (political democracy) and micro-democracy (organizational democracy)? The sharp distinction between public and private sectors in liberal democracies may cause problems. Sometimes the connection between the two levels of democracy is regarded as positive. The individual learns about democracy in the organization and transfers his knowledge to political democracy (Pateman, 1970, 1975). But sometimes the two kinds of democracy are regarded as competitive: if internal democracy is allowed to influence the political decisions. The question is topical in Sweden where the law stipulates that provision be made for employee participation in state and local government administration. Agne Gustafsson has forcefully argued for the primacy of political democracy (Gustafsson, 1978; cf. Westerståhl and Persson, 1975). Internal democracy in public organizations has also been discussed in American public administration studies. The positive effects of public 'industrial democracy' are noted, for instance that the employees, because of their increased responsibility, work more efficiently (cf. Smith, 1976: 281f.). It is tempting to relate this discussion to Weber's model of bureaucracy. The American results indicate that it is not self-evident that organizational democracy is incompatible with efficiency.

Citizen participation in administrative processes may be achieved through individual citizens or corporative representatives. The first means that individuals participate directly in the administration (preparation and implementation) of public policy. Various forms of 'grass-roots democracy' have been discussed in relation to planning processes on the local level. This phenomenon has been given a great deal of attention (cf. the bibliography in Alemann, 1975 and later editions). As a rule these studies have no distinct administrative aspect.

Possibly, participation analysis, more than anything else, has led input oriented political scientists into the field of administrative research. The participation of representatives of powerful social interests in administrative processes has been studied almost as much as individual citizen participation. This kind of representation is very frequent throughout Scandinavia, but seems particularly extensive in Denmark, at least it is exhaustively examined there (cf. Buksti, 1980; Fivelsdal et al., 1979; Valentin, 1981). Often this representation is analysed in terms of corporatism. The concept is used to describe a system whereby decisions are not made by parliament but by means of cooperation between top officials in public and private administration.

However, there is a wide gap between works on a general level of abstraction without any reference to the administration (cf. Kastendiek, 1980; Winkler, 1976; Schmitter and Lembruch, 1979) and specific investigations of interest representation in the administration. What is lacking are examinations of the real interest participation in administrative processes and without such information it is impossible to determine the real significance of the phenomenon.

A normative consciousness

Since the mid-sixties the question of norms and values has been widely debated. The nucleus of this debate is the attempt to formulate an operative theory of value. Such a theory must contain some fundamental values that may be operationalized in lines of action. An important source of inspiration for administrative analysis is Rawls's *A Theory of Justice* published in 1971 (cf. Frederickson, 1980: 40ff.; Price, 1981: 142).

The discussion on norms in administrative studies was an important element at the Minnowbrook conference in 1969 when the New Public Administration was outlined. The state of normative research was far from satisfactory as was clarified in a contribution from La Porte who maintains that the state of philosophical analysis in administrative science had reached a low-water mark. It is 'so scantily attended in Public Administration that I am ill-prepared and almost embarrassed to continue' (La Porte in Marini, 1971: 31). The importance of an explicit presentation of norms in research reports is often stressed. Argyris maintains that it is necessary for a normative view to be made explicit and to be seen as an objective to approximate (Argyris, 1973: 264ff.). Lindblom argues that explicit statements for or against fundamental values are 'necessary to give coherence to any analysis. Otherwise one only randomly and aimlessly observes the phenomenon under study' (Lindblom, 1977: 6f.).

What more specifically does this imply? Often values are presented at a high level of abstraction. Lindblom mentions 'the traditional values of liberty, equality, democracy, and popular participation in policy-making'. In an enumeration of standards of theory construction Golembiewski also includes norms: 'it must be shown to deal with some relevant values defining "good administration" and its relationship to a "just state"' (Golembiewski, 1977/1:x). La Porte sketches a basic norm intended to be used as a point of departure, namely that 'the purpose of public administration is the reduction of economic, social, and psychic suffering and the enhancement of life opportunities for those inside and outside the organization' (La Porte in Marini, 1971:32). La Porte tries to transform his general norm into a few more precise norms:

— public organizations should be assessed in terms of their effect on the production and distribution of material abundance in efforts to free all people from economic deprivation and want;

— public organizations have a responsibility to enhance social justice by freeing their participants and the citizenry to decide their own way and by increasing the probability of shared political and social privilege;

— the quality of personal encounter and increasing possibilities of personal growth should be elevated to major criteria of organizational assessment.

These norms are valid for public activities in general. However, there are norms valid for public officials, a kind of ethical code. The title of a book (*Public Duties: The Moral Obligations of Government Officials*) is an indication of the meaning of these norms. The moral dilemma of the civil servant is that there are forces pulling him in different directions. Thus, Hart proposes that civil servants are 'constrained by the specific rules and goals of their public organizations, the professional code of their discipline, and the expectations of their clientele (the public)' (Hart, 1974: 4, cf. Rein and Rabinovitz, 1978: 308f.).

One has to look for 'moral principles that are . . . standards for adjudicating the competing moral claims arising in the exercise of administrative discretion' (Warwick, 1981: 111). Standards of this kind are necessary in order to answer questions about administrative behaviour. Warwick presents two opposite schools of administration: 'administrative Darwinism' and 'Weberian idealism'. In the first school the officials are seen as 'players in games of self-interest' and in the other one is committed to 'a combination of conformity with directives from above and an internalized understanding of proper behaviour for career officials'.

In Scandinavian administrative studies further schools are presented (cf. Rylander, 1969; Olsen, 1978: 45ff.). Different schools stress different norms which are sometimes carefully specified. Also, there may be different norms in different situations as for example the officials' relations with their clients may be oriented in terms of 'universalism, specificity, and affective neutrality' (Katz and Danet, 1972). As has been already mentioned, there are norms on different levels of abstraction and complexity. The 'Rechtstaat' has its norms which are complemented by the democratic rules of the game in Western democracies. Generally speaking, normative administrative research is underdeveloped.

A prescriptive ambition

In a situation where there is a normative consciousness and a lot of empirical results, it is natural to start constructing a prescriptive theory. Such a theory prescribes lines of action for the public administration, the substance of administrative activities (the subject area of the administrative unit) but the administrative organization, processes and personnel. The ambition does not amount to an innovation of administrative analysis, because American studies in the 1920s and 1930s tried to shape an optimal public administration as regards effectiveness — an ambition that disappeared in the behaviouralist wave of the 1950s and 1960s. Now it has returned. As Caiden maintains, administrative reform has not played such a prominent role in practical politics since the New Deal. All over the world governments are starting inquiries into problems in their administrative systems (Caiden, 1979: 456).

Relevance is an increasingly frequently raised demand made on the social sciences. An ideal state is administrative research as a 'Beratungswissenschaft'. The trend may be illustrated by such titles as 'Policy Analysis in Government: Alternatives to "Muddling Through"' (Beckman, 1977: 221ff.). Governments aim at 'Verwissenschaftlichung der Politik' (Mayntz and Scharpf, 1973: 7, cf. Weiss and Barton, 1979). This means parallel lines of development: governments are looking for information in research reports, and administrative research increasingly works on prescriptive theory.

There are a great number of approaches focusing on a prescriptive administrative theory. Four of these will be briefly presented below: organizational development, policy sciences, administrative reform and management sciences. Furthermore, there are such things as the ethics of civil servants which have been discussed under the heading 'Normative consciousness'. It should also be mentioned that many of the main approaches include prescription on their programmes. One example of this is implementation research, where influential authors have policy relevance as a primary criterion for the value of their analysis: 'At basic issue is the extent to which implementation studies can yield "pertinent, sound, timely" information to aid those who formulate and execute public policies' (Williams, 1982:1).

Organizational development is an extensive approach and embraces a number of separate 'movements'. At one extreme, there is little interest in 'interpersonal relations', while the other extreme stresses the human component of an organization. The latter is most peculiar. It consciously tries to improve the properties and results of the organization by improving the standards of its members, using psychology and social psychology (cf. Waldo, 1972: 240ff.). In order to delineate the characteristics of this approach its intellectual basis will be elucidated. The individual orientation is an outgrowth of Maslow's humanistic psychology with its attempts to help the individual towards self-realization. Concerning the group it has its roots in the 'human relations school': 'Organizational development is oriented towards *process*; it stresses interpersonal competence, collaboration, teamwork, and group dynamic skills' (Thayer, 1981: 22f.). The approach focuses on the inner dynamics of the organization. Typical characteristics are various methods of education such as 'Laboratory training' and 'Sensitivity-Training' (Kirkhart and Gardner, 1974: 97ff.). The organizational development approach has both passionate protagonists and antagonists. The question is whether it is to be understood as 'cynical manipulation, a passing fad that cannot last much longer, or an important profession' (Thayer, 1981: 20).

Policy sciences started with Harold Lasswell's book of the same title (1951). Yehezkel Dror, in particular, has maintained the necessity of the approach in a number of books and articles since the late 1960s (Dror, 1968, 1971, 1971a). In Dror's version, the policy sciences have several characteristics. The approach is a 'supra-discipline', one aimed at improving policy making; integrating a good many disciplines, it accepts tacit knowledge, brings about an instrumental-normative knowledge, will construct an operative theory of values and it works with a long time perspective. Moreover, it stresses metapolicies and it includes extra-rational and irrational processes such as creativity (Dror, 1970: 135f.). In his editorial in the first number of the journal, *Policy Sciences*, Quades asks: 'Why Policy Sciences?' His answer is that the public sector has not adapted procedures, techniques and instruments from management and decision sciences. The idea is not that public administration should adopt methods such as operation analysis, simulation, game theory and so on, but that the knowledge of behavioural sciences should be placed in a framework of systems engineering (Quade, 1970: 1f.). Dror has the same objective in stressing that the problem is to integrate the social sciences and decision sciences and on this basis build 'a new additional approach to the uses of systematic knowledge and structured rationality for the conscious shaping of society' (Dror, 1970a: 137).

Administrative reform is another approach in the prescriptive genre. Its objective is 'induced and directed change in the machinery of government'. The measures to be used fall into four categories: structural, procedural, technical, and people-changing (Dunsire, 1976: 7). Social and administrative developments are the background to this new approach. Administrative reform wants to modernize the machinery of government in order to make the administrative state capable of keeping pace with the expansion and complexity of state activities. In the long run, the aim is the transformation of the public administration into a dynamic force for national development. Improved productivity and efficiency in the public sector and improved control to guarantee that governments serve the public interest are important sub-goals (Caiden, 1979: 457; cf. Leemans, 1976). Administrative reform is very close to the process of change. It is not enough to prescribe possible and appropriate methods of change. They must also be properly implemented.

Management sciences includes those advanced techniques which have been introduced in public administration during the last two decades in the name of rationality and efficiency. The efforts in this direction have 'become a major concern, almost an obsession, of modern governments' (Self, 1975: 178). What are the management sciences? Gorpe makes a division into methods of knowledge-seeking (methods of prognosis, delphi technique, systems analysis, evaluation, social indicators), methods facilitating decision making (social cost-benefit analysis, operation analysis, policy analysis), and steering methods (programme budgeting, zero-base budgeting, steering on objectives, management information systems, planning, planning systems) (Gorpe, 1978).

While the earlier prescriptive approaches trace their origin to the social sciences with the exception of the synthetic ambition of policy sciences, management sciences have their roots in mathematical approaches: 'optimization theory, probability, linear algebra, and others' (White, 1979: 128). The question is whether administrative research in the social sciences can contribute to the development of administrative techniques. Perhaps it is more useful in analysing the impacts of the techniques to ask: What are the impacts on political decision making? Do the impacts cause problems for political democracy? etc. (cf. Gorpe, 1978; Self, 1975).

Towards a post-Weberian theory of administration?

This study presents eight topical trends in administrative research over the last ten to fifteen years. The trends seem rather diverse, but is it possible to discern a common perspective? One possible point of departure is postbehaviouralism that is anchored in administrative science as well as in other social sciences. This circumstance may possibly support one fundamental supposition in this study: changes in the social sciences reflect social change. The study of public administration is conducted on three levels of analysis: empirical, normative and prescriptive. One problem is that there is a distinct difference in the general direction of these levels. While important empirical approaches have more or less abandoned rationality, prescriptive analysis — in its eagerness to be relevant — has often but not always a rationalist perspective.

The general thesis is that there is an orientation away from the traditional Weberian model with its rationality, hierarchy, etc. Leaving the prescriptive and normative trend aside, we find within the empirical trends a number of characteristics that are not stressed in Weber's theory of bureaucracy. Sometimes they are quite the opposite of Weber's categories, as is evident from the following table:

Weber	*New characteristics*
rationality	'garbage can'
intraorganization	interorganization
hierarchy	mutuality
central coordination	spontaneous, decentralized coordination
substantive steering	form steering
static	dynamic
bureaucracy	democracy

Is the conclusion that we just have to replace the Weberian categories with the new ones? No doubt, such a step would mean a real revolution in the study of public administration, where Weber's influence has been fundamental. However, such a conclusion is doubtful, because the solution is to be found elsewhere. Another possibility is to view the problem from the point of view of dynamic models. Is it possible to construct dynamic models (models with *time* as an explicit variable) merely for the administrative level? The answer must be no, because organizational changes depend on so many conditions which the organization is unable to control, for instance fundamental social and economic changes. It is unlikely that it will be possible to distinguish regularities isolated at the level of organization. What is the alternative?

One solution is to construct situational typologies for organizations. The result is 'conditional generalizations — statements that specify the limits of their applicability to particular situations or types of organizations' (Scott, 1981: 67). The background to this is that 'different environments place different requirements on organizations: specifically, environments characterized by uncertainty and rapid rates of change in market conditions or technologies present different demands — both constraints and opportunities — on organizations than do placid and stable environments' (Scott, 1981: 114). If we apply this reasoning to the relationship between the two types of categories — Weberian and post-Weberian it is conceivable that Weber's model fits some environments and the new model others. The two sets of categories simply relate to different situations. The new instruments of analysis represent attempts to describe, explain and understand a reality that the old instruments were not able to make intelligible. Both sets of categories may be included in a situational typology and we may search to find the property space that encompasses them and other relevant categories of public decision making and implementation.

REFERENCES

Abrahamsson, Bengt (1977) *Bureaucracy or Participation: The Logic of Organization*. Beverly Hills: Sage.

Abrahamsson, Kenneth (1972) *Samhällskommunikation. Om kontakten mellan myndigheter och medborgare*. Lund: Studentlitteratur.

Abrahamsson, Kenneth and Strömblom Bengt (1979) *Förvirrande förvaltning. Medborgaren i den byråkratiska labyrinten*. Stockholm: Liber Förlag.

Agersnap, Torben and Fivelsdal, Egil, (eds.) (1978) *Demokrati i organisationer*. Copenhagen: Nyt Nordisk Forlag Arnold Busck.

Alemann, Ulrich von (ed.) (1975) *Partizipation — Demokratisierung — Mitbestimmung*. Opladen: Westdeutscher Verlag.

Allison, Graham T. (1971) *Essence of Decision. Explaining the Cuban Missile Crises*, Boston: Little, Brown and Co.

Anckar, Dag and Ståhlberg, Krister (1980) 'Assessing the Impact of Politics: A Typology and Beyond'. *Scandinavian Political Studies*, 3.

Argyris, Chris (1973) 'Some Limits of Rational Man Organizational Theory'. *Public Administration Review*.

Armstrong, John, A. (1973) *The European Administrative Elite*. Princeton NJ: Princeton University Press.

Beck Jørgensen, Torben (1977) *Samspil og Konflikt mellem organisationer*, Copenhagen: Nyt fra Samfundsvidenskaberne.

Beck Jørgensen, Torben (1981) *Når staten skal spare*. Copenhagen: Nyt fra Samfundsvidenskaberne.

Beckman, Norman (1977) 'A Symposium. Policy Analysis in Government: Alternatives to "Muddling Through"'. *Public Administration Review*.

Behn, Robert D. (1978) 'How to Terminate a Public Policy: A Dozen Hints for the Would-Be Terminator'. *Policy Analysis*, 2.

Benson, J. Kenneth (1975) 'The Interorganizational Network as a Political Economy'. *Administrative Science Quarterly*, 22.

Benson, J. Kenneth (ed.) (1977) *Organizational Analysis. Critique and Innovation*. Beverly Hills: Sage Publications.

Benson, J. Kenneth (1977) 'Organizations: A Dialectical View'. *Administrative Science Quarterly*.

Buksti, Jacob A. (1980)*Organisationer under forandring*. Århus: Politica.

Caiden, G. (1969) *Administrative Reform*. Chicago: Aldine Publishing Company.

Charlesworth, James C. (ed.) (1968) *Theory and Practice of Public Administration: Scope, Objectives, and Methods*. Philadelphia: Monograph 8, The American Academy of Political and Social Science

Cockburn, Cynthia (1977) *The Local State. Management of Cities and People*. London: Pluto Press.

O'Connor, James (1973) *The Fiscal Crises of the State*. New York: St. Martin's Press.

Damgaard, Erik (1972) 'Politisk output analyse'. *Statsvetenskaplig Tidskrift*.

Downs, Anthony (1967) *Inside Bureaucracy*. Boston: Little, Brown and Co.

Dror, Yehezkel (1968) *Public Policy Re-Examined*. San Francisco: Chandler.

Dror, Yehezkel (1970) 'Prolegomena to Policy Sciences'. *Policy Sciences*.

Dror, Yehezkel (1971a) *Design for Policy Sciences*. New York: American Elsevier.

Dror, Yehezkel (1971b) *Ventures in Policy Sciences. Concepts and Applications*. New York: American Elsevier.

Dunn, William and Fozouni, Bahman (1975) *Towards a Critical Administrative Theory*. Sage Professional Papers in Administrative and Policy Sciences 3, 26. London: Sage.

Dunsire, Andrew (1973) *Administration. The Word and the Science*. London: Martin Robertson.

Dunsire, Andrew (1976) *Structural and Behavioral Obstacles to Administrative Reform*. Tampere Conference: European Group of Public Administration (mimeo).

Dye, Thomas R. (1976) *Policy Analysis. What Governments Do, Why They Do It, and What Difference It Makes*. University, Alabama: University of Alabama Press.

Ekecrantz, Jan (1975) *Makten och informationen*. Lund: Studentlitteratur.

Enderud, Harald (1976) *Beslutninger i organisationer i adfaerdsteoretisk perspektiv*. Copenhagen: Fremad.

Enderud, Harald (1977) *Four Faces of Leadership in an Academic Organization*. Copenhagen: Nyt Nordisk Forlag.

Etzioni, Amitai (1980) 'Mixed-Scanning: A "Third" Approach to Decision-Making' in Faludi, Andreas (ed.) *A Reader in Planning Theory*. Englewood Cliffs, NJ: Prentice Hall.

Fesler, James W. (1980) *Public Administration. Theory and Practice*. Englewood Cliffs NJ: Prentice Hall.

Fivelsdal: Egil et al. (1979) *Interesseorganisationer og centraladministration*. Copenhagen: Nyt fra Samfundsvidenskaberne.

Frederickson, H. George (1980) *New Public Administration*. University, Alabama: The University of Alabama Press.

Garner, Roberta Ash (1977) *Social Change*. Chicago: Rand McNally.

Golembiewski, Robert T. (1977) *Public Administration as a Developing Discipline* 1 and 2, New York: Marcel Dekker.

Gorpe, Peter (1978) *Politikerna, byråkraterna och de nya styrformerna*. Stockholm: Liber Förlag.

Gortner, Harald F. (1977) *Administration in the Public Sector*. New York: John Wiley.

Grauham, Rolf Richard and Hickel, Rudolf (eds.) (1978) *Krise der Steuerstaats*. Opladen: Westdeutscher Verlag.

Grottian, Peter and Murswieck, Axel (eds.) (1974) *Handlungsspielräume der Staatsadministration. Beiträge zur politologisch-soziologischen Verwaltungsforschung*, Hamburg: Hoffmann und Campe.

Grumm, J. G. (1975) 'The Analysis of Policy Impact', in Greenstein and Polsby (eds.), *Handbook of Political Science* Vol. 6. Menlo Park, California: Addison-Wesley.

Gustafsson, Agne (ed.) (1978) *Företagsdemokratin och den offentliga sektorn*. Lund: Studentlitteratur.

Hanf, Kenneth and Scharpf, Fritz W. (eds.) (1978) *Interorganizational Policy Making. Limits to Coordination and Central Control*. Beverly Hills: Sage Publications.

Hargrove, Erwin (1975) *The Missing Link. The Study of the Implementation of Social Policy*. Washington DC: The Urban Institute.

Hart, David K. (1974) 'Social Equity, Justice, and the Equitable Administrator'. *Public Administration Review*, 34.

Heclo, Hugh (1972) 'Review Article: Policy Analysis'. *British Journal of Political Science*, 2.

Henry, Nicholas (1975) 'Paradigms of Public Administration'. *Public Administration Review*, 35.

Henry, Nicholas (1975) *Public Administration and Public Affairs*. Englewood Cliffs NJ: Prentice Hall Inc.

Hernes, Gudmund (ed.) (1978) *Forhandlingsøkonomi og blandningsadministrasjon*, Oslo: Universitetsforlaget.

Hjern, Benny and Lundmark, Kjell (1979) 'Blandekonomi och post-Weberiansk förvaltningsteori'. *Statsvetenskaplig Tidskrift*.

Hjern, Benny and Porter, David O. (1981) 'Implementation Structures: A New Unit of Analysis'. *Organization Studies*.

Hofferbert, Richard (1974) *The Study of Public Policy*. Indianapolis, NY: The Bobbs-Merril Co.

Hoffman-Riem, Wolfgang (ed.) (1980) *Bürgernahe Verwaltung. Analysen über das Verhältnis von Bürger und Vervaltung*. Neuwied und Darmstadt: Luchterhand.

Hood, Christopher (1976) *The Limits of Administration*. London: John Wiley and Sons.

Häussermann, Harmut (1977) *Die Politik der Bürokratie. Einführung in die Soziologie der staatlichen Verwaltung*. Frankfurt: Campus Verlag.

Jaques, Elliot (1976) *A General Theory of Bureaucracy*. London: Heineman.

Kastendiek, Hans (1960) 'Neokorporativismus'. *Prokla*, 38.

Katz, Elihu and Danet Brenda (eds.) (1973) *Bureaucracy and the Public. A Reader in Official-Client Relations*. New York: Basic Books.

Kaufman, Herbert (1976) *Are Government Organizations Immortal?* Washington DC: The Brookings Institution

Kaufmann, Franz-Xaver (ed.) (1977) *Bürgernahe Gestaltung der sozialen Umvelt. Probleme und theoretische Perspektive eines Forschungsverbundes*. Meisenheim am Glan: Verlag Anton Hain.

Kaufman, Franz-Xaver et al. (1976) 'Soziologische Probleme publikumsbezogenen Verwaltungshandelns'. *Zwischenbilanz der Soziologie. Verhandlungen des 17. Deutschen Soziologentages*. Stuttgart: Ferdinand Enke Verlag.

King, Anthony: 'On Studying the Impacts of Public Policies: The Role of the Political Scientist' in Holden, M. and Dresang, D. (eds.) *What Government Does*. Beverly Hills: Sage Yearbooks in Politics and Public Policy, Vol. 1.

Kirkhart, Larry and Gardner, Neely (eds.) (1974) 'A Symposium. Organization Development'. *Public Administration Review*, 34.

Klages, Helmut (1973) 'Assessment of an Attempt at a System of Social Indicators'. *Policy Sciences*, 5.

Leemans, A. F. (ed.) (1976) *The Management of Change in Government*. The Hague: Martinus Nijhoff.

de Leon, Peter (1978) 'Public Policy Termination'. *Policy Analysis*.

Lerner, Daniel and Lasswell Harold D. (eds.) (1951) *The Policy Sciences*, Stanford, California: Stanford University Press.

Levine, Charles H. (1978) Organizational Decline and Cutback Management'. *Public Administration Review*.

Lindblom, Charles E. (1965) *The Intelligence of Democracy*. New York: The Free Press.

Lindblom, Charles E. (1977) *Politics and Markets*. New York: Basic Books.

Lipsky, Michael (1980) *Street-Level Bureaucracy. Dilemmas of the Individual in Public Services*. New York: Russel Sage Foundation.

Lundquist, Lennart (1971) *Förvaltningen i det politiska systemet*. Lund: Studentlitteratur.

Lundquist, Lennart (1972) *Means and Goals of Political Decentralization*. Lund: Studentlitteratur.

March, James G. and Olsen, Johan P. (1976) *Ambiguity and Choice in Organizations*, Bergen: Universitetsforlaget.

Marini, Frank (ed.) (1971) *Toward a New Public Administration*. San Francisco: Chandler.

Mayntz, Renate (1979) 'Public Bureaucracies and Policy Implementation' *International Social Science Journal*.

Mayntz, Renate and Scharpf Fritz (eds.) (1973) *Planungsorganisation. Die Diskussion um die Reform von Regierung und Verwaltung des Bundes*, München: R. Piper.

Meyer, Marshall W. (1979) *Change in Public Bureaucracies*. Cambridge: Cambridge University Press.

Milward, H. Brinton (1982) 'Interorganizational Policy Systems and Research on Public Organizations'. *Administration and Society*, 13.

Nakamura, Robert T. and Frank Smallwood (1980) *The Politics of Policy Implementation*. New York: St Martin's Press.

Nelson, Barbara (1980) 'Help-Seeking from Public Authorities: Who arrives at the Agency Door?' *Policy Sciences*, 12.

Niskanen, William A. Jr (1971) *Bureacuracy and Representative Government*. Chicago: Aldine Atherton.

Offe, Claus (1972) *Strukturprobleme des kapitalistischen Staates*. Frankfurt am Main: Suhrkamp Verlag.

Olsen, Johan P. (1972) 'Public Policy-Making and Theories of Organizational Choice'. *Scandinavian Political Studies*, 7.

Olsen, Johan P. (1978) *Politisk organisering*. Oslo: Universitetsforlaget.

Ostrom, Vincent (1973) *The Intellectual Crises in American Public Administration*. University, Alabama: The University of Alabama Press.

Palumbo, Dennis J. 'Organization Theory and Political Science' in Greenstein and Polsby (eds.) *Handbook of Political Science Vol. 2*. Reading, Mass.: Adison-Wesley Publ. Co.

Pateman, Carole (1970) *Participation and Democratic Theory*. London: Cambridge University Press.

Pateman, Carole (1975) 'A Contribution to the Political Theory of Organizational Democracy'. *Administration and Society*.

Premfors, Rune (1979) 'Social Research and Public Policy Making'. *Statsvetenskaplig Tidskrift*.

Pressman, Jeffrey and Wildavsky, Aaron B. (1973) *Implementation*. Berkeley: University of California Press.

Price, David E. (1981) 'Assessing Policy: Conceptual Points of Departure' in Fleishman, Joel L., Liebman, Lance and Moore, Mark H. (eds.) *Public Duties: The Moral Obligations of Government Officials*. Cambridge, Mass.: Harvard University Press.

Prottas, Jeffrey Manditch (1979) *People-Processing. The Streetlevel Bureaucrat in Public Service Bureaucracies*. Lexington Mass.: Lexington Books.

Quade, E. S. (1970) 'Why Policy Sciences?' *Policy Sciences*.

Rawls, John (1973) *A Theory of Justice*. London: Oxford University Press.

Rainey, Hal G. (1983) 'Public Organization Theory: The Rising Challenge'. *Public Administration Review*.

Rein, Martin and Rabinovitz, Francis F. (1978) 'Implementation: A theoretical Perspective' in Burnham, Walter Dean and Weinberg, Martha Wagner (eds): *American Politics and Public Policy*, Cambridge, Mass.: The MIT Press.

Ridley, F. F. (1975) *The Study of Government. Political Science and Public Administration*. London: Allen and Unwin.

Ronge, Volker and Schmieg, Günther (1973) *Restriktionen politischer Planung*. Frankfurt am Main: Athenäum.

Rose, Richard (1979) 'Ungovernability: Is there Fire behind the Smoke?' *Political Studies*, xxvii.

Rose, Richard (ed.) (1980) *Challenge to Governance. Studies in Overload Politics*. Beverly Hills: Sage.

Rossi, Peter H, Freeman, Howard E. and Wright, Sonia E. (1979) *Evaluation: A Systematic Approach*. Beverly Hills: Sage.

Rylander, Staffan (1969) 'Om demokrati och statsförvaltning' in Hessler, C. A. (ed.) *Idéer och ideologier*. Stockholm, Almqvist and Wiksell.

Schmied, Günther and Treiber, Hubert (1975) *Bürokratie und Politik. Zur Struktur und Funktion der Ministerialbürokratie in der Bundesrepublik Deutschland*. München: Wilhem Fink Verlag.

Scott, W. Richard (1981) *Organizations. Rational, Natural and Open Systems*. Englewood Cliffs NJ: Prentice Hall.

Self, Peter (1975) *Econocrats and the Policy Process. The Politics and Philosophy of Cost-Benefit Analysis*. London: The Macmillan Press.

Shonfield, Andrew and Shaw, Stella (eds.) (1972) *Social Indicators and Social Policy*. London: Heinemann.

Simeon, Richard (1976) 'Studying Public Policy'. *Canadian Journal of Political Science*.

Simon, Herbert (1945) *Administrative Behavior*. New York: Macmillan.

Smith, Michael P. (1976) 'Barriers to Organizational Democracy in Public Administration'. *Administration and Society*.

Spadoro, Robert N., Dye, Thomas R., Golembiewski, Robert T., Stedman, Murray S. and Ziegler, L. Harmon (1975) *The Policy Vacuum*. Lexington, Mass.: Lexington Books.

Ståhlberg, Krister (1976) *Utvecklingsdrag inom den offentliga förvaltningen 1960–75*. Helsinki: Research Reports, Institute of Political Science, University of Helsinki.

Tarschys, Daniel (1978) *Den offentliga revolutionen*. Stockholm: Liber Förlag.

Thayer, Frederick C. (1981) *An End to Hierarchy and Competition: Administration in the Post-Affluent World*. New York and London: Franklin Watts, 2nd ed.

Thompson, Victor A. (1975) *Without Sympathy or Enthusiasm. The Problem of Administrative Compassion*. University, Alabama: The University of Alabama Press.

Tullock, Gordon (1965) *The Politics of Bureaucracy*. Washington DC: Public Affairs Press.

Valentin, Finn (1980) *Fordelningen af påvirkningsmuligheder*. Copenhagen: Lavindkomstkommissionen.

Waldo, Dwight (ed.) (1971) *Public Administration in a Time of Turbulence*. San Francisco: Chandler.

Waldo, Dwight (1972) 'Developments in Public Administration'. *The Annals of the American Academy of Political and Social Science*, 404.

Waldo, Dwight (1976) 'A Symposium. Comparative and Development Administration: Retrospect and Prospect'. *Public Administration Review*.

Wamsley, Gary L. and Zald, Mayer N. (1973) *The Political Economy of Public Organizations*. Lexington, Mass.: Lexington Books.

Warren, Roland L. (1977) *Social Change and Human Purpose: Towards Understanding and Action*. Chicago: Rand McNally.

Warwick, Donald P. (1975) *A Theory of Public Bureaucracy. Politics, Personality and Organization in the State Department*. Cambridge, Mass.: Harvard University Press.

Warwick, Donald P. (1981) 'The Ethics of Administrative Discretion' in Fleishman, Joel L., Leibman, Lance and Moore, Mark H. (eds.): *Public Duties: The Moral Obligations of Government Officials*. Cambridge, Mass.: Harvard University Press.

Weiss, Carol H. and Barton, Allen H. (eds.) (1979) *Making Bureaucracies Work* Beverly Hills: Sage.

Werner, Rudolf (1975) *Soziale Indikatoren und politischer Planung. Einführung in Anwendungen der Makrosoziologie*. Hamburg: Rowohlt Taschenbuch Verlag.

Westerståhl, Jörgen and Persson, Mårten (1975) *Demokrati och intresse-representation*. Stockholm.

White, Michael (1979) 'Observations on Management Sciences in Government'. *Policy Studies Journal*.

Williams, Walter (1980) *The Implementation Perspective. A Guide for Managing Social Service Delivery Programs*. Berkeley: University of California Press.

Williams, Walter (1982) 'The Study of Implementation: An Overview' in Williams, Walter et al., *Studying Implementation. Methodological and Administrative Issues*. Chatham, NJ: Chatham House Publ.

Winkler, J. T. (1976) 'Corporatism'. *Archives Européennes De Sociologie*.

Wollmann, Hellmut (1980) 'Implementationsforschung – eine Chance für kritische Verwaltungsforschung?' in Wollmann, Hellmut (ed.) *Politik im Dickicht der Bürokratie*. Opladen: Westdeutscher Verlag.

Wollmann, Helmut and Hellstern, Gerd-Michael 'Sozialwissenschaftliche Untersuchungsregeln und Wirkungsforschung' in Haungs, Peter (ed.) *Res Publica. Studien zum Verfassungswesen*. München: William Fink Verlag.

Yin, Robert K. and Yates, Douglas, (1975) *Street-Level Government. Governments Assessing Decentralization and Urban Services*. Lexington, Mass.: Lexington Books.

10

The Logic of Public Sector Growth

Aaron Wildavsky
University of California, Berkeley

This is a radical thesis: the growing proportion of national product spent through governments in the twentieth century cannot primarily be explained by their growing wealth or industrialization. Nor can it be attributed, as a few recent authors do, to the political changes that follow from concomitant modernizations. Except in the tautological sense that citizens in a democracy must in some way approve of rising expenditure, we are no wiser about why government grows even when there are parties in power opposed to this very result. On the contrary, it is precisely the very wealth and technological capacity of these countries that would make it possible, were they otherwise inclined, to diminish the proportion of state activity.

Consider in this context of economic and technological determinism the rationales most often given for the increasing role played by the state in poorer countries. Since private entrepreneurship is weak, some authors say, the state must step in to accumulate resources for investment. Since vital data would not otherwise be collected, government must do so. But richer nations have all sorts of private data collection. Though the susceptibility of poor nations to international economic fluctuations is frequently cited as a source of governmental protectionism, the relative security enjoyed by richer nations should (and sometimes does) enable them to engage in freer trade. Where the lack of political legitimacy in poorer nations, combined with the severity of internal conflict over a smaller 'pie', encourages governments to mitigate disruption by subsidizing consumption, why does not the largesse of richer nations lead to less need to placate protest? If it is the relative degree of poverty that leads to enhanced spending on welfare programmes, why do poor countries do proportionately less? And if it is their absolute level of income that constrains the poor, why do they spend so much more than they used to at comparable levels? Why is it that the one thing the poor and rich share is a devotion to increasing state activity? Turning the poor country (Caiden and Wildavsky, 1980) literature against the rich country explanations, we find that the same reasons for larger government are applied to governments operating under opposite conditions.

I do not deny that over time every democratic, industrial, rich nation spends proportionately more on social welfare and on government as a whole. Nor do I doubt the validity, as far as they go, of the equations that try out a number of variables on government spending as a proportion of national product and conclude that wealth is by far the most important. I do deny that this outcome is predetermined, existing apart from and despite human will. My argument is not that we know economic-technological explanations to be wrong, but rather that they need not be right. For every proposition supporting the inexorable growth of government, there is another pointing in the opposite direction, both intuitively plausible.

Conceive, by contrast, of a world in which competitive individualism was the dominant culture. When the economy was on the upswing, its achievements would be attributed to the wondrous workings of markets. When there were periodic depressions, the fault would be found in violations of market principles — too high subsidies or income transfers, too restrictive trade practices. As the nation became wealthier, it would indeed be easier to spend more. But information gathering is relatively inexpensive and relief of poverty, while it might well expand, would be consigned to private charities and local bodies, by then (viz. mid-nineteenth-century Britain) better able to afford remedial action. Surpluses would be used to reduce taxation, fuelling the forces that were believed to create wealth in the first place. Hard luck would be rationalized by rules enabling individuals to begin again. 'Person blame' rather than 'system blame' would be the norm. Every adversity that might be used to justify governmental intervention — an industry weakened by foreign competition, an abundance of illegitimate children with only one responsible parent — would be countered by an anti-interventionist rationale: 'creative destruction' à la Schumpeter makes everyone better off by moving money to more productive uses, whereas subsidizing illegitimacy will only produce more of it.

Arguments taken for granted today as requiring state subsidy, such as the increased interdependence of people in industrialized societies, can just as well be cited by individualists as reasons — social complexity, individual capacity — for private people to do more and government to do less.

Especially interesting is a pattern in the data — a gradual or rapid acceleration, a plateau or, occasionally, a tiny decline, and another advance. Why, in plain words, does spending in constant currency sometimes go up as a proportion of gross national product but go down only rarely and then only a little? For one of the few obvious aspects of the situation is that if moves to drive spending up are sometimes halted but seldom reversed, the end result over time must be a continuous increase in the relative share of government. Nor is there any evident stopping place.

The placement in power of parties and associated interest groups that favour larger domestic government, especially expansion of welfare programmes, does make a difference. But, by itself, a pro-welfare orientation by certain parties some (or most) of the time does not explain why their opponents maintain or even expand these programmes rather than reducing them. The growth of the welfare state has to be explained not only by the impetus upwards, but also the resistance downwards. If it is said that there is a general consensus among all important parties and political elites that welfare programmes will either rise or remain stable, then it is that underlying consensus rather than the surface flux of political events that requires explanation.

When we observe that government spending continues to increase in regard to national product, we know that someone must want this to happen. In whose interest, according to whose values and practices does this occur? Which regime would reject ever-greater governmental growth and which regime perpetuate it? My hypothesis is that the relative size of spending is a function (consequence, if you prefer) of regime, namely, the relative strength of hierarchies and sects versus markets.

Regimes are different types of rule. These relationships between rulers and the ruled not only include but exclude certain kinds of behaviour, much as in the impossibility theorems of science. Extensive public ownership is incompatible with competitive individualism, abolition of distinction with hierarchy, trust in authority with sectarianism. A deeply egalitarian labour party or a Catholic party concerned with obligation to the worst off, when they are in power, will try to spend more. Socialists, Catholics, and conservatives, though they differ on many issues, however, are all hierarchically oriented. Should the dominant regime be hierarchical, coopting sectarian support along the way (see pp. 263–65 for discussion of regimes), government will continue to expand, whether or not more conservative parties are in power. It is the nature of the regime that controls the relative size of government.

I agree with Forsman and his colleagues that 'the rise of the public sector is the most important single change in twentieth-century socioeconomic development' (Forsman, et al., 1979: 191). I shall pursue the question of why Western governments have grown in regard to their societies (as well as why the United States has 'lagged behind') by examining the types of explanations offered by scholars of the subject.

Wagner's law

The first and still the most important effort to explain why public expenditures kept growing at a rate faster than that of the economy is Adolf Wagner's 'law of increasing state activity' (Larkey et al., 1981). Wagner does not claim that the richer nations will spend more proportionately than less rich nations. He does claim that as per capita real income increases in particular nations, they will spend a higher proportion of national product through government. And whatever the limitations of spending and taxing data, which are often missing or inconsistent or differently conceived from one place to another, there is unanimous agreement that this is exactly what has happened.[1] The differences, and they are profound, occur over why this unrelenting pattern continues to occur. My interest in Wagner's law is justified because it raises the kinds of explanations that have received widespread acceptance, explanations with which I disagree.

There is in Wagner's work, as in much of the literature, a teleological element in which one imagines a certain unspecified, ever-present but powerful logic of industrialization that ineluctably tends but in a single direction. The density of urban living, Wagner believed, would exacerbate social frictions that government would be called in to ameliorate. As people lived closer and closer together in urban life, the need would arise for enhanced police protection and for other forms of government regulation. It is surprising, to me at least, that no one appears to have thought of countering this argument with its opposite, namely, that density would provide opportunities for economies of scale. Thus, though the danger of epidemic may be greater in urban concentrations, the cost per person of inoculation may be considerably lower than among sparsely settled people. The same is true for the provision of transportation, communication, and sanitary services. Under some circumstances, at least, the proximity of people to one another should or could result in networks of personal support, lessening the need for public services.

Wagner may have been on firmer ground when he wrote about the additional complexity of legal relationships introduced by the increased specialization and division of labour that accompanies industrialization. Certainly, the spread of the rule of law to regularize relationships, together with the keeping of files and the emphasis on uniformity and predictability, does extend the sphere into which the law that may be enforced by the state extends. But it is also true that specialization brings with it professional associations that help resolve disputes among members. Thus many cases that might formerly have been subject to state adjudication are resolved within the proliferating new associations that also accompany industrialization (Larson, 1977; Jackson, 1970; Gilb, 1967, Freidson, 1975).

Now professionalization is not only an alternative to government, it is also part of government. Since governments are generally organized in a hierarchical manner, depending as this form does on expertise, it is not surprising that professionals are given wide leeway. When we discover an enormous increase in lawsuits that question professional judgement, as has occurred in the United States in recent decades in regard to medical practice and consumer product liability, we know at once that hierarchical norms have broken down. In most other Western nations, by contrast, the prevailing rules make it difficult for patients to challenge doctors. Such American devices as the contingency fee for lawyers are not made available precisely in order to limit the challenges to the professional judgement on which these hierarchies depend. If sectarians are encouraged to challenge authority and competitive individualists to make money by bringing suits on all sides, this does not appear to be inherent in the logic of industrialization, whatever that might be, but in choice of way of life. It would seem, then, that beyond a certain minimum, the legalization of relationships need not be a function of industrialization per se, but rather of how a people choose to organize themselves.

As industry grew, Wagner believed that certain investments would require so much capital that the state would have to provide it. At the same time, there would be certain facilitating investments, which today are called public goods, that it might not be in the interest of any one entrepreneur to provide, because the benefits could not be strictly appropriated to the investor. Preeminent among these was education. Like most of the arguments of Wagner (and his innumerable successors), this thesis is intuitively appealing because it has some merit; the question is how much? For every example one can cite of an indispensable activity that just has to be funded by the state, one can show other countries that either do without it or provide for user charges, thus shifting the burden from general revenues to those who benefit most directly. Governmental transportation networks may be financed by toll roads or by user charges from gasoline taxes. If the idea is not what the state should do but whether it faces inexorable demands that cannot be resisted, the evidence is against that claim. That governments tend to take over losing industries depends on political rather than technological arguments. It well may be that private enterprise would not provide certain scientific facilities, though industry does provide some, but research centres are not normally listed among the major recipients of governmental funds. The view that provision of luxuries, such as opera, puts government in the position of a natural monopolist hardly deserves refutation.

Education is a major object of government spending. And it may be that a better educated, or at least a more literate population, is a requirement of an industrial society. Yet, not only are some aspects of education provided privately, but in a number of countries, such as Japan, industry itself provides the kind of education it thinks its employees need. Since the proportion of secondary school graduates in higher education differs from something like 8 to 45 percent among Western industrial democracies, it appears that there is considerable leeway in whatever necessity there is for collective provision of this good.

The idea that certain goods were income-elastic, in that the desire for them to be provided by the state grew with increasing income, is one of Wagner's major contributions. Here his ideas merge with Maslow's hierarchy of wants (Maslow, 1954) in which (after basic needs are satisfied) non-material needs, such as art and theatre or the desire to help one's fellow man through income redistribution, continue to increase. The sociologists' view of 'relative deprivation' is turned on its head so that as people become relatively affluent their tastes change to collective goods. It would indeed be fortunate if, as people became richer, they became nicer. We do not know what evidence can be cited in support of this remarkable viewpoint. For one thing, there have been people throughout history whose material needs, however one conceives them, were satisfied many times over without their necessarily wanting to share more of it with others. For another, the idea of relative deprivation begs the question of what sort of culture justifies envy of others rather than rejecting such feelings as unworthy.

More to the point is Tarschys' gloss on economic development leading to social demands — the demonstration effect. 'The revolution in social communications, particularly the coming of television,' he writes, 'has led to increased awareness of the standard of living enjoyed by other segments in society and even in other parts of the world. As a consequence, expectations and pretensions mount, and people get increasingly sensitive to injustices in the distribution of public goods' (Tarschys, 1975: 21). The word 'injustices' hides a multitude of meanings. Why, if people become aware of goods they would like to have, do they not undertake strategies for working harder or differently in order to obtain the necessary resources? While it is understandable that people in various regions might become aware that others have more, this feeling need not be automatically translated into a sense that government has to redistribute income in its favour; it might, under other circumstances, be translated into the view that the region might make itself more attractive to income-producing ventures. What is taken for granted, the feeling of injustice, the belief that competition won't work because regions lack relevant resources, is exactly what has to be explained.

The belief that wealth leads to generosity dies hard. Thus Tarschys says that 'when subsistence needs have been satisfied, citizens are more likely to part with their surplus resources. The government of an advanced society would then be in a better position than that of a poor nation to raise money for public programmes' (Tarschys, 1975: 24). As long as real incomes are rising, taxation is certainly less onerous. Prosperity makes it easier to tax. But then, when economic conditions are worse, the cry goes out, as Wagner anticipated, for the state to compensate people for suffering through bad times. If all signs lead to Rome, whatever direction they point, we certainly know why most people arrive there.

The proposition that government has certain natural advantages in the provision of public goods conflicts with the contention, also made by Wagner, that the cost of governmental provision of services tends to rise over time. When applied to military armaments, as Wagner did, it makes more sense, because the competition tends to reach to quality as well as quantity of armaments. But it lacks force when applied to the civilian sector. In its modern garb, sometimes called 'Baumol's disease', the labour-intensiveness of the service sector drives up the price of a given volume of services. The conclusion — 'to secure stable output, one would therefore need to increase the transfer of resources to the public sector, provided that the wage structure is to be maintained' (Tarschys, 1975: 26) — assumes a prior decision to maintain and increase the relative size of the public sector. Generally, if a certain good costs more, one is likely to buy less of it. Yet the argument is the same about any increase in factor prices: the multiplications in the price of oil, say, may lead that factor to increase dramatically but, without an increase in the supply of money, its consumption must decline or other prices must go down, thus leaving the general price level unchanged. The relative price effect (Heclo and Wildavsky, 1981) may raise the cost of a given amount of governmental activity. Nevertheless, without a willingness to raise the sum of spending, these increases would have had to be offset elsewhere.

The sheer size of technology, already visible at the end of the nineteenth century, led Wagner to predict that increasing industrialization would lead to state intervention. As the size of the capital required led to private monopolies, government would intervene either through regulation or by taking over a private power that seemed all too powerful. In Galbraith's hands (1967) this thesis is expanded: technological development drives all industrial societies toward the same ends, namely, greater government power to counteract greater private monopoly as industrial firms divide markets and administer their own prices. The implicit functionalism of these explanations is made explicit by Wilensky and Lebeaux (1958), who explain how industrialism places burdens on families as women work, the elderly can no longer be supported at home, children are delinquent, and other difficulties arise for which state action — control of juvenile delinquency, pensions, welfare provisions — are made necessary.

My reply is that 'it ain't necessarily so'. While I do not object in form to functional explanations, it is precisely the question of whether human needs are best met by the state that is at issue. What reason is there to believe that families in the past several hundred years were able to deal with sickness, old age, poverty, and all that, better than they are in this century? They were much poorer, thus had far fewer resources of any kind. Housing, for instance, was smaller and unhealthier. Being crowded in with large, multi-generation families, so far as we know, made every relationship — husband and wife, parents and children — much more difficult (Wright, 1981; Fish, 1979; Beyer, 1965).

Pryor (1968), whose careful empirical work remains the standard for this field, refuses to be concerned by charges of rank functionalism, insisting 'that the policy dilemmas facing decision-makers of public consumption expenditure are quite similar in all nations, regardless of system', so that 'it should not be too surprising that the decisions are roughly similar.' Perhaps, but the direction of causality could conceivably go the other way — from a common political culture to a common policy response. Starting from an assumption of cultural bias, so that there are 'solutions looking for problems', would be a better approach, I believe, to explaining the growth of government.

Although Wagner evidently thought that capitalism must increase economic growth, for otherwise his law would not apply, he also maintained that the cycle of 'boom and bust' was built into its very nature. Hence, in times of depression, government would step in to maintain its legitimacy by alleviating human distress. Since he also believed that, at a high stage of development, capitalist ventures would become increasingly unprofitable, Wagner expected government to provide the missing employment. (This may be the origin of the Marxist claim that defence spending rises in capitalist countries so as to make up for unemployment.) Suppose one observes that social disturbances, such as mass unemployment, give rise to larger government expenditure. No trouble with that, except that at certain times and places — the United States in the 1920s, Britain in the 1930s — the expected relationship does not hold. Why, then, in periods of peace and prosperity, does spending not decline at all, let alone to previous levels? The period following the second world war, one with unparalleled increases in governmental growth, fits that description exactly.

State control of industry can be justified both on the grounds of efficiency and on the grounds of inefficiency, the former claim being that private companies do not provide adequate economic performance, and the latter that the state must use broader social criteria rather than narrow economic ones. Both arguments may, at times, be valid. Whichever way the argument goes, however, the result is expansion of the size of government.

The strongest statement of economic determinism comes from Harold Wilensky (1975); after doing a cross-sectional analysis of some 64 poor and rich nations, he concludes that

> alternative explanations collapse under the weight of such heavy, brittle categories as 'socialist' versus 'capitalist' economies, 'collectivistic' versus or even 'democratic' versus 'totalitarian' political systems . . . These categories are almost useless in explaining the origins and general development of the welfare state (p. xiii).

The differences in levels of funding for various aspects of social welfare among the richest nations, however, are sufficiently dissimilar so that Wilensky thinks there may be particular social or political factors determining these gaps. As with Wagner, there is no doubt about the conclusion, but only about the theory on which it is based. Presumably, the richer the nation, the higher its proportionate level of public spending, but empirical evidence is against this conclusion. Why should level of economic development be so important if it cannot distinguish among nations at the same or similar levels? Saying that, in addition, some nations have strong socialist parties and others weak trade unions, or vice versa, is correct and important but detracts from the grandeur and simplicity of the economic determinism with which we are dealing.

No doubt demographic changes may be responsible for some of the increases in public spending. The question is why these changes always appear to operate in an upward rather than a downward direction? Given the large place that pensions play in state spending, for instance, the aging of the population, which has proceeded at a rapid pace as life expectancy continues to rise, appears inexorably to increase the cost of government. But where, we ask again, are the offsetting savings? Presumably, lesser sums should be spent on children or other sectors of the population that must, comparatively speaking, be smaller. Such spending may drop but not in proportion to the fall in clientele. Higher spending is a result of deliberate decisions to do certain things and not to do others that would alter the situation.

Take the notable rise in the proportion of the population that receives some form of disability pension. Is this occurring because there are more accidents or because modern life is more stressful? However difficult modern life might or might not be, the evidence in all industrial nations (with the possible exception of the Soviet Union) is that accident rates and sickness rates are in substantial decline, for otherwise the population would be living shorter lives, so to speak, rather than longer. Workmen's Compensation is undoubtedly a development of industrialization. Nevertheless, the hypothesis that higher levels of disability are due to the opportunities provided by governmental legislation cannot be disregarded. Though precise numbers are difficult to come by, given the situation, there appears considerable circumstantial evidence that many of these 'walking wounded' are, in fact, working, despite their disability (Haveman, et al., 1983).

All over the world, whether nations are industrial or not, they undertake a variety of neomercantilist measures to protect national industry. There exists some empirical support for the view that nations more susceptible to fluctuations in international trade are more likely to subsidize national industry. The point of such policies is to enable some of the recovery processes, like redeployment of labour, to work without causing undue hardship. The strongest argument on this subject has been made by Cameron (1978), who states that the openness of economies generates certain structural changes: industry becomes concentrated, so does unionization, leading to an expansion in the scope of collective bargaining to include industrial and individual subsidies, that is, collective provision. Thus state spending is said to vary with the openness or vulnerability of economies. The state not only provides some investment capital but unemployment compensation, pensions, and subsidies to maintain employment, and so on (Cameron, 1978; Larkey, et al., 1981).

Part of this state support is used to subsidize the cost of domestic production for export purposes. Yet it might be supposed that the two desires — higher standards of living and dampening domestic fluctuations by lowering export prices — would at some level, conflict. One might think, following classic economic formulations, that the strength of international competition, which cannot be controlled by any one nation (hence the emphasis on vulnerability), would lead over time to a levelling of rewards for labour among nations. Alternatively, fearing assaults on their economic boundaries, states might throw up ever-higher tariff barriers, thus exchanging greater income equality for higher living standards. That one choice rather than another is made, my thesis goes, is not part of any 'logic of industrialization' but of the values shared by the elites making the decisions.

Economic wisdom on taxation is aptly summarized by Tarschys (1975: 23):

> The 'extractive capability' of a political system is closely linked to the structure of production. Large-scale taxation is possible only where there is large-scale economic exchange, and the amount of extractable resources are related both to the mode and to the volume of this exchange. As external trade is easier to tax than domestic trade, a substantial part of government revenue in less developed countries is derived from this source. Urban trade is easier to tax than rural, which was a reason for certain restrictions on commerce in the past. And finally, a far-reaching division of labour which follows from the expansion of the market economy and the public sector at the expense of home production is an obvious boon to the tax collector. When more goods and services are traded, there is a better opportunity for the government to intervene and intercept a share of the benefits that accrue to the trading partners (p. 23).

Since this reasoning applies equally well to more industrialized nations, it appears that open economies, characterized by having a higher proportion of activity in international trade, also give government an opportunity to collect a larger proportion of resources through taxation. Is it, then, the dependence of the economy or the relative independence of the government that constitutes the best explanation for higher state spending in open economies? Which is only to suggest that governments could, given the ease of resource mobilization, lower rates and spend less rather than increase rates and spend more. The very increase in trade could conceivably lead to doing more, not less, of the same.

Turning from the demand for public spending to the supply of public revenues, Peacock and Wiseman (1961) have proposed their 'displacement effect hypothesis': spending, in their view, is limited by available revenues. Casting about for an explanation of substantial increases in revenue, they observed that after the first and second world wars the level of taxation, though it receded from the enormously high levels in wartime, did not quite recede back to the old level. In general form, their hypothesis is that major crises expand public tolerance for higher levels of taxation, after which spending floods in to make up the difference between older and newer levels of revenue. In finer detail, Peacock and Wiseman believe that elites can always find good causes on which to spend public money. Their problem is to persuade the people to pay. The missing link in this argument is the change in elite ideology explaining why no great surge of spending occurred after the first world war but did after the second, or, for that matter, why elites did not demand even greater tax reduction after the second world war.

The advantage of Peacock and Wiseman's theory is that it would explain (by arguing that spending tends to use up the available revenues) not only why spending might rise with revenue but also why spending would be 'sticky' on the down side. The weakness of their theory is that it does not simultaneously explain why spending is so quick to fill the vacuum unless spending itself is considered a law of nature. Wagner himself was cognizant of this possibility but argued that 'in the long run the desire for development of a progressive people will always overcome these financial difficulties,' and who, in light of the trends, will say that he was necessarily wrong (Bird, 1971). Empirical evidence on this question is mixed but certainly does not unambiguously confirm the displacement hypothesis. It is certainly plausible to argue that a people's attitude toward taxing and spending may be altered by severe shocks, though as Bird says: 'The whole question of fiscal psychology . . . clearly requires much closer study . . .' (Bird, 1971).

The continental historian, Henri Pirenne, saw alternation between laissez-faire and collective control lasting several centuries at a time. He would place the nineteenth century, or at least large parts of it, together with the eleventh, twelfth, fifteenth, and sixteenth as periods in which, if not private enterprise, then, at least private governments, were dominant whereas the thirteenth, fourteenth, seventeenth, eighteenth and twentieth centuries were more disposed to public control (Pirenne, 1914; Crowley, 1971). Roughly speaking, the centuries Pirenne characterizes as competitive economically also were competitive in their political and social structures. Psychologies of budgeting might therefore be traced to their constituent cultural elements, putting some flesh on what would appear to be overly generalized hypotheses.

Among Frederick Pryor's many contributions to the study of expenditure growth in industrial nations is his awareness that all authors, whatever their main hypothesis, bolster it by the ad hoc use of special explanations. Whether an author refers to sudden economic crises, such as the great depression, or gradual political changes, like the extension of the ballot to larger groups of citizens, or the methods of spending (say, the increasing use of income transfers versus spending by governmental agencies), variants of Wagner's law are supplemented by something quite different. What we want to know is why all these special explanations only work one way — upward, to higher spending?

Having given prominent place to one of these myself, namely, incrementalism (Wildavsky, 1975), I am hardly in a position to complain. No one denies that in periods of stability most budgetary changes are small, varying from the past year by only a few percent. Probably, also, due to the complexity of the environment, decision makers consider only a few alternatives and these differ but marginally from the programme already in existence. This budgetary base, built up by slow accretion over decades, not only simplifies calculations by reducing the scope of decision, it also, by virtue of accepting most past programmes, limits the scope of conflict. So far so good. If one wishes to explain why certain programmes are larger than others, for instance, incrementalism points to a truth: the earlier a programme was established, the longer it has had the opportunity to build up increments, the larger it will be in relation to comparable programmes that began later. Henry Aaron says that the best explanation of the relative size of twenty-two large social security programmes was the time they had to develop (Aaron, 1967). 'Once a programme is launched', Wilensky (1975) concludes, 'precedent is the major determinant of who gets what the government has to give, and how much goes to the programme or agency depends on what it got the last time around.' Agreed. But what is it that makes incrementalism a one-way street? There is nothing in the theory of the subject that requires positive rather than negative increments. And there is something — the suggestion of adaptation via successive small steps — that suggests decremental changes might, on occasion, also be desirable. Were that so, were increments and decrements to offset each other, there would be no law of increasing state activity. What factors are operating in the environment of government, then, apart from incremental processes, that leads to selection of increases and rejection of decreases?

Since pensions and medical care are the largest items of expenditure in the welfare state, the aging of the population does indeed contribute to higher levels of spending. Yet an increase in certain items cannot explain why other items are not reduced so as to maintain a desired proportion of spending to the size of the economy. The elderly themselves might be required to retire later or to save toward their retirement. Should it be said that other programmes cannot be reduced — defence is life-and-death and education is sacrosanct — all that has been done is to restate the problem: why, when some items go up, do others not go down proportionately?

Wilensky (1975) says that '. . . social security programs simply do not appear without sufficient national surplus to make them a policy option, or if, as in many poor countries these programs are enacted, they remain weak paper programs or are severely restricted in coverage until such surplus is produced.' This is a truism; if there are insufficient resources, these missing monies cannot be spent. Indeed, if one were to imagine a different set of values guiding decision making, the very surplus that makes social security spending possible might make the economy rich enough to permit most people to invest for their own retirement.

According to David Cameron (1978), author of one of the major recent studies of the determinants of public spending:

> Contrary to Wagner's 'law', the rate of growth in the economic affluence of a nation does not contribute to the expansion of the public economy. Apparently citizens' demands for services and their willingness to accept higher levels of taxes, or both, are not income-elastic. Instead, the analysis supports Wildavsky's argument that the public economy grows, in relative terms, when economic growth is modest . . . (p. 1251).

The size of spending in relation to the size of national product increases when economic growth declines, not, according to Wagner's law, when it rises. Again, we rephrase the critical question: this 'counter-Wagner's' law might explain why, when rates of economic growth declined in the West as a whole, state spending continued its proportionate rise. But it does not necessarily explain why, as their real income declined, people were willing to pay higher taxes.

Perhaps the people, in view of the diversity of tax sources, do not realize how much they are paying. Known as 'fiscal illusion' (named, possibly, after the (in)famous 'money illusion' in which it is face amount and not purchasing power that matters), this doctrine contends that indirect taxes hide the total amount paid so citizens are misled into paying more than they otherwise would (Wildavsky, 1980). Perhaps, but a closer connection between tax revolts and a high proportion of direct taxes has been noted by Wilensky (1975). Another empirical analysis by Cameron (1978) denies that spending increases go along with reliance on 'invisible' taxes (social security contributions, sales and value-added taxes). 'Instead', he concludes, 'the public economy expanded most rapidly after 1960 in nations which relied heavily, and to an increasing degree, on wealth-elastic taxes, such as those on personal and corporate incomes.' To us, like Lincoln, it is possible to fool some of the people some of the time but we are made incredulous by the thought of fooling all of the people all of the time. How might we explain a century, if not of foolishness, then, at least, according to the doctrine of fiscal illusion, of being fooled? Could it be that citizens are so easily 'duped' because they *want* to spend more?

Public opinion

Different levels of public spending have been accompanied by different patterns of politics. Among the welfare state leaders — the Scandinavian countries, Austria, and the Netherlands — the expansion of public services has fluctuated little; while generally one party has been dominant throughout this period, changes in the ruling party, such as in Sweden in 1976, have had little effect. We may suspect a basic consensus, among both governing elites and the mass public, on the relation between state and society embodied in state guarantees of a wide variety of social services. This does not mean that taxes can rise forever; at some point, even in these countries, people may feel they are getting less than they pay for. But it suggests that tax revolts, if they take place, would occur at a higher level of government consumption of product than in countries with different values. In the old European powers, benefit growth has been associated with more left-wing governments, but has also been strongly related to government attempts to control the economy. Governments, especially in France and Italy, have been concerned with maintaining the support of various sections of society, both in order to and as a condition of manipulating the economy, and this support has been viewed as problematic. In Britain, France and Italy, business and labour are sharply divided; they fight for control of the state while the state attempts to control them. There is no consensus on what the state should do, but there is consensus on an activist role for the state. In America, state activity is less widely accepted. Neither state responsibility for individual security nor state responsibility for the economy is as thoroughly accepted as in Europe. Yet there are social forces which favour expansion of the public sphere.

These differences in relationships between the state and the citizenry might be expected to be reflected in different structures of public opinion. It is not easy, however, to separate interests from values. Further, the prospective popularity of a programme may be determined by the seriousness of the perceived problem and the availability of alternatives, while the popularity of an existing programme may be judged instead by reports as to its performance. Problems of inference are made more difficult by a general lack of cross-national surveys. The best collection of relevant data and analysis is Richard M. Coughlin, *Ideology, Public Opinion, and Welfare Policy* (1980), and even he has to compare countries using different questions asked at different times. Nevertheless, following Coughlin's analysis, we can express broad tendencies of public attitudes toward the welfare state and its programmes.

First of all, people everywhere like the generally available social programmes: pensions, child allowances, and health care. 'Public efforts in the area of pensions for the aged', writes Coughlin (1980: 95–101), 'enjoy a level of approval uncommon in the normally contentious area of social and economic policy.' People are particularly likely to support increases in this area, and there is virtually no doubt anywhere as to the worth of the programme. Family allowances are also popular in nations as diverse as Australia, Canada, France and Sweden (Coughlin, 1980: 105–6). In Britain, however, support is at best lukewarm, and increases are opposed unless associated with a redirection of the programme to those with greatest need. Health care is popular everywhere that it exists, and even in America, support for the idea of a national health plan is substantial. In the United States and Britain, however, Coughlin also finds support for private care. First, private health insurance plans are much more highly developed in the US than anywhere else, so an equivalence in public support for the two ideas does not express as much of a private bias. The questions about allowing private health care in addition to the public system in Britain are about providing an option; Coughlin contrasts that to a German question about whether people would opt out if possible. The substantial difference between findings for the two countries may reflect the difference between keeping options open (always a good thing) and making a particular choice. The Australian case indicates that a distrust of private enterprise may coexist with a desire for the possibility.

There is general suspicion of abuse and (grudging) support nonetheless for unemployment insurance. Americans favour providing work rather than paying benefits; however, the tilt of government policy towards providing jobs in Scandinavia indicates that this is not unusual. In 1965, 69 percent of the US population wanted to make requirements more strict, while a 1968 Canadian survey found 65 percent wanting to make cheating more difficult (Coughlin, 1980: 108).

Public assistance — the set of programmes directed solely at the poor and generally means-tested, that is, according to ability to pay — is subject to much the same doubts. In comparing attitudes towards the causes of poverty and appropriate government spending responses in six countries, Coughlin suggests that

> the most salient feature of European beliefs uncovered . . . was the exceptional attribution of the blame for poverty to 'individual laziness and lack of willpower' among the British. In contrast, French and West German samples emphasized the impact of 'social injustice' in the etiology of poverty, while the Danes focused on the fatalistic elements of 'bad luck' and 'inevitability'. British beliefs about poverty more closely resemble those of Americans and Canadians than those of any other Common Market nation . . . the three Anglo-American nations stand apart from the French, West Germans, and Danes in the common emphasis on the role of individual initiative (or, rather, the lack of it) as the main cause of poverty (p. 111).

The data suggest a combination of ideological and instrumental attitudes towards specific programmes. Coughlin argues that what individualistic attitudes exist are overwhelmed by collectivist attitudes in the cases of health care and pensions (p. 121). Individualistic attitudes are more important to disapproval of unemployment compensation and public assistance. One explanation, not offered by Coughlin, is that individualism, when it comes to policy, is 'individualism for the other guy'. Were this so, the difference between nations would be a difference not in the sense of egalitarianism, but in the sense of *solidarity* — 'we are all in the same boat'. Coughlin thinks that the difference is due to perceptions of risk: whether a problem is conceived as beyond individual control (aging, illness) or related to individual behaviour (unemployment, poverty) (Coughlin, 1980: 122). He is suggesting, therefore, that 'individualism' is not only a preference, but a perception of how the world works.

Everywhere people like the idea of social guarantees, but support is weakest in the United States. People everywhere value individual mobility and enterprise; even in Sweden there is little popular support for increased government control over business (Coughlin, 1980: chapter 2). France has a history of 'individualistic' sentiment in regard to taxes; as Coughlin points out:

> Collectivism that entails more willingness to receive the benefits of government programs does not mean much; true collectivism entails a willingness to sacrifice disposable individual income for wider public purposes. In this the French have shown a reluctance to forego the individualism of the pocketbook to pay taxes for the collectivism of the welfare state (Coughlin, 1980: 30).

An intriguing aspect of Coughlin's findings is that the best predictor of attitudes toward public spending is occupation. People who are part of the economic system, such as small entrepreneurs, like to keep the state small (Coughlin, 1980: 138–42). Unfortunately, the only data we have on public employees comes from the state and local level in the United States. Compared to other citizens of comparable social and economic standing, public employees are markedly but not hugely likely to prefer higher spending. Since they turn out to vote with much higher frequency than other citizens, they may make a difference at the polls (Gramlich and Rubinfeld, 1982).

Political explanations

It should not be difficult, the layman might imagine, to determine whether governments controlled by political parties favouring higher spending gain support from the citizenry. If they are voted in and maintained in office, presumably that — higher spending — is what the voters want. Now everyone would like an ideal world of painless spending in which economic development exceeds governmental growth. Most parties promise to do both. Faced with a choice, however, parties may choose welfare spending, even if at the cost of reducing citizen's private consumption. Socialist parties, certainly, being dedicated to governmental growth, provide a test of the hypothesis of whether 'the people' are getting what they want.

Wrong again. For one thing, non-socialist, liberal, Catholic or conservative parties, when they are in power, often spend proportionately as much (or more) as do avowed socialists. One reason state spending does not decline is that non-socialist parties, at a minimum, do not substantially reduce the level of spending they inherit. There is, it appears, consensus (with but few, short-lived exceptions) that there will not be cuts below existing levels. Some programmes, to be sure, such as defence in the 1960s and 1970s, decline as a proportion of GNP and of state spending, though, in the presence of economic growth, they may maintain their absolute level of expenditure. Evidently, if some programmes remain the same and others are increased, the result will be higher spending.

Even the question of whether socialist parties in power undertake measures that do increase economic equality is hotly debated. Hewitt (1977) says they do, while Jackman (1975) and Parkin (1971) argue they do not. It turns out that there are many measures of economic equality and the ones chosen affect findings (Wilensky, 1981: 350). Suppose a programme begins by being targeted at the worst off. Those who pay the most taxes, send their money, in effect, to the poorest people. Suppose, however, that in order to broaden political support or to spread more of a good thing around, so that there can be higher benefits, a broader spectrum of beneficiaries are included. Then the difference between those who are taxed most and those who benefit most is narrowed, thus decreasing the egalitarian effect of the programme. Shall equality depend on the *degree* of redistribution for smaller numbers of beneficiaries or the *scope* of redistribution, even if at a lower level, for a larger number? The closer to narrower income inequality the measure used, the more important political, as contrasted to economic, variables become (Hewitt, 1977).

The considerable differences between the political institutions of industrial nations make it difficult to say conclusively whether a particular measure of strength – control of the executive, representation in the legislature, proportion of the popular votes — is the most appropriate measure of socialist (or, more generally, 'left' or 'welfare statist') political tendencies. I would follow Wilensky in choosing control of the executive because, especially in parliamentary forms of government, that is the crucial indicator of ability to rule. In general, as Pryor (1968) and Wilensky (1975) argue, economic capacity is more powerful than political leftism in correlations with state spending. Always, of course, the United States remains anomalous, being wealthier and spending less proportionately. Nevertheless, Wilensky (1975: 45) argues that political ideology has virtually no effect.

In later work, however, Wilensky asserts some political influence over social spending connected not so much with socialist but with Catholic parties. While Catholic social doctrine is anti-socialist, opposing direct governmental control of enterprise, it is also collectivist. Catholic parties see the state as securing an organic consensus by bringing all segments of the population together through social welfare legislation. Family policy is particularly important to Catholics as they support allowances for children. Related to Catholicism is corporatism,

> the capacity of strongly organized centralized economic interest groups interacting under government auspices within a quasi-public framework to produce peak bargains involving social policy, fiscal and monetary policy, and incomes policies — the major interrelated issues of modern political economy. The measure is *corporatist-technocratic linkages* indicated by the centralization of government and the centralization of labour federations and, by inference, the centralization of employer federations. Such structure for policy deliberation is a relatively effective consensus making machine; it permits high levels of taxing and social spending with only weak or moderate political protest (Wilensky, 1981: 345).

Harold Wilensky and Frank Castles have both proposed political explanations of differences in welfare state growth. Wilensky (1981) argues that Catholic party power is more important than Left party power as a determinant of welfare effort. Castles (1978; and Borg and Castles, 1981) contends that both Social Democratic power and Right party power (the latter negatively) correlate strongly with welfare effort, but Right party power, or the lack of it, is more important. I think they have discovered the same phenomenon.

What is important is not whether the 'right' or 'left' of a particular country's spectrum is winning, but the range of attitudes represented on that spectrum; in particular, whether there is a strong anti-statist party.[2] Wilensky's analysis defines the American Democratic Party and Swedish Social Democratic Party as similarly 'left'. Yet in Sweden none of the 'right' parties are similar to (that is, as 'right' as) the American Republicans. He also divides his sample into 'strong corporatist' and 'weak corporatist' nations, succeeding in the process in throwing much of the 'left', that is, Social Democratic, parties into one box and not the other. Further, corporatism is itself characterized by an activist state, usually bargaining with centralized employer and labour federations. One should not be surprised, therefore, by the absence in the 'strong corporatist' group of any of the polities which have proven to be relatively low spenders. Castles argues:

> If the welfare state is seen largely in T. H. Marshall's terms as conferring 'equality of status', it is not merely in the interests of the industrial working class, but also of the vast majority of wage earners to secure as great a reduction of 'risk and uncertainty' as possible . . . The only stratum that has a clear interest in opposing welfare initiatives, in so far as they involve a redistribution of wealth will be that which is extremely privileged compared with the majority of the population. In absolute numbers, such a social stratum is likely to be relatively small, but its political influence will depend on the historical and structural forces which have shaped the party system. My hypothesis is that to the degree that such forces have led to the emergence of a large and united party of the Right which can act as the political instrumentality of the privileged stratum, there will be a strong impediment to welfare (Castles, 1978: 75).

While specific conditions will influence the level of cohesion and strength of whatever party best reflects 'Capital's' interests, for that party to gather a substantial base, it must be able to make some appeal to the 'masses'. Therefore an anti-state party (unlike, say, France's Gaullists) must have an ideological base in free markets.

In Scandinavia and the Benelux countries, party systems are fragmented. In Belgium and the Netherlands, Catholic parties tend to lead coalition governments. But in none of these countries is the party that Castles defines as that of the Right usually included in government, and in all of them (in part due to the number of parties), its total vote is small. In the Netherlands, especially, cross-cutting religious cleavages retard the emergence of a large party defined by free-market ideology.

Canada, the United States, Australia and Britain, in contrast, all have virtual two-party systems in which one party represents more or less free-market forces. They also do not have Catholic parties (unless one counts the Quebecois), and in spite of occasional efforts, centring around wage restraints, have difficulty being 'Corporatist'. For these countries, then, the Castles and Wilensky analyses converge.

In Germany, Italy, and France, the tale is more varied. In France, the Right has been strong and not Christian Democratic; 'income maintenance expenditure', the variable Castles wished to explain, grew very slowly. In Germany, the Right was strong *and* Christian Democratic; public income maintenance expenditure still grew (relatively) slowly. In Italy, the Right was strong and always in office; however, it was usually in coalition with the social democrats (here, socialists). Expenditures on income grew at roughly the OECD average rate. Since in these nations welfare state expenditure was high at the beginning of our period, the overall totals remained high. Therefore, in Wilensky's analysis, they provide evidence for the advantages of Christian Democracy, while for Castles they indicate the inhibitions on welfare state development created by a strong Right.

Perhaps it is not only state ideology but state structure that matters: what do we know about the relationship between centralization, decentralization and state spending? Intuitively speaking, the outcomes could go either way — centralized states, because they are believed to be better able to exert control from the top, may spend less per capita; contrariwise, because the cost of spending programmes per capita is diffused over the largest number of taxpayers, none has sufficient interest in reducing expenditure to lower total costs. Less centralized political systems, federal in structure, might spend more because there are so many more spending spigots to turn on. Alternatively, they might spend less per capita because the multiplicity of local governments makes the connection closer between taxing and spending.

Where rival intuitions clash, it is not surprising that the scholarly battle has raged with the mantle of higher or lower spending resting now on one (centralized or non-centralized) side or the other. As experience cumulates, however, centralization seems to be associated with higher spending. All highly centralized governments are high on social service spending, with only Israel and the Soviet Union spending less for these purposes than they might, no doubt due to higher levels of defence outlays (Wilensky, 1975: 52ff.). The neatest research comes from a comparison of the American states of Maine and Vermont, one of which taxes and spends largely from the centre while the other diffuses these activities among both state and local governments. Spending per capita, it turns out, is considerably higher in the more centralized of these two neighbouring states (Giertz, 1981).

Seeking to generalize this explanation, Wilensky contends that internal social cleavages (between economic, ethnic, religious and geographic groups) slow down state spending only when they are accompanied by a fragmented political structure as in the United States and, to a lesser extent, Switzerland (Wilensky, 1975: 53–4). Is it their centralized or less centralized political structures that inhibit or expand spending, we may ask, or the preferences of their peoples for governmental involvement that shape their political institutions? Canada and the United States, which share federal structure but differ in political culture, offer us the opportunity to examine the case point-counter-point. At one and the same time, Canada is like the United States in spending less on social welfare than European democracies do and different in that it spends more than its neighbour to the south on a wider variety of programmes (Canada, for instance, has family allowances). Canada is recognizably in the mould of the European welfare state and the United States is not. Thus there is no 'welfare backlash' in Canada nor any disposition to dismantle any part of the panoply of welfare programmes. Why not?

'Canada', as Robert Kudrle and Theodore Marmor (1981: 89) tell us, echoing, as they say, existing literature, 'was originally settled by people with a different structure of values from the Americans, and the distinctions persisted.' In Canada, I would say, succinctly, there were criminals but not, as in the United States, outlaws. Desperadoes who rode outside the law in the West might be pursued by vigilantes or local sheriff's posses. Their neighbour to the north would dispatch the Northwest Mounted Police, a centralized organization serving a central hierarchy. Whether French or English in origin, Canadians came from established hierarchies and were joined by the American Tories who lost the revolutionary war in defence of the English king. Though, for evident historic and geographic reasons, it emerged with a federal structure: 'There is', as all observers agree, 'great centralization of power within the federal and provincial levels of government in Canada' (Kudrle and Marmor, 1981: 90).

The cultural difference is that the United States has had strong markets and weak hierarchies, while both hierarchies and markets have been strong in Canada (Lipset, 1968), though hierarchical norms weaken as one travels west in Canada. 'The larger the percent of the labor force who have had a taste of self-employment,' Wilensky argues, 'the greater the economic individualism and concomitant resistance to the welfare state' (1975: 61). The consequences for legislation have been that Canadian public policy has been more egalitarian and redistributive than in the United States, reflecting the hierarchical concern of the parts for the whole, while maintaining a greater interest, due to market influence, in limiting total spending than in Europe. By combining the capacities of strong central governments with a desire to leave scope for private enterprise, Canada, since 1980, by limiting spending to the proportionate increase in national product, has been more successful at expenditure control than has the United States (Kudrle and Marmor, 1981; Wildavsky, 1982; Doern, 1980 and 1981).

After observing that the trades union movement in Canada has been much more socialist than in the United States, Kudrle and Marmor go on to make my point in different words: 'In sum, the ideological differences . . . between Canada and the United States appears to have made a considerable difference in welfare state development' (1975: 113). If, instead of a disembodied concept of ideology, as pure thought, one substitutes the meatier cultural expression — shared values legitimating desired social practices — differences in policy may be seen to stem naturally from differences in ways of life.

The economy and the polity

Let us remind ourselves of what we wish to explain: (1) the continuous rise of public spending as a proportion of national product among industrial democracies; (2) the resistance to downward movement, that is, the absence of countervailing forces; and (3) despite the applicability of (1) and (2), the large difference in state spending that still separates the United States from other nations. In posing the grand question, I would associate myself with Hinrichs's formulation (except that today his upper bound might well be doubled):

> A complex democratic industrialized state could function with a public sector, say, between 20 and 40 percent. The point where it settles within (or above) this range is most likely to be determined not by structural needs (which would demand, say only 20 percent) but by ideological commitments, toward a 'Welfare state' and/or toward the 'security and defense' of an existing ideological system (1966: 9–10).

Since, up to the present time, 'welfare' continues to dominate 'warfare' spending in the democracies by more than two to one, it is to their 'ideological systems', their values and practices, that I would look for explanations of the growth of government.

The social mobilization-cum-industrialization thesis can hardly be disproved. There are rough objects of spending that parallel industrialization — 'infrastructure', transportation, public health, natural resources in the nineteenth century, social welfare in the twentieth. It is not the kinds of spending, however, but the totals to which they add up that is my main concern. From that perspective, Hinrichs can hardly be faulted — why the maximum rather than the minimum over time?

Nor can economic growth be invoked again, if only because it has slowed down in the 1970s and 1980s. At a quarter of GNP, government, with a spending increase of eight percent, as Guy Peters shows (1980: 42), can be supported by a two percent expansion of the economy. At half of GNP, with an eight percent annual spending increase, however, a four percent increase in growth is required to service government with nothing left over for additional private consumption or investment. Yet many European governments are near or past 50 percent of GNP, while their economic growth is less than four percent. The decline in take-home pay revealed the difficulties of supporting governmental growth at an average of 131 percent of economic growth in the 1970s. Concern with 'ungovernability' in Western democracies proceeds directly from the gap between the growth of government and of the economy. If, as Wilensky says: 'Over the long pull, economic level is the root cause of welfare-state development . . .' (1975: 47–48), does that mean state spending will decline proportionately? Apparently not.

Perhaps economic explanations are faulty or perhaps they have not been carried far enough. To explore the latter alternative — large-scale economic determinism — we should consider Marxist theories.

At the outset, however, I should say a word about two other theorists who provide hypotheses about broad, historical relationships between the economy and the polity. The first of these — Rudolf Goldscheid (1967) — does not explain why government grows because he thinks it is (or was, in his time, at the end of the nineteenth century) too small. Recall the 'poor' kings of the early modern era. They could live off their own without requiring financial support from the citizenry. Alas, capitalism changed all that. It created the 'tax state', where governmental income depended on taxes raised through the private sector. Unfortunately, the private sector liked its private income, which it was reluctant to give up. Hence, in an inversion of both capitalist and Marxist claims, the private sector exploited the public, which had to work for it (Lindblom, 1977). This unfortunate separation of capital from government should be reconstituted, Goldscheid contended, by giving government its own property. Then there could really be a mixed society. Instead of sacrificing the present to an unreal future classless society, as Marxists suggested, as if there need be no government, or sacrificing public authority to private property,

Goldscheid would resolve the contradictions of capitalism by overcoming the alienation of the state from property. No doubt he had in mind nationalizing 'winners', that is, profitable concerns, rather than 'losers' as has been the custom.

Do not sell Goldscheid short: in historical perspective, over hundreds of years following the demise of feudalism, government no longer lived off its own. The distinction between public and private that is accepted today could not have arisen if the lord and ruler owned it all. In the modern era, a state came into being that had to raise revenues from other people, people they did not control or, better still, own. If spending other people's money is the hallmark of modern government, this estrangement between ownership and control of productive resources, which is widely acknowledged to be a hallmark of corporate capitalism, actually had a more profound predecessor in the postfeudal split between state and society.

'The crisis of the tax state', according to Joseph Schumpeter (1954), is that capitalism sets the stage for its own destruction, not, as Marxists would have it, because it has failed but rather because it is too successful. Affluence leads to disparagement of the profit motive on which productivity depends. As revenues increased so would social sympathies in spending other people's money. Eventually, governmental taxation would become excessive so that the economy declined and with it the 'tax state'. Here, also, as in the literature on governmental overload, the defects of capitalism are inherent in its political organization: affluence leads to moral collapse as the bourgeoisie ceases to believe it is worth defending.

So long as Marxist theorists maintained that the state was merely and only the repressive arm of the capitalist class, they did not have to confront the growth of welfare programmes. Whatever it was, welfare was exploitative. The expansion of welfare programmes eventually became anomalous, for if welfare programmes helped those worst off, they could not be entirely exploitative and if workers approved of them, as they evidently did, then the demise of capitalism might not necessarily be inherent in its operations. If the state (as government is sometimes called) was paying people off but couldn't keep these bribes up, however, it would be doing good for bad reasons, reasons that would eventually catch up with it. This is how deficit spending and governmental growth became signs of capitalist contradiction for Marxists as well as for conservatives.

Capitalist contradictions, James O'Connor (1975) holds, arise as the state simultaneously seeks to increase the profits of capitalists, including big union labour, by rigging markets, and to dampen discontent through welfare services. Social welfare and economic investment compete for the same resources, resulting in decline on both sides.

Put another way, as Alan Wolfe (1977) does, authority and democracy are placed at odds by the welfare state. He traces democratic (sometimes called liberal) political structures to the ideology of the market place. Government seeks to facilitate accumulation of capital, reducing along the way impediments to the mobility of labour. As alternatives from prior eras are used up, that is, as welfare spending increases faster than economic growth, government gets exhausted (Wolfe's term for 'overload'). Bureaucracy, he believes, is good at distribution but not at accumulation, a criticism previously confined to opponents of the welfare state as undermining the incentive to produce (see Straussman's review of Wolfe, 1981).

I could go on to cite work by Marxist scholars — Poulantzas (1978, 1975), Miliband (1977, 1969), Habermas (1979, 1975) — in which an effort is made to say that the state is more than a mouthpiece for the capitalist class without calling it good. If the state was, to some degree at least, independent of social forces and economic classes (Marx can be quoted on both sides), then it would be possible to account for its behaviour in sponsoring welfare programmes.

In return, other Marxists argued for an underlying 'logic' of capitalist relations that would bridge the apparent contradictions in Marxist analysis by showing that everything was being done to further capitalist interests, however ultimately unsuccessful. According to Marxist doctrine, capitalism depends on exploitation, that is, surplus value or profit. Thus Picciotto and Holloway (see Gough, 1978 and 1979) write of how the state shifts its function at different times, according to whether capitalist accumulation is strong or, as they think today, the rate of profit starts to slow down. But has it? Evidence is inconclusive (Musgrave, 1981: 375ff.).

Can government expand so as to take up the slack in the private economy, or will this very expansion threaten private production? Ian Gough's (1979) efforts to forge a synthesis of Marxist thought on this question is worth quoting:

> A growing level of welfare expenditure need not interfere with the accumulation of capital, so long as the higher 'social wage' could be financed out of total labour costs (the value of labour power) rather than from profits (surplus value) . . . The social

> contract may provide a means of achieving this and thus of resolving, albeit temporarily, the contradiction within the welfare state analysed earlier. By securing an overall agreement on wages, prices, taxes *and* social benefits, the state may be able to ensure a growing level of welfare expenditure without generating excessive inflationary pressures or harming profitability. The social contract permits the private wage, the 'social wage' and 'collective consumption', plus the level and direction of taxation, to be simultaneously negotiated on a tripartite basis between business, union leaders and the state. This could dampen down some of the conflicts over financing welfare expenditure that have proved harmful to the stability of the capitalist economies in recent years . . .
>
> If this analysis is correct, the implications for the welfare state are profound . . . Social policy would become part and parcel of a social contract between capital, labour and the state. The welfare state would be harbinger to the corporatist state (pp. 149–50).

Capitalism saves itself by corporatism. The welfare state legitimizes the acquisitive state. Since relationships between the state and society are no longer predetermined, detailed empirical study is required to assess what is happening. What, then, is the difference between Wilensky and Gough, an empirical analysis of the relationship between government policy and interest group activity by a Marxist and any other social scientist?

The difference is that Gough thinks corporatism cannot succeed. Slow growth prohibits all groups from gaining more: 'The material bases for reformism disappears' (Gough, 1979: 151). Consequently, union leaders and party politicians cannot deliver the goods to their supporters. Social life, Gough believes, is a fixed sum; more for labour means less for capital and vice versa (1979: 150). The conclusion is always the same: capitalism cannot cohere because it is built on internal contradictions.

I agree with Guy Peters:

> What is perhaps most remarkable about these discussions of the fiscal crisis of the state is the degree of similarity between the market and radical reformers [i.e. Marxists]. They both see a direct connection between the political and economic factors in determining the current condition of the welfare state. The downward spiral which both sets of analysts conceive of as almost inherent in these systems is the result of the need of the systems to legitimate themselves. For the 'radicals', this need is inherent in the capitalist system and its structural deficiencies, while for the market reformers the need is based more upon specific political considerations and commitments such as the pledge to full employment, or the fear of the political consequences of high unemployment (1980: 30).

If government grows in order to legitimate itself, the question remains of why legitimacy (the belief that institutions have the right to make the decisions they do) depends on the growth of government?

Forsman and his collaborators (1979) attribute state corporatism in Sweden to a variety of motives. In line with Wagner, they claim that capital costs are too large for private firms. But their evidence concerns state intervention in order to prevent declining industries (shipbuilding, textiles) from disappearing altogether. Is this a deliberate state policy, or a functional necessity or both? Their second rationale is the common one of maintaining employment in declining geographic areas. Their third rationale for forming state enterprises is 'to maintain societies' interests in development branches and growth industries,' such as nuclear energy. These activities, which Forsman claims are 'system preserving' (pp. 230–31), are evidently designed to prevent people from suffering losses in employment or income. Because a region or industry does not produce enough to justify continuance on economic grounds, is no reason why its peoples should receive less than others. Equality, not productivity, is the dominant value in all three causes of state enterprise.

Less use of welfare policies, as Herbert Tingsten said long ago, signifies willingness to accept inequality of results. It is not, as Offe (1976, 1975) and Wolfe (1978, 1977) maintain, along with a host of reactionaries, that state planning is incompatible with capitalism. Hierarchy and markets have coexisted for a long time. Insisting that there be no uncompensated failures, intervening to guarantee everyone against loss so as to maintain equality of result, however, would be incompatible with capitalism because it would destroy the rationale for competition.

Other theories

One alternative explanation, already mentioned, is that the median voter will vote for expansion unless and until his income is reduced. I think that interest group activity under democratic conditions is a better explanation of why spending does not decline, once it has reached a certain level, than why it goes up in the first place. It could be argued that enough people will believe that big government reduces their income to vote against it. Should the proportion of public spending to national product decline in a number of countries in the coming decades, we would evidently wish to reexamine this hypothesis. But I doubt it. Unless and until there is a decline in the desire for more equal outcomes, spending, I believe, will not go down.

The displacement hypothesis of Peacock and Wiseman (1961) has been found wanting; a new and powerful version has, however, been advanced by Mancur Olson (1982) who argues the opposite side of the street: Japan and Germany reach record levels of growth, while Britain and the United States, among others, do not, he contends, because the wars destroyed the complex of interests that, by gaining excessive benefits, slowed down growth. He sees in the political organizational mechanisms of modern democracies, especially the desire of broad spectrums of the population for goods available to all without being willing or having to pay for them (an extension of his seminal *Logic of Collective Action*) a gradual but pervasive cause of economic decline. Though it had facetiously been suggested before that nations might be better off to lose than to win wars, this is the first time a general hypothesis has been made out of such aspersions. The Olson thesis subsumes those theorists of government overload and of capitalist crisis who claim that in order to legitimate itself the state must take so much out of the private economy that economic growth declines.

I would be more inclined to credit Olson's brilliant thesis of the inadvertent decay of capitalism if there were not significant elements in these communities who make a point out of urging what he considers disaster as desirable national policy. The proponents of welfare programmes, at least in the period after the second world war, used Keynesian analysis to defend the position that government was good for the private economy. Still others defended social welfare programmes as a mechanism of maintaining these political systems, which otherwise, in their view, would have collapsed, so that the question of a level of economic growth would not have arisen. And there are still others who rail against economic growth as being undesirable or who prefer distribution to cumulation. Olson's latent functions, to use the language of sociology, are their manifest functions. From their point of view, which as a whole has been dominant in Western democracies, the only thing wrong with the current situation is that there has been insufficient governmental growth.

Another alternative explanation, best stated by Hugh Heclo (1981) is that governmental growth is a product of certain historical circumstances. The implication is that as the adverse aspects of this growth become evident, there will be a change. Heclo divides the growth of the welfare state quite reasonably into three stages. The first, beginning at the end of the nineteenth century, he calls the era of 'experimentation' in which a variety of proposals for social insurance, especially pensions, are tried out. No one is certain whether everyone should have the same pension or they should be income related or only the poor should receive them or whether everyone should have them as a matter of right. Whether security, the desire to be protected against adversity, was compatible with liberty or either could go with equality was what the debate was about. During the period of consolidation, lasting through the 1950s, new programmes on housing, education, health and unemployment were established and old ones became politically sacrosanct. In a series of elections, those who opposed these programmes were uniformly defeated and they became part of what every government was pledged to spend. The depression of the 1930s was especially important in beating down the view that matters of security and equality could be left entirely to the private sector. Government, it was everywhere believed, had to be intimately involved. Both political legitimacy and economic growth would be served by a variety of programmes for income maintenance and social services, policy commitments that led some to speak of an end of ideology as if everyone were agreed. The third period, which Heclo calls 'expansion', was one in which 'government tax extractions grew faster than economic resources; total expenditures grew faster still. In every country the result has been a gradually increasing share of national economic product absorbed by the public sector' (Heclo, 1981: 394). The substantial economic growth that occurred after the second world war was, as Heclo rightly reminds us, largely unexpected. He believes that this bounty reduced the perceived need to maintain political support for welfare spending. 'Instead of shared risks and vulnerability, its ethic was based on piecemeal compensation for anyone who lagged behind others' gains . . . Virtually everyone could claim to be entitled to one or another kind of compensation.' The 'unsettling rediscovery of inequality' at the end of the 1960s, together with decline in economic growth, led to disillusion (Heclo, pp. 398–99).

Why, I ask, was inequality of results so suddenly discovered in the 1960s and 1970s? There seems to be nothing inherent in the situation, indeed a great deal running in the opposite direction. People were better off, not worse off. Welfare spending had been growing, not declining. Why, in the face of this improvement, would there be still greater demand for equality of results? The alternative explanations either fail empirically or assume the very thing that needs to be improved, namely, the increased value given to equality of results.

The explanation for why government grows, as I have insisted, must deal with two trends: it must explain why spending goes up and also why it does not go down. Economic growth, so long as it lasts, provides a facilitating condition; without money to spend, aspirations are limited by resources. Once these resources are available, however, the question is whether they will be used to expand the private sector, thus increasing state spending absolutely but not relatively, or to expand the public sector at the expense of the private. Sustained economic growth makes the choice unnecessary. When it does become necessary in times of adversity, spending does not decline because the commitment to equality of result requires even greater governmental effort to maintain prior social welfare programmes. Government intervenes in markets in an effort to increase equality of result. Things could be different but they are not because critical choices are made only in a single direction.

A cultural hypothesis

Observing that a particular conception of equality grows in importance as a rationale for public policy is only the beginning of analysis. What we want to know is what sort of people, following which way of life, believe in and practise equality of result as a solution to their own problems? Now few nations even approximate income equality. The observable trend is a movement in that direction but by no means achievement of that objective. There is opposition as well as support. Let me reformulate: what culture (or combination of cultures) moves toward but does not necessarily achieve equality of results?

Competitive individualism (expressed economically as capitalism) supports equality of opportunity to facilitate perpetual bidding and bargaining. Without the chance of gain, people would lack incentive to compete; without the possibility of loss, there would be no gain for taking risks. Equality of result, which requires redistribution, undoes the consequences of competition. At some level, of course, inequality, if it became cumulative, would also destroy competition. The dilemma of capitalism is that government intervention to promote sufficient equality to preserve competition may become a threat to viable markets.

Hierarchies are held together by the rule of law, which guarantees to people the appropriate role, status, and position that they have been selected to fill. By obliterating these differences, equality of result, pushed to its ultimate end, would nullify hierarchy. The principle of differentiation could no longer be used to solve the problem of social order.

Hierarchy is institutionalized inequality. It justifies inequality on the grounds that specialization and the division of labour enable people to live together with greater harmony and effectiveness than alternative arrangements. The belief that hierarchy creates a caring collective, the rulers caring about the ruled, is essential to its continuance. Hence hierarchies, in full vigour, are animated by a sacrificial ethic on all sides — the parts sacrificing for the whole. This explains the mildly redistributive policies of governments in societies with strong hierarchies. Why, in recent years, have they gone further?

Equality of result is the preference of a sectarian regime. Committed to a life of purely voluntary association, a life utterly without coercion or authority, sectarians place all their moral fervour on what Mary Douglas calls the 'wall of virtue' separating them from groups organized on an inegalitarian basis (Douglas, 1970, 1982). The best indicator of sectarian practices is reduction of differences— between races or income levels or men and women, parents and children, teachers and students, authorities and citizens. Sectarian moralism is invoked to diminish differences. Lacking authority, sectarian regimes find it difficult to control envy or collect taxes or deal with conflicts of views. Equality of result makes their internal life easier by decreasing envy.

At long last, I am able to offer my explanation of the continual growth of government. 'The time has come', as Anthony King (1973) said, 'to let the cat out of the bag. . . . The State plays a more limited role in America than elsewhere because Americans, more than other people, want it to play a limited role.' My contribution extends King's analysis in two directions — geographically, to cover industrial democracies, and organizationally to identify the precise social forms responsible for the differences between Europe and the United States and the similarities among European countries. America has marched to its own drummers, a combination of weak hierarchy and strong markets, leading to less welfare spending.

European nations share strong hierarchies and moderate to strong sectarianism, leading all of them to increase welfare spending and some, being more sectarian, to spend more than others. Britain, Canada, and Australia are in between because, while hierarchy remains strong, so do market relationships.

If spending patterns in European social democracies and Soviet-style governments on welfare is similar, as it is, that must be because of factors they share rather than those, like democratic decision-making, that differentiate them. Whatever else might be said about Eastern and Western Europe, they share strong hierarchies. They differ increasingly in another dimension — sectarian groups, which were destroyed in the Soviet Union after the Bolshevik revolution (Shapiro, 1965; Daniels, 1969), are growing stronger in the West. Therefore I predict that by the twenty-first century it will become clear that equality of result has been more nearly achieved in Western rather than Eastern Europe.

Sectarianism, standing for equality of results, leads the charge for state spending on welfare. Or so I hypothesize. If this hypothesis were correct, it would predict that movements toward economic equality would pre-date major redistributive efforts by government: sectarianism grows before redistribution. As long as other differences diminish, state spending will continue to increase as a proportion of GNP. And as sectarianism spreads, patterns of spending among European governments will converge. The larger their public sectors grow, the more they will look alike.

Peltzman's law, or culture reconsidered

Were there to be an empirical test of the cultural theory I have been propounding, it would have to include the reverse causal sequences to that postulated by the broad camp of followers of Wagner's law: increased inequality of result would have to precede growth in proportion of public expenditure. The rise of hierarchical and sectarian political cultures would first lead to an increased desire for redistribution through government, which would secondly provide facilitating political institutions, soon (say, in a generation) leading to higher public spending on welfare and in total. Fortunately for us, Peltzman has provided exactly the kind of test we require. His findings pose a direct challenge to those who argue the primacy of economic development.

Peltzman's law, as I will call it, states that 'reduced inequality of income stimulates the growth of government' (Peltzman, 1980: 263). His contribution lies in showing more precisely how equality affects spending. The greater the inequality between taxpayers in a prior period, Peltzman argues, the less inclined they are to support redistributive spending in a later period. The greater the income equality, earlier, in other words, the more it is desired later on.

Using wage (in)equality as a surrogate for general economic trends, Peltzman summarizes the data and relates it to his theory:

> The broad outlines of the British, American, and Canadian twentieth-century experience hold almost everywhere in the developed world. Some time around World War I, wage and salary inequality began to decline and some time around 1950, the decline flattened or stopped . . . Around World War I the top 5 percent of income recipients in the typical developed country account for around 30 percent of the national income . . . However, by about 1950 this share falls to just under 20 percent . . . In broad outline, the growth of government follows a similar path . . . For many countries a major part of the growth of government has occurred in the last twenty-five years, or after the main force of the trend toward equality had been spent. If equality is indeed a major determinant of the equilibrium size of government, a lagged-adjustment process has been dominating recent experience. Thus recent *growth* of government would be more closely related to the level of inequality than absolute size.
>
> Size of government and inequality were essentially uncorrelated in the late 1950s. But there is a very strong negative correlation between inequality then and subsequent growth (pp. 262–63).

Testing the theory on a set of data for countries outside Europe, Peltzman concludes that: 'The international data seem to say something even stronger. Nothing much besides income inequality is needed to explain the growth of government. We are able to pretty much write the history of government growth in the next fifteen years from what we know about income inequality in 1960' (p. 265).

It is worth noting that Mancur Olson's historical, developmental theory reinforces Peltzman's. Since Olson believes groups seek special advantage by limiting competition, he contends that government is a greater source of inequality than markets (Olson, 1982: 173). It follows that (with special force after the early 1960s), '. . . the longer a state has been settled and the longer the time it has had to accumulate special-interest groups, the slower its rate of growth' (Olson, 1982: 97). Lower growth rates, combined with efforts to redistribute income, lead to a larger size government.

The part that level of education (used as a surrogate for human skill) plays in stimulating state expenditure receives special consideration. As the middle class grows, and with it both higher educational attainment and a general equalization of incomes with the class, the kind of people interested in (because they stand to benefit) and able to (because they are articulate) sponsor redistributive policies also increases (Olson, 1982: 285).

I cannot but agree with 'the larger message' of Peltzman's seminal paper: '. . . there is nothing inevitable or inexorable about the growth of government' (Peltzman, 1980: 287).

Following the public-choice literature, Peltzman's general 'argument is that the size of government responds to the articulated interests of those who tend to gain or lose from politicization of the allocation of resources' (p. 287). Once we abandon the fiction that it is possible for people to live as isolated individuals, we can refer to the 'interests' of public choice theory in two ways. One would be 'local advantage' or, as psychologists call it, 'secondary gain', as when a person's income is directly determined by a governmental action. The other sense of interest, explicitly recognizing the social character of social interaction, refers to shared values legitimating various ways of life. This is culture. So Peltzman's law (with a dose of incrementalism) may be broadened to say that cultural change precedes and dominates budgetary change: the size of the state today is a function of its political culture yesterday.

NOTES

1. See Larkey et al. (1981) for a sophisticated statement of the methodological difficulties.
2. I am indebted to Joe White for ideas about the differences between Wilensky and Castles.

REFERENCES

Aaron, Henry (1967) 'Social Security: International Comparisons' in Eckstein, Otto (ed.) *Studies in the Economics of Income Maintenance*. Washington, DC: Brookings Institution.

Beyer, Glenn H. (1965) *Housing and Society*. New York: Macmillan.

Bird, Richard (1971) 'Wagner's "Law" of Expanding State Activity'. *Public Finance*, 26, 1: 1–26.

Borg, Sten G., and Castles, Francis G. (1981) 'The Influence of the Political Right on Public Income Maintenance Expenditure and Equality'. *Political Studies*, 29, 4 (December): 604–21.

Caiden, Naomi, and Wildavsky, Aaron (1980) *Planning and Budgeting in Poor Countries*. New Brunswick, NJ: Transaction Press.

Cameron, David R. (1978) 'The Expansion of the Public Economy: A Comparative Analysis'. *The American Political Science Review*, 72, 4 (December): 1250–60.

Castles, Francis G. (1978) *The Social Democratic Image of Society*. London: Routledge and Kegan Paul.

Coughlin, Richard M. (1980) *Ideology, Public Opinion, and Welfare Policy*. Research Series, No. 42. Berkeley, Calif.: University of California Institute of International Studies.

Crowley, Ronald W. (1971) 'Long Swings in the Role of Government: An Analysis of Wars and Government Expenditures in Western Europe Since the Eleventh Century'. *Public Finance*, 26, 1: 27–43.

Daniels, Robert Vincent (1969) *The Conscience of the Revolution: Communist Opposition in Soviet Russia*. New York: Simon and Schuster.

Doern, G. Brude (ed.) (1981) *How Ottowa Spends Your Tax Dollars*. Toronto: James Lorimer.

Doern, G. Brude (ed.) (1980) *Spending Tax Dollars: Federal Expenditures 1980–81)*. Ottawa: Carleton University School of Public Administration.

Douglas, Mary (1970) *Natural Symbols, Explorations in Cosmology*. London: Barrie & Rockliff.

Douglas, Mary (1982) 'Cultural Bias' in *In the Natural Voice*. London: Routledge & Kegan Paul.

Fish, Gertrude Sipperly (ed.) (1979) *The Story of Housing*. New York: Macmillan.

Forsman, A., Rodriquez, E., Waara, L. and Wickman, K. (1979) 'Appendix: The Expansion of the Public Sector in Sweden in the Postwar Period' in Gustafsson, Bo (ed.) *Post-Industrial Society*. New York: St. Martin's Press.

Freidson, Eliot (1975) *Doctoring Together: A Study of Professional Social Control*. New York/Oxford/Amsterdam: Elsevier.

Galbraith, John Kenneth (1967) *The New Industrial State*. New York: New American Library.

Giertz, J. Fred (1981) 'Centralization and Government Budget Size'. *Publius*, 2, 1 (Winter): 119–28.

Gilb, Corinne Lathrop (1967) *Hidden Hierarchies: The Professions and Government*. New York: Harper and Row.

Goldscheid, Rudolf (1967) 'A Sociological Approach to Problems of Public Finance' in Musgrave, Richard A. and Peacock, Alan T. (eds.) *Classics in the Theory of Public Finance*. New York: St. Martin's Press.

Gough, Ian (1978) 'Theories of the Welfare State: A Critique'. *International Journal of Health Services*, 8, 1: 27–40.

Gough, Ian (1979) *The Political Economy of the Welfare State*. London and Basingstoke: Macmillan Press.

Gramlich, Edward M., and Rubinfeld, Daniel L. (1982) 'Voting on Public Spending: Differences Between Public Employees, Transfer Recipients, and Private Workers'. *Journal of Policy Analysis and Management*, 1, 4 (Summer): 516–33.

Habermas, Jurgen (1975) *Legitimation Crisis*. Boston: Beacon Press.

Habermas, Jurgen (1979) *Communication and the Evolution of Society*. Boston: Beacon Press.

Haveman, Robert, Habberstadt, Victor and Burkhauser, Richard V. (1983) *Public Policy Toward Disabled Workers*. Institute for Research on Poverty, University of Wisconsin, Madison (Manuscript).

Heclo, Hugh (1981) 'Toward a New Welfare State?' in Flora, Peter and Heidenheimer, Arnold J. (eds.) *The Development of Welfare States in Europe and America*. New Brunswick, NJ: Transaction Books.

Heclo, Hugh, and Wildavsky, Aaron (1981) *The Private Government of Public Money* (2nd ed.). London: Macmillan.

Hewitt, Christopher (1977) 'The Effect of Political Democracy and Social Democracy on Equality in Industrial Societies: A Cross-National Comparison'. *American Sociological Review*, 42, 3 (June): 450–63.

Hinrichs, Harley H. (1966) *A General Theory of Tax Structure Change During Economic Development*. Cambridge, Mass.: The Law School of Harvard University.

Jackman, Robert (1975) *Politics and Social Equality: A Comparative Analysis*. New York: John Wiley and Sons.

Jackson, J. A., (ed.) (1970) *Professions and Professionalization*. Cambridge: Cambridge University Press.

King, Anthony (1973) 'Ideas, Institutions and the Policies of Governments: A Comparative Analysis: Part III'. *British Journal of Political Science*, 3, 4 (October): 409–23.

Kudrle, Robert T., and Marmor, Theodore R. (1981) 'The Development of Welfare States in North America' in Flora, Peter and Heidenheimer, Arnold J. (eds.) *The Development of Welfare States in Europe and America*. New Brunswick, NJ: Transaction Books.

Larkey, Patrick D., Stolp, Chandler and Winer, Mark (1981) 'Theorizing About the Growth of Government: A Research Assessment'. *Journal of Public Policy*, 1, 2, (May): 157–220.

Larson, Magali S. (1977) *The Rise of Professionalism: A Sociological Analysis*. Berkeley: University of California Press.

Lindblom, C. E. (1977) *Politics and Markets*. New York: Basic Books.

Lipset, Seymour M. (1968) *Agrarian Socialism: The Cooperative Commonwealth Federation in Saskatchewan*. Garden City, NY: Anchor Books.

Maslow, Abraham H. (1954) *Motivation and Personality*. New York: Harper.

Miliband, Ralph (1969) *The State in Capitalist Society*. London: Wiedenfeld and Nicolson.

Miliband, Ralph (1977) *Marxism and Politics*. Oxford: Oxford University Press.

Musgrave, Richard A. (1981) 'Leviathan Cometh — Or Does He?' in Ladd, Helen F. and Tideman, T. Nicholas [eds.] *Tax and Expenditure Limitations*. Washington, DC: Urban Institute Press.

O'Connor, James (1975) *The Fiscal Crisis of the State*. New York: St. Martin's Press.

Offe, Claus (1975) *Wolfahrtsstaat und Massenloyalität*. Köln: Kiepenheuer and Witsch.

Offe, Claus (1976) *Industry and Inequality: The Achievement Principle in Work and Social Status*. London: Edward Arnold.

Olson, Mancur (1982) *The Rise and Decline of Nations: Economic Growth, Stagflation and Social Rigidities*. Cambridge, Mass.: Yale University Press.

Parkin, Frank (1971) *Class Inequality and Political Order*. New York: Praeger.
Peacock, A. T., and Wiseman, J. (1961) *The Growth of Public Expenditures in the United Kingdom*. Princeton.
Peltzman, Sam (1980) 'The Growth of Government'. *The Journal Law and Economics*, 23, 2 (October): 209–88.
Peters, B. Guy (1980) 'Fiscal Strains on the Welfare State: Causes and Consequences' in Levine, Charles H. and Rubin, Irene [eds.] *Fiscal Stress and Public Policy*. Sage Yearbooks in Politics and Public Policy, Vol. 9. Beverly Hills/London: Sage Publications.
Pirenne, Henri (1914) *Les periodes de l'histoire social du capitalisme* Bruxelles: Hayez, Imp. de l'Academie Royale de Belgique.
Poulantzas, Nicos (1975) *Classes in Contemporary Capitalism*. London: NLB.
Poulantzas, Nicos (1978) *Political Power and Social Classes*. London: Verso.
Pryor (1968), quoted in Castles, Francis G. and McKinlay, R. D. (1979) 'Public Welfare Provision, Scandinavia, and the Sheer Futility of the Sociological Approach to Politics'. *British Journal of Political Science*, 9, 2 (April): 157–72.
Pryor, Frederick (1968) *Public Expenditures in Communist and Capitalist Nations*. Homewood, Ill.: Irwin.
Schumpeter, Joseph A. (1954) 'The Crisis of the Tax State'. *International Economic Papers*, 4. London: Macmillan. (Translated by Stolper, W. F. and Musgrave, R. A.)
Shapiro, Leonard (1965) *The Origin of the Communist Autocracy: Political Opposition in the Soviet State: First Phase, 1917–1922*. New York: Praeger.
Straussman, Jeffrey (1981) 'Spending More and Enjoying It Less: On the Political Economy of Advanced Capitalism'. *Comparative Politics* (January): 235–52.
Tarschys, Daniel (1975) 'The Growth of Public Expenditures: Nine Modes of Explanation'. *Scandinavian Political Studies*, 10: 9–31.
Wildavsky, Aaron (1985) *Budgeting: A Comparative Theory of Budgetary Process*, second edition. New Brunswick: Transaction Press.
Wildavsky, Aaron (1980) *How To Limit Government Spending*. Berkeley, Calif.: University of California Press.
Wildavsky, Aaron (1982) 'The Limits of Government Spending'. Paper prepared for Carleton University's School of Public Administration Thirtieth Anniversary Conference on 'The Limits of Government Intervention'. October.
Wildavsky, Aaron (1984) *The Politics of the Budgetary Process* (4th ed.). Boston: Little, Brown.
Wilensky, Harold L. (1981) 'Leftism, Catholicism, and Democratic Corporatism: The Role of Political Parties in Recent Welfare State Development' in Flora, Peter and Heindenheimer, Arnold J. (eds.) *The Development of Welfare States in Europe and America*. New Brunswick, NJ: Transaction Books.
Wilensky, Harold L. (1975) *The Welfare State and Equality*. Berkeley/Los Angeles: University of California Press.
Wilensky, Harold L. and Lebeaux, C. N. (1958) *Industrial Society and Social Welfare*. New York: Russsell Sage Foundation.
Wolfe, Alan (1977) *The Limits of Legitimacy*. New York: Free Press.
Wolfe, Alan (1978) *The Seamy Side of Democracy: Repression in America* (2nd ed.). New York: Longman.
Wright, Gwendolyn (1981) *Building the Dream: A Social History of Housing in America*. New York: Pantheon.

11

The Post-Industrial City in Transition from Private to Public

Ted Robert Gurr
University of Colorado, Boulder
Desmond S. King
University of Edinburgh

The vitality of cities in advanced industrial democracies is increasingly determined by the allocative decisions of national, regional, and local governments. This is particularly true of post-industrial cities, those which lost jobs, population, and tax revenues because of the process of industrial disinvestment which began in parts of northwestern Europe and northeastern America during the 1960s. Some of these cities are in absolute decline, others have stabilized decline by shifting away from an industrial base to new financial, administrative, and service activities. The economic dynamics of this process are well understood: because of changes in the structure of national and international capitalism, most old industrial cities in North America and northern Europe have lost their comparative advantage to other regions and to third world countries. Less closely scrutinized is the role of the state and its policies in reshaping the private and public economies of these and other cities. The general tendency in EEC countries throughout the post-war period has been a growth in the size of the public sector and the state's regulatory powers, nationally and in cities. The growth of cities' financial, administrative, and service activities, which are increasingly important to their survival in an era of deindustrialization, is the aggregate result of private and public decisions about the location of investments and contracts, jobs and services. In some post-industrial cities the threshold has probably already been passed, without notice, from primary reliance on the private economy to primary dependence on the public economy. This chapter develops a conceptual argument about the ways in which the power and resources of the national and regional state are being used in response to the problems of declining cities in advanced industrial societies.

Theoretical assumptions about urban policies

The theoretical argument which underpins the research is a state-centred one. Unlike the pluralist and neo-Marxist traditions of urban political analysis, we assume that state officials have interests in the vitality of cities which are substantially independent of private interests (a perspective influenced by treatments of state autonomy by Block, 1981; Nordlinger, 1981; and Skocpol, 1982). Pluralist approaches treat urban-related policies of the state as a vector of contending private interests. The specifics of urban policy decisions and policy implementation are a function of shifting coalitions of organized economic, political and social interests, some pursuing conceptions of the general welfare, others seeking to enhance sectoral and individual interests (see Guterbock, 1980). Neo-Marxist perspectives assume a class-conflict model of political action and regard the capitalist state, even if relatively 'autonomous', as concerned with the maintenance and legitimization of the capitalist mode of production. Urban growth and decline are understood as the product of economic dynamics. The siting and structure of large industrial cities followed from the needs of capital in the nineteenth and early-twentieth centuries for socially controlled concentrations of labour, housed in systematically segregated districts (Gordon, 1976). The contemporary crisis of American cities results from the fact that: 'In a capitalist society the circulation of surplus is constantly shifting to new channels as new opportunities are explored, new technologies achieved and new resources and productive capacities are opened up. Correspondingly, the prestige and vitality of individual cities come to rest largely upon their location with respect to the geographic circulation of the surplus' (Hill, 1977: 77; see also Castells, 1977; Mollenkopf, 1975; Smith, 1980).

Our argument (developed more fully in Gurr and King, 1984) is that elective and appointive officials have concrete interests in maintaining the political institutions and relationships from which they derive their authority, status, and privileges. While elective officials are recurrently preoccupied with their short-term interest in renewal of office, both they and, especially, higher-level administrators also pursue longer-term interests in the perpetuation of state authority. The most essential conditions to that end are the maintenance of public order and the capacity to secure public compliance by invoking legitimacy. Further conditions are the establishment and maintenance of centralized, effective, well-financed, durable institutions of state authority. In Western democracies, and elsewhere, officials may also use the powers of the state to promote their conceptions of the general welfare, but they cannot do so effectively without securely establishing public order and state authority.

In the pursuit of these interests officials operate within constraints. Prevailing ideology — including their own — may require them to rationalize actions by reference to the general welfare. Usually there are institutionalized limits on their powers such that they must modify their own preferences to take into account the preferences of groups not directly controlled by the state (Nordlinger, 1981). And, if they do not control the means of production directly, they must cooperate with those who do in order to obtain revenues enough to maintain the state. The state can become the instrument of a dominant economic class outside the state, as happened during the ascendant stages of capitalism in some Western countries, but there is a strong long-run tendency for the state to attempt to (re)establish its autonomy from economic and other social forces. The twentieth-century experience is that the absolute and relative scope of public authority in European states have continued to grow, the acquisition of new resources and responsibilities being particularly associated with domestic crises (such as the Great Depression) and war (Tilly, 1975). New powers and revenues once gained are seldom ceded.

In advanced industrial democracies the maintenance of public order, legitimacy, and a significant level of well-being in urban populations are crucial. The majority of the population in contemporary Western states lives in cities; so do almost all officials. Most of the economic activity upon which states depend for revenue is centred on cities. Urban populations provide the basis for the coalitions of political support for incumbents and contenders alike. For all these reasons and more, it is imperative for political elites to maintain the vitality of some, though not necessarily all, cities. The state's policies with respect to cities are constrained, but not determined, by private economic and other interests. Ultimately it is in the interest of state officials and managers to subordinate economic activity to state authority, either indirectly through regulation or by direct state control of the means of production, first to minimize constraints on state power, secondly to ensure ample revenues. In general, we suggest that the logic of the contemporary democratic welfare state, confronted with urban decline, propels it not toward 'autonomy' in some absolute sense, but rather toward a state-dominated partnership with private economic forces in which the state increasingly assumes primary responsibility for the character and vitality of post-industrial cities and of urban systems generally.

Some cities are more important to the managers of the national and regional state than others (managers of the local state are of course invariably interested in the viability of their city). As a result, some cities receive substantially more from the national and regional state than others: some are chosen as centres of regional growth programmes or as 'model cities', others suffer from 'benign neglect'. Some of the variation is due to the differential 'political salience' of cities; those which are politically more salient to the national and regional state tend to get more, and are more likely to be eased successfully through the process of deindustrialization.

Our concern is with economically based urban decline and its political consequences. The declining cities of particular interest are those with both (1) declining productivity, reflected in declining per capita income relative to the performance of other cities and regions in the same national economy; and (2) shrinking total population. Urban decline caused by structural economic change creates or exacerbates a complex set of social stresses, which in turn pose severe problems for municipal governments and increase the political salience of cities for the national and regional state.[1] Official attention and resources are not allocated among cities in strict proportion to the severity of decline, however. The salience of declining cities to the state varies according to their political and administrative primacy, and in proportion to the current urban-based demands, disorder, and political mobilization centred on issues of urban change. Moreover, from the political perspective of this study it is declining *central* cities which are vital to the state's interests. There are good reasons why economically oriented analyses should concentrate on larger functional regions or metropolitan areas (as in the work of Hall and Hay, 1980 and the Urban Europe project). This chapter, however, is concerned with the political implications and consequences of decline *at the urban core*.

The national and regional state in advanced industrial societies have a great many instrumentalities which can effect urban change. A complete profile of changing 'state presence' in cities must take into account not only grants-in-aid to municipal governments and programmes for stimulating private-sector growth but also social transfer payments, the siting of public institutions and public employment, private-sector contracts, and investment in public enterprises. The net effect of state resources allocated through all such instrumentalities potentially can stabilize and reverse the malign conditions associated with urban decline: unemployment, decaying housing and infrastructure, deteriorating municipal services, and social pathologies. This is not to minimize the role of the private sector in determining the outcomes of state intervention. From a state-centred perspective, however, the question is the extent to which the private sector follows up or complements the public initiatives upon which post-industrial cities are increasingly dependent.[2]

The preceding argument can be summarized diagrammatically in this causal model of the consequences of urban decline:

urban decline → increased political salience → increased state presence → stabilization of decline

To the extent that the state does assume primary responsibility for economic and social wellbeing in deindustrializing cities, the causal sequence above is paralleled by this shift in the economic basis of urban systems:

cities dependent on private industry and services → cities dependent on private services and public sector activities

In fact the sequence of changes set in motion by urban decline is problematic. The political salience of urban decline is variable between countries as well as within them. Americans seem to be prepared to abandon their older cities more readily than continental Europeans, while conservative administrations on both sides of the Atlantic, even if politically sensitive to urban decline, may be ideologically disposed against assuming primary responsibility for urban survival. Thus the arguments which are fleshed out below identify tendencies, not inevitabilities.

The extent and nature of urban decline

Approximately half the larger cities of Europe and the United States were losing population during the 1970s. Urban development trends in fourteen Eastern and Western European countries have been examined in the Urban Europe project. The study includes 150 functional urban regions (cities and their peripheries) of which 19 percent experienced absolute population loss during 1970–75, while these plus another 29 percent lost population in their core cities. Three-quarters or more of the urban regions in Britain, the Netherlands, Belgium, and Switzerland were in these two groupings (van den Berg et al., 1982: chapter 7). In the United States the incidence of urban decline during 1970–75 was quite similar. Of 121 Standard Metropolitan Statistical Areas (SMSAs) 26 (21 percent) lost population during these five years and 51 (42 percent) of SMSAs had core cities with shrinking populations. As in Europe, declining American urban regions are concentrated in old industrial areas. In the northeastern United States, 23 of 24 metropolitan areas had absolute or core-city decline and in the north central region 29 of 33 (Bradbury, Downs, and Small, 1982: chapter 3). Deindustrialization was not the only factor contributing to population decline in these regions and cities, but clearly was the most important one.

Studies of the trends and correlates of urban population decline in the United States show that the reversal of a century of urban growth began in the late 1950s and gathered momentum in the 1960s and 1970s (Berry, 1973). One fundamental shift is from the core areas of cities to the suburbs (Schwartz, 1976; Berry, 1977; Kasarda, 1976). There also have been significant movements from urban to rural, from larger to smaller cities, and regionally from the industrial northeastern and midwestern cities to the South and West (Perry and Watkins, 1977; Harvey, 1975; Gluck and Meister, 1979; Gordon, 1976; Bluestone and Harrison, 1982). The latter two regions have enjoyed dramatic population growth over the last two decades, principally due to net in-migration from the northeast and north central regions. Per capita personal income and employment levels have tended to rise significantly faster in the South and West during the same period, partly the result of migration trends that favour the South and West. The economic development of the Sunbelt region has now become largely self-sustaining.

The underlying dynamics of urban decline in the United States arise from structural economic changes. The natural resources and locational advantages of the Northeast have declined in economic significance. The region's highly developed transportation network and financial institutions proved sufficiently flexible and responsive to short and long-term economic changes until the 1960s and 1970s (Greenberg and Valente, 1975). The falloff in primary and secondary industries in major northeastern and midwestern cities has been partly replaced by the rise of tertiary ones. These cities are being functionally transformed — some of them — from centres of industrial production and distribution to administrative, information-exchange, and higher-order service centres. Paralleling this transformation are changes in the demographic composition of declining urban areas, from predominantly white residents of European heritage to a predominantly black and Hispanic population. Employment opportunities and aggregate personal income levels have declined significantly for residents in these cities (Greenberg and Valente, 1975; Kasarda, 1982; Sternlieb and Hughes, 1975). The drop in per capita income levels also reflects the suburban migration of those employed in the new tertiary and service industries. Core city residents tend to be those in the least well paid industries. This resident population, combined with the decline of traditional manufacturing industries, has made serious inroads on the tax base of northeastern and midwestern cities (Gluck and Meister, 1979). However the same factors have placed increased demands on urban services, resulting in varying degrees of municipal fiscal stress, a condition in which cities have a chronic excess of expenditures over revenues.

Recent work on growth and decline in European urban systems identifies a superficially similar pattern of declining core-city population, especially in larger cities (Hall and Hay, 1980). Britain offers the closest parallels with the US situation: the major urban areas have experienced substantial population decline due to out-migration and very significant declines in industrial employment (McCallum, 1980; Hall and Hay, 1980). Preliminary analysis of the 1981 census show that 'the bigger the city the bigger the loss'. Simultaneously, a number of smaller cities in environmentally more appealing areas have gained both in population and employment: examples are Bristol, Oxford, and Norwich (Young and Mills, 1982: 83). As one consequence the larger British urban areas have growing concentrations of unemployment, of lower socio-economic groups, of workers with both parents born outside the country. And, as in declining US industrial cities, employment in low-wage service industries has increased (McCallum, 1980; Cameron, 1973).

In continental Europe the trend of declining core cities is also widespread, but with the exception of Belgium and some industrial regions of France and West Germany, the process through the mid-1970s was largely the result of the appeal of suburban living rather than declining urban economic opportunities resulting from deindustrialization (van den Berg et al., 1982; Hall and Hay, 1980). This pattern is paralleled by the distribution of urban crisis: Britain is the only industrial European state (with the anomolous exception of Italy) where the social and fiscal stresses of urban decline are comparable to the experience of the older industrial cities in the United States (Sharpe, 1981). On the other hand it is evident that the 'filtering out' of more prosperous inner-city migrants to suburbs leads to increased concentrations of lower-income groups and the unemployed in inner cities even where core cities retain their economic viability. In West Germany, where foreign workers in 1976 were 6.5 percent of total population, in some larger cities made up 12–15 percent of the population and in some inner-city districts, well over 20 percent (Gude, Heinz and Rothammer, 1981).

The political salience of urban decline

This portmanteau concept refers to a set of state-centred arguments about why the national state and regional governments, in Europe and North America, can be expected to devote more attention and resources to some cities than to others. The main issue is what determines differential allocation of state resources among declining cities, but some of the arguments are more generally applicable and can be expected to be relevant to all cities. We identify six such factors.

Administrative status. The location of a city in the national state's administrative network affects its political salience: the greater a city's administrative role for the national and regional state, the greater its political salience. The managers of the national state can be expected to be especially concerned about the viability and amenities of the national capital, not only for symbolic reasons but because, concretely, they want to live and work in a pleasant urban environment. The effects of such concern are obvious in 'government towns' like Bonn and Washington; the case of London is more instructive. Greater London from 1951 to 1974 had the greatest proportional population loss of any British conurbation, and also the most substantial percentage loss of manufacturing employment — both conditions associated elsewhere with economic decline and fiscal stress (McCallum, 1980). But on most indicators of decline and stress London fared better than other large British cities, a factor attributable to the large and growing size of London's public administration sector (Cameron, 1980: 64–5) and exceptionally high rates of increase in local government expenditure per capita (Kirwan, 1980: 78–81).

Similar effects should be evident in regional administrative centres in both unitary and federal systems. In a preliminary study of federal US assistance to state capitals, for example, we found weak but significant correlations showing that in 1970 and 1980 the municipal governments of state capitals report receiving more federal aid per capita than non-capital cities (King and Gurr, 1983). We expect stronger relationships for cities which are major regional administrative centres for the national state. Unlike the other dimensions of political salience, below, 'administrative status' is usually the cumulative result of historical policies which have increased the status of a city in the state's administrative network. Thus administrative status is unlikely to increase in short-run response to urban decline; rather, cities which have significant administrative roles are less likely to experience decline (because of sustained public-sector growth) and are more likely to get special policy consideration when they do.

Fiscal stress. Urban fiscal stress or 'crisis' has two principal meanings (Dearborn, 1978): first, it refers to an immediate condition whereby a city cannot meet its obligations owing to lack of cash and credit (Tabb, 1982); secondly, it refers to the culmination of the long-term economic and social dynamics responsible for urban decline, whereby revenues chronically fall well short of municipal expenditure budgets (Gluck and Meister, 1979; Alcahy and Mermelstein, 1976). In the old American industrial cities, urban fiscal stress reflects the structural, demographic, and economic changes of the last 25 years. It also reflects the enormous growth of expenditures, particularly for social welfare and education (Pettengill and Uppal, 1974). In one of the few comparative studies of urban fiscal stress, Sharpe (1981) concludes that the fiscal condition of European local government varies widely, with those of Britain and Italy being in greatest difficulty. The causes of stress are similar to those in the United States: insufficient revenues for municipal expenditures, exacerbated by inflationary pressures (Kirwan, 1980).

National or regional governments in advanced industrial societies have some legal and political obligations (the specifics varying among countries) to ensure the provision of minimum levels of local services, or at least to ensure the solvency of local governments. Therefore the greater is local fiscal stress in a city, the greater its salience to the responsible higher level of government. In some instances the national and regional state's response has been to oblige local governments to retrench as the price of bailout, as was the case in New York City in 1975 (see Tabb, 1982; a comparative US study of retrenchment is Levine, Rubin, and Wolohojian, 1981) and in the German city of Duisburg in 1976 (the only such German case, according to Gude, Heinz and Rothammer, 1981). The prevailing response, however, has been increased funding from national and regional governments. An analysis of local government expenditures in six countries during the 1970s shows consistent increases in the percentage share obtained from national and regional governments (King and Gurr, 1983: Table 3). In the United States the percentage of local government expenditures provided by higher levels of government increased from 38.6 to 48.6 (1972–79), in Britain from 39.3 to 44.6 (1971–80), and in West Germany from 27.5 to 30.4 (1970–79).

Crime. High and rising rates of personal and property crime constitute a threat to the state in two senses: first, they are evidence of underlying social stresses and deprivation which potentially threaten the state's capacity to exercise legitimate authority; and, secondly, the perception of disorder calls into question the capabilities, ultimately the legitimacy, of the state because of its perceived inability to protect law-abiding citizens. It follows that the greater the short-term increase in a city's rates of common crime, the greater the city's salience to the national and regional state. An obvious instance of empirical evidence in point was the creation of the US Law Enforcement Assistance Administration in the late 1960s. It was established in response to ghetto-based crime and collective violence, its purpose to improve the training, equipment, and community relations programmes of municipal police forces (Button, 1978).

Substantial empirical evidence links rising crime to urban decline. For example Skogan (1977), examining differential rates of increase in serious offences for 32 US cities between 1948 and 1970, found that cities with the greatest levels and rates of suburbanization had the greatest increases in known offences. The reason is that suburbanization drains off the middle class that is less prone to common crime, leaving potential criminals and their victims, most of them also poor, concentrated in the urban core. More generally, any process of urban decline which leads to the immiseration and proletarianization of city populations is likely to be associated with rising crime. In a more recent study of crime trends in 396 US cities from 1950 to 1975, Jacob and Lineberry find that cities with the most rapidly declining populations experienced greater increases in *violent* crimes than others (1982: 14–17). It is plausible to suggest that the levelling-down associated with core-city decline in American cities leads both to decreased opportunities for economic crime and to increased frustrations, which are expressed in increased interpersonal violence.

There are European parallels to the American connection between urban decline and rising crime. High rates of increase in personal and property crime characterized almost all advanced industrial democracies (but not Japan) during the 1960s and early 1970s (Gurr, 1977). The association with urban decline is illustrated by comparative historical studies of crime in London and Stockholm: both cities had substantial population declines after 1950, accompanied by crime rates which increased more rapidly than national rates (see Gurr, Grabosky, and Hula, 1977). In summary, the proposition is that increases in common crime have been greatest in declining cities, and constitute one more set of reasons for the national state to increase its presence in such cities — specifically in the form of policies aimed at reestablishing social control.

Unconventional politics and collective action. Cities are traditionally the foci of radical political action and less structured collective violence in Western societies. Such activities not only pose a diffuse threat to the state's authority and its citizens' sense of security, they may actively and directly challenge the authority and policies of the local and national state. The general proposition is that the greater the extent of unconventional political action in a city, the greater its political salience to the state. The relation between urban decline and the various forms of political action is less than exact, however. Three kinds of unconventional political action should be distinguished.

(1) Violent and unstructured actions like racial riots, street brawls, youth rampages, and mass looting have little or no explicit political content, but they often signal potential class or segmental disaffection which is capable of mobilization for more structured political challenges. These violent forms of collective action tend to

occur among the poor and ethnic minorities, groups heavily concentrated in declining inner cities in the United States, Britain, and West Germany. Studies of the structural correlates of ghetto rioting in American cities during the 1960s have yielded relatively few positive results but Downes (1970: 354–55) found that declining population was one of the stronger factors discriminating between riot and non-riot cities; others were mainly indicators of the proportional size and wellbeing of the black population (see also Spilerman, 1976). In Britain's episodes of urban racial and youth rioting in spring and summer 1981 the correspondence between youth unemployment, poverty, and rioting was unmistakable (see the Scarman report, 1981; and Kettle and Hodges, 1982).

(2) More politicized but episodic forms of collective action include strikes, campaigns of civil disobedience, rent strikes and building occupations, and political demonstrations aimed at those holding political and economic power. Strikes tend to be a function of the status and composition of cities' workforces, both public and private. There is a general tendency in industrial democracies for strike activity to increase in times of prosperity and decrease during hard times. An unanswered empirical question is whether there is a correlation between the inter-urban distribution of economic malaise and strike activity. Political demonstrations generally are organized in response to specific government policies; they may be expected to concentrate in capitals, and to a lesser extent in cities undergoing major political and policy changes (including retrenchment).

(3) A newer and more enduring form of urban-based political participation is the mobilization of issue-oriented action groups which work outside conventional parties and interest associations to pressure for, or against, particular kinds of urban change. Urban citizens' action groups are usually of middle-class inspiration and leadership, though there are significant categories of exceptions, for instance, the participatory groups associated with the Community Action Programs promoted by the US Office of Economic Opportunity (Greenstone and Peterson, 1973) and the organizations of squatters in such cities as London, Amsterdam, and West Berlin (on squatters' groups in London see Cockburn, 1977, especially chapter 3). Studies of citizen community participation in US cities suggests that community interest groups tend to be more effective, and more widely representative, than the institutionalized modes of participation sponsored by municipal agencies (Steggart, 1975; Dommel et al., 1982). But Margit Mayer (in Hellstern, Spreer,

and Wollmann, 1982, vol. 2) suggests that government-sponsored neighbourhood movements have had to restrict their efforts to what officials define as 'negotiable' issues, thus defusing or deflecting more explosive conflicts. Heinz says that citizens' action groups in German cities are primarily defensive — opposing bureaucratic projects and planning — and over-represent professionals and students. Such groups in declining inner-city neighbourhoods rarely include low-income groups or foreign workers (in Gude, Heinz and Rothammer, 1981). In Britain government-sponsored local Community Development Projects in the 1970s sought to provide a unified base for class action on urban problems but, in Kraushaar's interpretation (1981), largely failed because state responses preempted or deflected collective action. Such examples suggest that the presence of citizens' groups may prove to be more a reaction to the interests and expansion of state activities in declining cities than an independent reflection of local concern about urban decline.

None of the foregoing comments is a threat to the validity of the general proposition that unconventional political action increases the salience of a city to the national and regional state. But they do suggest that the ordinary residents of the most seriously declining cities may be politically more quiescent — except for unstructured violence — than people of other cities.

The local state as political actor. Cities in Britain, West Germany, and the United States have traditions of political autonomy, however much the legal and political practices of local autonomy have been constrained by the growth of the relative power of the national state (for theoretical discussion of local autonomy in advanced industrial states see Cockburn, 1977; Dear, 1981; and Elliot and McCrone, 1982). This means that local officials, and national representatives of urban constituencies, can be effective advocates in pressing the national and regional state for greater resources. The first general proposition is that the greater is urban decline, the more intense the level of local bureaucratic and political efforts aimed at obtaining more resources from the national and regional state. In this instance 'political salience' increases because of institutionalized political action.

The bureaucratic skills and political influence of the agents of the local state vary considerably. In the United States it is widely recognized that some municipal administrations have become more adept more quickly at federal 'grantsmanship' than others. The relative success of some Congressional delegations in securing greater federal resources for their constituencies is equally well known. A journalistic account of the renaissance of Portland, Maine, from a condition of economic stagnation cites as relevant factors a 'united and effective Maine Congressional delegation that succeeded in squeezing an uncommon amount of urban renewal money' from the Carter and Reagan administrations; new Navy contracts which helped revive a ship-repair industry; and the simultaneous attraction of new private investment (Coakley, 1983). In Britain and West Germany, where legal and fiscal obligations of the national state to local governments are more rule-bound, bureaucratic relationships might be expected to be more influential than political ones as determinants of the allocation of national and state resources among cities.

To the extent that allocative decisions are based on legally and administratively determined formulae, it will be more difficult for any one local state to gain a competitive edge in seeking outside public aid. But to the extent that electoral politics play a significant role, a second general proposition becomes relevant: cities whose mayors (if partisan) and national representatives support the ruling party or coalition at the national level will be at least marginally favoured in current allocative decisions. This should be especially evident with regard to new initiatives in public investment and regional growth plans.

Economic centrality. The national and regional state in advanced industrial society have large and expanding revenue requirements. The urban-based private sector provides the bulk of such revenues. Therefore the more important a city's role in the productive process, the greater its political salience. From a state-centred perspective this argument follows from revenue considerations, but its general implications for patterns of state policy are little different from neo-Marxist arguments that the state's urban policies aim at maintaining the dynamics of capital accumulation (Gordon, 1976; Castells, 1977; Friedland, 1983). The empirical question, which is testable in aggregate analyses, is the relative weight of indicators of 'economic centrality' vis à vis other dimensions of political salience as determinants of state presence.

Economic centrality can be conceptualized in alternative ways.

(1) It may be regarded as a function of a city's total private-sector production of goods and services. The empirical inference is that cities with the highest per capita productivity should attract the greatest state aid.

(2) Following both pluralist and neo-Marxist arguments, the economic centrality of a city is a function of its concentration of centres of economic decision making. This suggests the inference that state presence should vary as a function of numbers of corporate headquarters, total assets of banks, unionization of the local labour force, etc. Evidence in point is provided by studies of the allocation of federal funds for urban renewal and poverty programmes among American cities during the 1960s, showing them to correlate with the location of corporate and national labour union headquarters (Friedland, 1983).

(3) More sophisticated arguments can be derived from categorizations of cities according to their economic functions, such as those proposed by Gordon (1976), who distinguishes among commercial, industrial, and corporate/monopoly cities; and Duncan as elaborated by Castells (1977, chapter 1), who offers a seven-fold categorization: national and regional metropolises; sub-metropolitan regional capitals; diversified industrial centres with (a) substantial or (b) weak metropolitan functions; specialized industrial centres; and a residual category of 'particular types'. The Duncan/Castells typology is applied to American cities; it can readily be extended to those of other advanced industrial societies. We suggest that the economic centrality of cities for the state varies in descending order according to (a) whether they are national, regional, or subregional cities; and (b) whether they are industrially diversified or specialized.

Dimensions of state presence

There are four general dimensions of activity by the national and regional state which directly affect the economic and demographic viability of cities. Some consist of programmes designed specifically to meet urban problems. Examples in the United States include general revenue sharing, antirecession fiscal assistance, community development block grants, comprehensive employment and training programmes, and local public works (Cuciti, 1978; Glickman, 1980). The theoretical argument of this essay dictates a higher level of generalization. A full profile of the state's presence in any city (or other local government) needs to take account of the following.

Grants from national and regional governments. Of concern here are both general revenue sharing and grants targeted at specific programmes. Many such programmes in Europe and the United States are allocated on the basis of population rather than need. Even American programmes designed initially in response to the problems of declining cities experience a 'spread effect', with other jurisdictions soon seeking and getting entitlements. At the aggregate level, however, there is substantial variation around the norm of proportionate distribution. Our arguments about decline and political salience are centred precisely on those deviations from proportionality. In a preliminary empirical study of state and federal grants to US cities, for example, we find that substantially more grants per capita have gone to declining than to growing cities. In both 1970 and 1980, federal and state aid per capita to the most seriously declining quartile of cities was roughly three times as great as it was to the most rapidly growing cities (King and Gurr, 1983: Table 5).

Social transfer spending. Family allowances, disability payments, unemployment compensation, and publicly funded pensions are paid to 'people not places', but the people who receive most of these public payments are more concentrated in declining cities than elsewhere. Thus decisions by the national and regional state about which categories of people in need to help, and how much, inevitably affect the magnitude of public funds feeding into local economies. Moreover there is substantial US evidence that welfare expenditures under the federally financed AFDC programme increased in the 1960s in response to urban riots; the greater the number and severity of riots in a city or state, the greater the subsequent local expansion of AFDC rolls and payments (see Jennings, 1979 and Gurr, 1980 for reviews of the evidence). In other words this evidence suggests that both urban decline and political salience, in the form of collective action, can significantly affect the magnitude of transfer payments.

The state as employer and contractor. In welfare democracies, where general government expenditures range from c. 32 percent of GNP (the US and West Germany in 1979) to 46 percent (Britain in 1980), the state is both a major employer and a significant source of contracts for the private sector. Decisions about where to locate regional administrative offices, educational and cultural institutions, and where to place contracts, thus can and do have a major impact on the vitality of the favoured cities. This is most obvious with respect to capitals, which, as noted above, generally fare better than other large cities for 'obvious' reasons. The larger question is the extent to which declining cities like Glasgow and

Cleveland are favoured or disfavoured in the allocation of public sector jobs and contracts by contrast with growing cities like Oxford and Houston.

This is not merely or primarily an American concern. Young and Mills, in a recent analysis of urban economic decline in Britain, assess 'policies against the tide' (of decline) and comment that: 'There are also areas of public decision whose consequences for industrial cities tend to go largely unnoticed. There is a new interest in the analysis of the spatial distribution and impact of public expenditure programmes, and the 1980s are likely to see proposals for more finely tuned and impact-aware procedures in allocating resources and in the use of government purchasing power' (1982: 93). Both British and West German studies show public employment rising in cities, though usually without distinction between employment by the local state and higher levels. In Britain employment by local authorities increased between 1961 and 1980 from 1.87 to 3.01 millions, that is by 61 percent (Thomson, 1982: 111). Comparison of 1961 with 1971 census data for the large (and declining) British conurbations show that total employment in public administration proportional to population increased in them by one third while in the rest of Britain it remained proportionally constant (Cameron, 1980: 65).

Policies to stimulate growth. The fourth major mechanism at the disposal of the state in capitalist democracies for responding to urban decline is the (re)direction of private investment toward static or declining cities and regions. The general objectives of local and regional development policies are to increase private-sector employment, reduce the demand for some kinds of local services, and to increase local revenues. Such policies involve various mixes of incentives and disincentives and have been used particularly by centralized European states in response to regional decline, for example by the United Kingdom in the depressed Clydeside (Glasgow) and Tyneside (Newcastle) regions, and by the governments of France and Belgium in regions affected by the collapse of the textile industry. An Anglo-American equivalent at the municipal level is the creation of 'urban enterprise zones' with attendant tax advantages, designed to attract job-producing investment (Libassi and Hausner, 1977); British experiments, inaugurated in 1981, spurred similar efforts in the US (on Britain see Davies, 1981; Young and Mills, 1982). National and regional efforts to promote local economic revitalization have their parallels in the efforts of municipalities to keep or attract enterprises by providing infrastructure, tax incentives, and other relative advantages. But this kind of 'interurban competitive struggle' has potentially negative consequences noted in all three countries: intensification of inter-regional shifts from declining to growing cities and regions, potentially greater public investment in infrastructure than returns, foregone tax revenues, etc. The general European preference is that state efforts to stimulate urban and regional economic growth should be nationally planned (see especially van den Berg et al., 1982: chapters 11 and 12).

National patterns of policy and urban revitalization

The effects of aggregate public sector spending and programmes in declining cities are problematic for a variety of reasons. It follows from the 'political salience' arguments that, even if all urban-related programmes of the state are integrated in a comprehensive plan, not all declining cities are likely to be equally favoured. In fact, most urban policies are designed in response to particular problems and situations, therefore 'urban policy' in the industrial democracies is a mosaic of programmes, each with its own history, rationale, advocates, clientele, and bureaucratic momentum. There are also substantial differences among countries in the severity of urban problems, in the resources available to the state to deal with them, and in the political will do so. A brief comparative sketch of urban problems and public policy in the United States, Britain, and West Germany is illustrative.

There are significant variations among the three countries in local fiscal stress which, we infer, are systematically related to the ways in which national/regional states respond to urban needs. There are also variable economic constraints on the present capacity of national states to deal with urban problems, and variations in political orientations about the nature of state responsibility for urban vitality. Table 1 summarizes salient differences among the countries as of 1984; in-depth comparative research would be needed to substantiate it and round out the details.

In summary, the three national states differ markedly in approaches to urban decline. The US federal government could redirect more public resources to arrest urban decline but lacks the political will to do so. Britain, in the face of general economic

TABLE 1

	United States	Britain	West Germany
Distribution of urban decline	Regionally concentrated	Widespread	Localized
Local fiscal stress	Increasing	Stablized	Negligible
Political orientation to urban problems	Weak to moderate national/state support for local initiatives	Declining national support for local initiatives	Strong national/ laender support for local initiatives
Resource constraints on national state	Limited by tax resistance	Sharply limited by economic stagnation	Slightly limited by recession
Prospects for urban change under present economic, political conditions	Intensification of regional disparities between sunbelt and NE/Midwest	Continued decline but a few regional growth centres	Stabilization of decline?

stagnation and widespread urban decline, has lost the political will to do so under a Conservative government, but even under a future Labour government would lack reallocable resources. West Germany thus far has had both the political will and resources to respond effectively to urban decline. But whether the policies that have worked when dealing with localized problems will also be effective in responding to the stresses of more widespread structural economic changes now occurring, is problematic.

The central argument of this essay is that increased public-sector activity in declining post-industrial cities tends to stabilize decline, with the more or less unintended consequence that their primary dynamic shifts from the private sector to the public. Consideration of differential state responses to urban decline, between the three countries cursorily examined here and among cities within them, makes it clear that stabilization and reversal of decline is a potential rather than inevitable outcome of the process. We are certain that the intrinsic urban interests of state officials in advanced industrial societies, interacting with the political pressures associated with urban decline, generate strong pressures toward the 'nationalization' of postindustrial cities. But it is also evident that political conservatism and ideological preferences in favour of market forces being allowed to determine urban survival can restrain officials for a while from acting on the need and opportunity to take primary responsibility for the survival of cities in crisis.

NOTES

1. The relations among economic, demographic and fiscal variables have been thoroughly examined in comprehensive recent studies of urban growth and decline in the US (notably Bradbury, Downs and Small, 1982) and in Europe (the Urban Europe Project, cf. van den Berg et al., 1982 and forthcoming volumes). Another study, recently begun by Peter Hall and Paul Cheshire at the University of Reading (UK), takes a regional approach to the analysis of urban decline and policy responses in the EEC countries.

2. For a sharp debate about the responsibility of the public versus the private sector for urban change in the United States and Europe, see the exchange between John D. Kasarda and Peter Marcuse in Hellstern, Spreer, and Wollmann, 1982, vol. 1.

REFERENCES

Advisory Commission on Intergovernmental Relations (1975) *City Financial Emergencies*. Washington, DC: author.

Alcahy, R. and Mermelstein, D. (eds.) (1976) *The Fiscal Crisis of American Cities*. New York: Vintage.

Bahl, R. (ed.) (1978) *The Fiscal Outlook for Cities*, Syracuse: Syracuse University Press.

Berry, B. J. L. (1973) *Growth Centers in the American Urban System*, Vols. 1 and 2. Cambridge, MA: Ballinger.

Berry, B. J. L. (1977) *The Changing Shape of Metropolitan America 1960–1970*. Cambridge, MA: Ballinger.

Block, F. (1981) 'Beyond Relative Autonomy: State Managers as Historical Subjects', *New Political Science*, 2, 3: 33–49.

Bluestone, B. and Harrison, B. (1982) *The Deindustrialization of America: Plant Closings, Community Abandonment, and the Dismantling of Basic Industry*. New York: Basic Books.

Bradbury, K. L., Downs, A. and Small, K. A. (1981) *Futures for a Declining City: Simulations for the Cleveland Area*. Washington, DC: Brookings Institution.

Bradbury, K. L., Downs, A. and Small, K. A. (1982) *Urban Decline and the Future of American Cities*. Washington, DC: Brookings Institution.

Button, J. W. (1978) *Black Violence: Political Impact of the 1960s Riots*. Princeton, NJ: Princeton University Press.

Cameron, G. C. (1973) 'Economic Analysis for a Declining Urban Economy' in G. C. Cameron and L. Wingo (eds.) *Cities, Regions, and Public Policy*. Edinburgh: Oliver and Boyd.

Cameron, G. C. (1980) 'The Economies of the Conurbations' in G. C. Cameron (ed.) *The Future of the British Conurbations: Policies and Prescription for Change*. London and New York: Longman.

Castells, M. (1977) *The Urban Question*. Cambridge, MA: MIT Press.

Clark, T. N. and Ferguson, L. (1981) 'Fiscal Strain and American Cities: Six Basic Processes' in K. Newton (ed.) *Urban Political Economy*. New York: St. Martin's Press.

Coakley, M. (1983) 'Portland, Me., Has Still Another Rebirth'. *Chicago Tribune*, 4 September, Section 1: 15.

Cockburn, C. (1977) *The Local State: Management of Cities and People*. London: Pluto Press.

Cuciti, P. (1978) *City Need and the Responsiveness of Federal Grants Programs*. Washington DC: Report for the US House of Representatives Committee on Banking, Finance, and Urban Affairs, Subcommittee on the City.

Davies, H. W. E. (1981) 'The Inner City in Britain' in Schwartz, G. G. (ed.) *Advanced Industrialization and the Inner Cities*. Lexington, MA: Lexington Books.

Dear, M. (1981) 'A Theory of the Local State' in Burnett, A. D. and Taylor, P. J. (eds.) *Political Studies from Spatial Perspectives*. New York: John Wiley.

Dear, M. and Scott, A. J. (eds.) (1981) *Urbanization and Urban Planning in Capitalist Society*. London: Methuen.

Dearborn, P. M. (1978) 'Urban Fiscal Studies' in Peterson, J. E., Spain, C. L. and Laffey, M. F. (eds.) *State and Local Government Finance and Financial Management: A Compendium of Current Research*. Washington, DC: Government Finance Research Center.

Dommel, P. R. (1980) 'Distributional Impacts of General Revenue Sharing' in Glickman, N. J. (ed.) *The Urban Impacts of Federal Policies*. Baltimore: Johns Hopkins University Press.

Dommel, P. R. and Associates (1982) *Decentralizing Urban Policy*. Washington DC: Brookings Institution.

Downes, B. T. (1970) 'A Critical Reexamination of the Social and Political Characteristics of Riot Cities'. *Social Science Quarterly*, 50: 349–60.

Elliott, B. and McCrone, D. (1982) *The City: Patterns of Domination and Conflict*. New York: St. Martin's Press.

Friedland, R. (1983) *Power and Crisis in the City: Corporations, Unions, and Urban Policy*. New York: Schocken.

Glickman, N. (ed.) (1980) *The Urban Impacts of Federal Policies*. Baltimore: Johns Hopkins University Press.

Gluck, P. and Meister, R. (1979) *Cities in Transition*. New York: New Viewpoints.

Gordon, D. M. (1976) 'Capitalism and the Roots of Urban Crisis' in Alcaly, R. E. and Mermelstein, D. (eds.) *The Fiscal Crisis of American Cities*. New York: Vintage.

Greenberg, M. and Valente, N. (1975) 'Recent Economic Trends in the Major Northeastern Metropolises' in Sternlieb, G. and Hughes, J. (eds.), *Post-Industrial America*. New Brunswick, NJ: Rutgers University Center for Urban Policy.

Greenstone, J. D., and Peterson, P. E. (1973) *Race and Authority in Urban Politics*. Chicago: University of Chicago Press.

Gude, S., Heinz, W., and Rothammer, P. (1981) 'Urban Policy in the Federal Republic of Germany' in Schwartz, G. G. (ed.) *Advanced Industrialization and the Inner Cities*. Lexington, MA: Heath.

Gurr, T. R. (1977) 'Crime Trends in Modern Democracies since 1945' *International Annals of Criminology*, 16: 41–86.

Gurr, T. R. (1980) 'On the Outcomes of Violent Conflict' in Gurr, T. R. (ed.) *Handbook of Political Conflict: Theory and Research*. New York: The Free Press.
Gurr, T. R., Grabosky, P. N. and Hula, R. C. (1977) *The Politics of Crime and Conflict: A Comparative History of Four Cities*. Beverly Hills: Sage.
Gurr, T. R., and King, D. (1984) *The State and the City: A State-Centered Theory of Urban Policy*. Evanston, IL: Northwestern University Center for Urban Affairs and Policy Research, Working Paper.
Guterbock, T. M. (1980) 'The Political Economy of Urban Revitalization: Competing Theories'. *Urban Affairs Quarterly*, 15: 429–38.
Hall, P. and Hay, D. (1980) *Growth Centres in the European Urban System*. London: Heinemann.
Harvey, D. 1975. 'The Political Economy of Urbanization in Advanced Capitalist Societies: The US' in Gapport, G. and Rose, H. M. (eds.) *The Social Economy of Cities: Urban Affairs Annual Review*, Vol. 9. Beverly Hills: Sage.
Hellstern, G.-M., Spreer, F. and Wollmann, H. (eds.) (1982) *Applied Urban Research: Proceedings of the European Meeting of Applied Urban Research*, Essen, October 1981, Vols 1–3. Bonn: Bundesforschungsanstalt fuer Landeskunde und Raumordnung.
Hill, R. C. (1977) 'State Capitalism and the Urban Fiscal Crisis in the United States'. *International Journal of Urban and Regional Research*, 1: 76–100.
Jacob, H., Lineberry, R. L. et al. (1982) *Governmental Responses to Crime: Crime and Governmental Responses in American Cities*. Washington, DC: National Institute of Justice, US Department of Justice.
Jennings, E. T., Jr. (1979) 'Urban Riots and Welfare Policy Change: A Test of the Piven-Cloward Theory' in Ingram, H. and Mann, D. (eds.) *Why Policies Succeed or Fail*. Beverly Hills: Sage.
Kasarda, J. D. (1976) 'The Changing Occupational Structure of the American Metropolis: Apropos the Urban Problem' in Schwartz, B. (ed.) *The Changing Face of the Suburbs*. Chicago: University of Chicago Press.
Kasarda, J. D. (1982) 'Adapting Policy to New Urban Realities'. Unpublished paper read to a conference at the University of Chicago.
Kettle, M. and Hodges, L. (1982) *Uprising! The Police, the People and the Riots in Britain's Cities*. London: Pan.
King, D. and Gurr, T. R. (1983) 'State Fiscal Crisis and Urban Decline in Western Societies'. Paper read to the annual meetings of the American Political Science Association, Chicago.
Kirwan, R. M. (1980) 'The Fiscal Context' in Cameron, G. C. (ed.) *The Future of the British Conurbations: Policies and Prescription for Change*. London and New York: Longman.
Kraushaar, R. (1981) 'Policy without Protest: The Dilemma of Organizing for Change in Britain' in Harloe, M. (ed.) *New Perspectives in Urban Change and Conflict*. London: Heinemann.
Levine, C. H., Rubin, I. S. and Wolohojian, G. G. (1981) *The Politics of Retrenchment*. Beverly Hills: Sage.
Libassi, P. and Hausner, V. (1977) *Revitalizing Central City Investment*. Columbus, OH: Academy for Contemporary Problems.
McCallum, J. D. (1980) 'Statistical Trends of the British Conurbations' in Cameron, G. C. (ed.) *The Future of the British Conurbations: Policies and Prescription for Change*. London and New York: Longman.

Mollenkopf, J. (1975) 'The Post-War Politics of Urban Development'. *Politics and Society*, 5: 247–95.

Nordlinger, E. A. (1981) *On the Autonomy of the Democratic State*. Cambridge, MA: Harvard University Press.

Perry, D. and Watkins, A. (1977) *The Rise of the Sunbelt Cities*. Beverly Hills: Sage.

Pettengill, R. and Uppal, J. (1974) *Can Cities Survive?* New York: St. Martin's Press.

Scarmon, Lord (1981) *The Brixton Disorder 10–12 April 1981: Report of an Inquiry*. London: HMSO.

Schafer, G. (1981) 'Trends in Local Government Finance in the Federal Republic of Germany since 1950' in Sharpe, L. J. (ed.) *The Local Fiscal Crisis in Western Europe*. Beverly Hills: Sage.

Schwartz, B. (ed.) (1976) *The Changing Shape of the Suburbs*. Chicago: University of Chicago Press.

Sharpe, L. J. (ed.) (1981) *The Local Fiscal Crisis in Western Europe*. Beverly Hills: Sage.

Skocpol, T. (1982) 'Bringing the State Back In: A Report on Current Comparative Research on the Relationship between States and Social Structures'. *SSRC Items* 36 (June): 1–8.

Skogan, W. G. (1977) 'The Changing Distribution of Big-City Crime'. *Urban Affairs Quarterly*, 13: 33–48.

Smith, M. P. (1980) 'Critical Theory and Urban Political Theory'. *Comparative Urban Research*, 7, 3: 1–14.

Spilerman, S. 1976. 'Structural Characteristics of Cities and the Severity of Racial Disorders'. *American Sociological Review* 41: 771–92.

Steggart, F. X. (1975) *Community Action Groups and City Governments*. Cambridge, MA: Ballinger.

Sternlieb, G. and Hughes, J. (eds.) (1975) *Post-Industrial America*. New Brunswick, NJ: Rutgers University Center for Urban Policy.

Tabb, W. K. (1982) *The Long Default*. New York: Monthly Review Press.

Tilly, C. C. (1975) 'Reflections on the History of European State-Making' in Tilly, C. (ed.), *The Formation of National States in Western Europe*. Princeton, NJ: Princeton University Press.

Thomson, A. (1982) 'Local Government as an Employer' in Rose, R. and Page, E. (eds.) *Fiscal Stress in Cities*. New York: Cambridge University Press.

Van den Berg, L., Drewett, R., Klaassen, L. H. and Vijverberg, C. H. T. (1982) *Urban Europe Vol. 1: A Study of Growth and Decline*. Oxford: Pergamon.

Young, K. and Mills, L. (1982) 'The Decline of Urban Economies' in Rose, R. and Page E. (eds.) *Fiscal Stress in Cities*. New York: Cambridge University Press.

Subject Index

Author Index

Notes on Contributors

Wyn Grant is Senior Lecturer in Politics at the University of Warwick and Associate Editor of *Political Studies.* He is the author of *Independent Local Politics in England and Wales, The Political Economy of Industrial Policy* and co-author of *The CBI* and *The Politics of Economic Policy*. He has written over thirty contributions to books and articles in academic journals in the area of government–industry relations.

Ted Robert Gurr is Professor of Political Science and Director, Center for Comparative Politics, University of Colorado at Boulder. He is the author or editor of a dozen books and monographs on political conflict, governmental authority and performance, and criminal justice, including *Why Men Rebel, Patterns of Authority* (with Harry Eckstein), and, most recently, *Handbook of Political Conflict*. He is now working on a series of theoretical and empirical essays for a book on *The State and the City*.

Ernst Jonsson is Associate Professor in Economics at University of Stockholm, where he teaches public administration. His articles on cost–benefit analysis, budgeting and local government finance have appeared in several journals.

Desmond S. King is Lecturer in Politics at the University of Edinburgh. He took First Class Honours in Political Science from Trinity College, Dublin, in 1979 and recently completed a dissertation at Northwestern University on 'State Autonomy in Advanced Capitalism: National Penetration of the Local State in a Period of Fiscal Stress.' His articles have appeared in *Irish Studies in International Affairs* and *Global Perspectives*.

Manfred Konukiewitz is a Research Associate with Zentralinstitut fuer sozialwissenschaftliche Forschung, Freie Universität Berlin, and he is specializing in the field of administative studies, housing policies in particular.

Jan-Erik Lane is Professor of Public Administration at Umeå University. He is President of COCTA and has published within the fields of political theory, comparative politics, public administration and local government.

Lennart Lundquist is Professor of Political Studies at the University of Copenhagen, Denmark. He has written studies on public administration, decentralization, planning and democracy. His latest book is *The Party and The Masses*, an analysis of Lenin's model for the Bolshevik revolutionary movement.

Hans J.G.A. van Mierlo is Assistant Professor in Political Science and Political Economy at Erasmus University in Rotterdam. Specializing in welfare economics, public choice theory and policy analysis, he has published on these themes in various Dutch scientific journals and, recently, in *West European Politics* on Dutch elections. At the moment, he is preparing a thesis on the empirical testing of Downsian spatial models of electoral competition.

Professor Richard Rose, Director of the Centre for the Study of Public Policy, University of Strathclyde, has authored or edited more than 30 books in the field of comparative politics and public policy. His latest book is *Understanding Big Government*, a cross-national cross-time analysis of OECD nations.

Rune J. Sørensen (cand. polit. 1982) is Research Assistant at the Department of Political Science, University of Oslo. He has done research on game-theoretical applications in political science as well as a project on urban finances and public expenditure in general. He has published articles on these subjects.

Aaron Wildavsky, Professor of Political Science and Public Policy at the University of California, Berkeley, was Dean of the University's Graduate School of Public Policy from 1969 to 1977. He is author of *The Nursing Father: Moses as a Political Leader* (1984), co-author with Mary Douglas, *Risk and Culture* (1982), *How to Limit Government Spending* (1980), *Speaking Truth to Power* (1979), co-author with Nelson Polsby, *Presidential Elections* (1983, 6th ed.) and co-author with Hugh Heclo, *The Private Government of Public Money* (1981, 2nd ed.)

Oliver P. Williams is Professor at the University of Pennsylvania in Philadelphia. He has specialized in urban studies and has written a large number of articles and books in urban policy and in the study of urban outcomes.

SAGE Modern Politics Series sponsored by the European Consortium for Political Research/ECPR

1

Interorganizational Policy Making
Limits to Coordination and Central Control
Edited by Kenneth Hanf and Fritz W Scharpf (1978)

2

Democracy, Consensus and Social Contract
Edited by Pierre Birnbaum, Jack Lively, and Geraint Parry (1978)

3

Power, Capabilities, Interdependence
New Perspectives on International Power
Edited by Kjell Goldmann and Gunnar Sjöstedt (1979)

4

Models of Political Economy
Edited by Paul Whiteley (1980)

5

Policy Analysis and Policy Innovation
Patterns, Problems and Potentials
Edited by Peter R Baehr and Björn Wittrock (1981)

6

The Withering Away of the State?
Party and State under Communism
Edited by Leslie Holmes (1981)

7

Patterns of Corporatist Policy-Making
Edited by Gerhard Lehmbruch and Philippe C Schmitter (1982)

8

Unemployment
Policy Responses of Western Democracies
Edited by Jeremy Richardson and Roger Henning (1984)

9

State and Market
The Politics of the Public and the Private
Edited by Jan-Erik Lane (1985)